ANZAC THE PLAY

ANZAC THE PLAY

AN EPIC ON WAR AND PEACE IN THE 20TH CENTURY

MARY ANNEETA MANN

authorHOUSE®

AuthorHouse™
1663 Liberty Drive
Bloomington, IN 47403
www.authorhouse.com
Phone: 1-800-839-8640

Published by AuthorHouse   12/13/2012

ISBN: 978-1-4772-9598-4 (sc)
ISBN: 978-1-4772-9599-1 (e)

Library of Congress Control Number: 2012922884

Providence calls

on some lives

to bear witness

to great events

and on others

to find

the Providence

within them

CONTENTS

Part 2

Note to the 2012 Publication

I am only one
But I am one
I cannot do everything
But I can do something.

And what I can do
That I ought to do.

And what I ought to do
By the Grace of God
I WILL DO!

Willie Augustus Mann,   Anzac

ANZAC the play, based upon real men of ANZAC was written in 1969 and first printed by Mithra Press, Berkeley, California in 1971. The scenes with the women of these men were originally in a play "Kate Kitchener" written in 1976. The two were combined for the 1984 production at the Globe Playhouse, Los Angeles, directed by Edward Ludlum.

In the 1960s the atrocities of World War II were vivid and the Nuremberg Trials were in living memory. Artists were struggling to comprehend the global significance of these events while also being embroiled in the tumultuous social upheavals of the great country of America, virtually untouched by the physical devastation of World War II but finally coming to grips with its own issues of racial and gender inequality.

The United Sates of America had been a reluctant warrior in World War I, coming in late, in 1917.

It did not enter World War II until it was attacked at Pearl Harbor in December 1941. At the end of that war while Europe was in ashes, America was strong and powerful and the Vietnam War broke the pattern of the reluctant warrior and enraged artists and students alike in the 1960s.

It was in the environment of the 1960s in Berkeley that the play, percolating for so long, was finally written. Much that was relevant in the 1960s in Berkeley, was not relevant in 1984 in Los Angeles, the hub of the motion picture industry. It ran two evenings but many of the original scenes were omitted in this production.

The world itself was changing. Some time after the **second world war** ended, the great nations of Europe that were the major combatants in these wars, England, France, Germany, Italy, Greece and many others entered into economic alliances and partnerships binding themselves together through commerce as peace loving democracies. But war is not yet obsolescent globally. Regional wars have besotted the 20th century timeline, the Korean war, the Vietnam war, the Falklands, perpetual Israeli and Palestinian conflicts, ongoing Balkan wars, numerous wars and genocide in Africa and South American atrocities.

Then at the beginning of the 21st century when hopes were high that human beings were beginning to understand their interconnectedness, a **rogue** attack on the Twin Towers in the city of New York in the great democratic country of the United States of America, brought the whole world to its knees—again.

While the attack was made by human beings and the greatest sufferers were human beings, it was called an act of **terrorism**. The flood gates of anger and revenge were opened wide again, the Pied Piper returned again to call on young men around the world to fight, not to simultaneously dig into the **motives** that propelled the attack but to perform the age-old ritual of search and destroy where their idealistic soldiers' young bodies were again hurled at an enemy often personified by other young bodies obeying **orders,** sacrificing themselves to this mayhem that is now too familiar to comment upon any further.

Just as the Alsace Lorraine annexation had been a harbinger for the **first world war** so was an invasion of Iraq in 1992, where men were also mowed down, a precursor to the events that followed the 911 attack on the Twin Towers. The Iraq war claimed many more lives than were lost in the Twin Towers, civilians in the valleys of the Euphrates and the Tigris rivers were dispossessed by the thousands.

The **rogue** perpetrator and his band of discontents were followed into Afghanistan coming upon the ferocity of the Taliban still mired in the isolation of the middle ages in a countryside as impenetrable as civilization' efforts to reach its inhabitants. Many more young men perished there with their bereaved families spread all over the globe.

So what changed in the one hundred years since 1915 when it comes to the methods used to prevent the hurling of the bodies of young men and now women into the bloody fray of supposedly resolving conflicts?

There is still no great **global philosophy of life** that has taken hold of the imaginations and the will of human beings to rise above the mayhem of war to an understanding that **there are no enemies.**

The omitted scenes in the 1984 production of this play, marked with an * are the dream scenes as it were, the visionary, seemingly naively simplified sequences of an impossible ideal. They are very important to the totality of the epic as it moves through the 20th century.

In these scenes, the quest for understanding has penetrated reality and touched the essence of life in its origins. The natural harmony residing here is waiting to be described by language and committed to the covenants of human governance. These covenants will be ushering in a new age of full participation for all of humanity in its greatest challenge, that of harmonizing with the life force of the universe itself. The great art of the silver screen may be the most appropriate medium for this experience.

Philosophically, the dream scenes are the precursors to *A Practical Philosophy of Life* presented in the book *There Are No Enemies*. **The work on a global philosophy of life has begun.**

SOURCE
GOD—by any name or no name
LIFE FORCE
INFINITY
UNDERSTANDING
F I E L D   O F   S P I R I T U A L I T Y
Religions
Mystical Experiences
Conscience
Reverence for Life
Values

BELONGINGNESS
Female strength

female

BIRTH _____

male　　　　Outer limits of KNOWLEDGE

Goodwill
F I E L D   O F   S C I E N C E
Conscience-in-Action

(MONEY—inorganic construct)

HUMAN ACTIVITY
KNOWLEDGE
Facts

Ethics　　　　　　　　　　　　　　　　LAWS
　　　　　　　　　　　　　　　　　　Male predominance

_____

Integrating Religion, Spirituality and Science

Explanation of Philosophy Diagram

The **SOURCE** of all life has been given many names by humans since we seem to communicate best with language. Religions called it **GOD—by any name or no name**, Yahwah, Allah, etc. Natural philosophers call it the **LIFE FORCE**, scientists, **INFINITY**.

In the *F I E L D   O F   S P I R I T U A L I T Y*, that which lies beyond the outer limits of **KNOWLEDGE**, there are the originators of all of the *Religions* as well as *Mystical Experiences* by poets and mystics. For humans also it is *UNDERSTANDING* where language is not yet adequate. In the *F I E L D   O F   S P I R I T U A L I T Y*, there is the *Conscience*, each individual's connection to the **LIFE FORCE**, a totally innate phenomenon, a gift as it were from the Creator or **GOD** which always reminds each individual of which actions are in harmony with pure organic life development. *Reverence for Life* is the absolute requirement, the primal impulse of the organic development of all life. The Universe *lives*.

BELONGINGNESS is an inherent female sensitivity, a gift of the womb.

BELONGINGNESS anchors the female in the *FIELD OF SPIRITUALITY* and since it is inherent she is unable to escape from it.

The **FIELD OF SCIENCE** is finite, forever gaining ground in its drive toward comprehending the infinite, always aware that there is a field beyond its borders.

HUMAN ACTIVITY takes place in the **FIELD OF SCIENCE,** pushing **KNOWLEDGE** to its outer limits and moving forward with each generation.

HUMAN ACTIVITY is anchored by the Conscience-in-Action, the innate phenomenon now compelled to act. In humans the will is free to choose whether to act in harmony with the guidance of the *Conscience* as in **GOODWILL** or to act otherwise as in turning away from the prime organic directive of *reverence for life*. The fracture here grew to ominous magnitude in the 20th and 21st centuries.

Ethics or the science of morals is the attempt to put into practice, the directives of the *Conscience*.

In advanced societies the temptations for the individual conscience are many and varied. **LAWS** have been enacted in most societies to ensure a certain social stability. To date they are primarily man-made and some lack the female attributes of *BELONGINGNESS*. This is very noticeable in the United States where the prison population is disproportionately high.

For (**MONEY—inorganic construct**), refer to the **Philosophy of Money.**

This diagram is a blueprint only.

Section 1

The Beginning

1

ANZAC—Australian and New Zealand Army Corps—Its Place in History

The formation of Anzac—that historical event which began on April 25, 1915 and ended on December 20, 1915.

Each age inherits the responsibility to record and interpret an historical event in the light of those events which followed as well as those that preceded it.

Winston Churchill had a grand vision in 1915. He would take allied forces through the Suez canal to Russia. But the Germans were waiting at the Bosphorus and the Dardanellses became a graveyard for so many ships. Undeterred he decided to send troops overland through Turkey to reach Russia and enclose Germany from the south and the east while the allied armies would advance thorough France. It was indeed a grand vision. Had he succeeded, there might not have been a western front and the war of attrition for both sides might not have happened.

Turkey however was a sovereign nation and reacted as sovereign nations react when they are invaded. They fought back with everything they had. They were fighting for their liberty. They were fighting to preserve their own country. They were fighting for the same reasons as the young men who came ashore in those fateful months from April 25 to December 20, 1915. The young men who came ashore were also supposedly fighting for their own liberty as it had been described to them. That was the great tragedy of the Gallipoli invasion. It pitted soul brother against soul brother. The decimation on both sides was awful and it was destined never to be forgotten as other battles have been forgotten and relegated to the history books.

The Australians and New Zealanders who fought on Gallipoli became known as Anzacs, members of the Australian, New Zealand Army Corps. Their heroism was so extraordinary that even the Turks whose land they were ordered to take, considered them their own and passed on the message to their loved ones in Australia that they were not buried on foreign soil but were considered native sons of Turkey and were *buried in native land*.

So many of them had rushed headlong into the "great adventure". Once into it, they could not go
back. They were half a world away from their homeland. They knew what freedom was. It was in their blood. They had experienced it in a vast virgin land with 'virgin' meaning land that was previously inhabited only by its indigenous peoples. Their parents or grandparents had traveled the world's oceans to make their way in unexplored land, mysterious in the ways of its native inhabitants, ferocious in its ability to alternate between floods and drought. It molded the character of all those who would try to love her and understand and yield to her relentless ways. Freedom was tough and always tempered by the mighty elements. Freedom in Australia could never be taken for granted as far as the land was concerned. The land exercised its own discipline on all those who trod upon her surfaces. This discipline forged the character of those who followed the pied piper in 1914 and 1915 and onward to the end of that **war to end all wars**.

All of the great religions were teaching that faith was the way to inner harmony, personal peace and reverence for life. Yet, those humans who became leaders, while clinging to their so-called religion, also bonded to nationhood as a way of finding and securing the peace through which humanity becomes civilized and self-actualization becomes real.

Philosophically, there is much more. Certain customs or mores had been accepted among nations concerning their national boundaries. In the past these would be changed as neighbors invaded each other and then called the annexed territories their own. People themselves bonded with each other in various ways of ethnicity or religion but nationhood seemed to be the most powerful

Its Place in History

What the Anzacs did was to bring the great continent of Australia as a nation with its tiny population on to the world stage as a player in contemporary affairs with morals and standards that were very close to the core of humanity at its deepest level. They did this while using the language of blasphemy and raucous humor as the way to survive, emotionally resilient, the most heinous ongoing affronts to humanity that have ever been inflicted. The Anzacs were not victims; they were ordinary men who were called upon to assert their humanity time and again in the face of brutal onslaughts ordered by uncomprehending fools who were vested with more brute power and authority than human or military diplomacy. Anzacs had, imbedded in their hearts, a vision of a lifestyle that was carefree and peaceful. What they won for Australia and what they helped win for the world, was *the right of human beings to live a good life in peace*. The book *Anzac to Understanding* is an effort to help us strive for remembrance of this vision with more intensity than we now expend on the glorification of their military deeds.

2

Original Anzacs—

What was the call and why did they heed it?

Who of us would want our contracts broken?
Who of us would trample down the weak?
ANZAC the play Scene 4

Preamble

From the beginning of our recorded civilization, the recognition of inherent human dignity and human rights has been a long, slow, and very uneven process. Brute force and the right of might has barreled its way through our history. Even into the 21st century, many people have been held in bondage to the few. Over the centuries, powerful personalities have risen up and won the services if not the loyalty of the many through whatever means necessary. Then 'sides' would fight each other. Poets would record the exploits where "ignorant armies clashed by night". The glories of the great battles would be sung and re-sung until they faded from memory as new battles took their place. But something different happened in 1914. In that year, and in those that followed, humanity itself was to make a stand for human dignity with a vision of generic human rights.

What *was* the call in 1914? What was it that men felt they *had* to respond to?

In essence, it really did come down to human rights and human dignity and there were enough people and particularly young men, prepared to sacrifice everything for this ideal, this vision for all of humanity which manifested their own innate and unfettered knowledge of what it really means to be a human being. In essence again, there were enough free people in the world to be able to take a stand and make a desperate bid for personal freedom for all even if those who answered the call were to give everything they had, their young, and for the Anzacs at least, *enthusiastic* lives.

They were all forced into 'sides' again but this time there was a 'free' side, or those who fought of their own free will for the 'imponderables' of the state of being human, and there were on the other side, people in different and various forms of bondage.

3

Every age has its own assumptions about the status quo which it is somehow necessary to preserve. Nation states were the norm or the state of the world in 1914. Australia had declared itself a nation in 1901. It shared its heritage with England since most of the settlers there had arrived from England during the previous century.

The Causes of the Great War

Europe in the nineteenth century was this continent of nations. Some were larger, some were smaller. Russia was a giant to the east. Poland was sandwiched between Russia and Germany. France was a great nation and one to be feared after the revolution of 1792 when it became a democracy and her people began to understand the full meaning of personal freedom. Comparative peace in Europe had been achieved by a balance of these powers, smaller nations assuring their existence through neutrality and larger nations aligning themselves together in such a way as to deter any major shift in geographical boundaries. Some nations were becoming democracies in various levels of development.

When the dual powers of Germany and Prussia merged in 1870, William of Prussia became the Emperor of Germany. The German armed forces were absorbed by the Prussian Army. After the Franco German War of 1870-71, Alsace and Lorraine were annexed from France despite the vigorous protests of its citizens that they were French and having tasted democracy, would never submit to German rule of heavy militarism. Germany redrew its boundary in 1871 to include Alsace Lorraine. It secured it for an army of a hundred thousand men, a military zone for Germany and the iron ore mines of Lorraine. The rest of Lorraine's iron ore mines were seized at the beginning of the Great War, in 1914.

The action of Germany was perhaps the first time citizens of a democracy were forcibly annexed by a foreign power and the brutality of German rule could never subdue them. The people of Alsace Lorraine cried out to all of Europe for redress finally declaring that Germany's act was 'a legitimate and permanent provocation to war'. In 1871 the world did not respond to their call but in 1914 when Belgium was overrun by Germany, the world did respond.

The philosophy behind a 'chosen people'

While so many of the European countries were primarily Christian, the old testament idea of a 'chosen people' had not been debated philosophically in such a way as to expose the unscientific nature of it in terms of the whole of humanity. This left an opening for a philosopher like Nietsche to build upon the great scientific advances that had occurred by that time to declare that 'God is dead' or in other words to declare there is no spirituality that goes beyond the realm of science, no generic humanity where all human beings are born equal, and certain minds proceeded to subjugate by persuasion or by force all of those people who did not fit a certain mold. Those of the Aryan race benefitted from it. It was so mesmerizing an idea that even after the abject defeat of Germany in that war, that country could still rise up again in the 1930s and wreak even greater degradation and mutilation of humanity itself.

Partly because of the Alsace-Lorraine annexation and the will of the people refusing to be broken by it, Germany and France were on opposite sides in the balance of power at the close of the nineteenth century. England, France and Russia formed the *Triple Entente* and Germany with Austria-Hungary and and Italy formed the *Triple Alliance*. England and France were the only free countries but by the end of that war, the dynasty of the Hohenzollern that ruled Germany, Prussia and Russia was swept away and the people of the world were scrambling to find ways to handle their own governance.

Egalitarianism was finding its feet. But no truly great philosopher emerged to describe it. The gut feeling of personal freedom embodied by the Anzacs was a phenomenon that was yet to be understood.

Providence in the tragic irony and the restless dead

Remembrance of what they fought for—WORLD PEACE

—and—

"Preventing the tribe from going into bondage and so destroying or stagnating its culture"

26-3-62
McKelligett St.,
Rockhampton

Dear Mary,

The good God that I worship gave me 5 talents not 1 or 10 just 5. In the exuberance of my youth I thought I could turn them into 50! I soon discovered that I had insufficient tools to accomplish this so set about to rectify same.

Then an enemy from without attacked the tribe to which I belonged. Having been born and bred a man, even if not a gentle one in the accepted term, I joined with many other men, many of whom were not gentle in the accepted term, but I soon found out that basically 99.5% of them were in that fundamentally basic art of defending their tribe and their culture (and those who prided themselves in the knowledge of the latter), were born gentlemen and acted accordingly, and in my very humble opinion no man can claim this distinction if the very base of this pyramid is not composed of that ingredient which is essentially man.

Having completed the job of preventing the tribe from going into bondage and so destroying or stagnating its culture, those who returned had to lick their wounds, for which they required no sympathy, before setting about the task their master God had given them of making use of the talents he had given them. In my case as you know, having protected the tribe, I then had to re-establish my family within the tribe, by the time much of the exuberance of youth had evaporated and cold hard facts had to be faced. I still had only my 5 talents. Would I live poor and die rich, or live rich and die poor?

I remembered a few lines I saw somewhere when I had time to enrich my mind (in a hospital bed). Some men are rich some men are poor, but only God can tell us which is which. To us who had seen the degradation and bestiality of war, had experienced the break down of most of the things we were taught were right, the disillusionment of things we thought inviolable, this was quite a problem, we had no anchor! We weren't tied to anything for 5 years, we had to make our own fun, we had to live each day in knowing that it probably was our last, we had to take what we could when we could, tomorrows were too horrible to contemplate. For 5 years we had only one loyalty, one burning desire, we had to win the dirty game into which we had been pushed. Unfortunately we were expendable! And we knew it. Go down we must, but that did not seem to matter so much provided you took as many as possible with you.

What a wonderful Cultured life we led? Burned into your Soul, Mind and Body. All good things generally come to an end, so fortunately do the other ones, sometimes!

Back, we drifted, Gentlemen of Hell into the Heaven of Peace? Or we often wondered if it wasn't the other way around after we had been back some little time!!

We had to learn a new life and unlearn as far as we could what we had learned and to try and winnow out of 2 lives the best of each, no easy task believe you me! Which wind we had to set our sails for or what current we had to follow, but more important what harbour we had to sail for?
Did you ever see the painting "Menin Gate" ghostly figures rising from the earth, seeking what? That guy knew and had experienced what we Knights of the stinking gutters (trenches) had with us always, when we slept or when we were awake, Tom, Bill, Jack, Harry coming back to us we knew not from where, with an incomprehensible look on their faces, which came to haunt us, why that look?

Slowly, it took a long time, the problem sorted itself out. Live rich and die poor. Matter, the scientists tell us is indestructible. Souls, the theologists tell us are immortal. Live poor in pursuit of what happiness you could grab as you went along life's way, or give Tom, Bill, Jack and Harry another chance? I decided on the latter. Bang went the last of my dreams! I had to become a materialist, by the sweat of my own brow, by the use of my own muscles, by everlastingly driving my own mind often against its own will, to make my 5 talents grow into 10 against the competition of those who had 10 to start with to ensure that those ghostly faces (only by the will of God mine was not one of them) would smile again and I would again be reunited with the Cultured Knights of the Gutters of War!

Willie Augustus Mann

Why poetry?

Throughout our heritage, heightened emotion has produced some form of poetry. Since the time of **Beowulf** for saga and the time of the great Greeks for drama, there has been the urge to create art with language describing the workings of human events or human beings in action. These actions for the most part have been the deeply emotional and highly charged ones of great human exploits and deep personal relationships and inner journeys as human beings endeavor to reconcile the mystery of the relationship between the individual and the great creator of the universe with man-made laws that sometimes reinforce but at other times threaten to contaminate, mutilate or destroy this eternal bond.

The Angles and the Saxons though fierce and merciless fighters were also very brave and loyal. They loved their freedom and they left their mark on English literature. From **Beowulf**,

> *Behold! In the Hall, many heroes lay sleeping,*
> *Brothers in battle, a band of one blood . . .*
>
> *They marveled the building withstood such an onslaught,*
> *And fell not in ruin, mere feat of man's hand.*

This is the language of thought.

Shakespeare deeply questions the assumptions in armed conflict but he does so in prose through a common soldier, Bates.

> *We know enough, if we know we are the King's subjects: if his cause be wrong, our obedience to the King wipes the crime of it out of us.*

Shakespeare's *poetry* about this comes from Henry V himself,

> *We few, we happy few, we band of brothers;*
> *For he to-day that sheds his blood with me*
> *Shall be my brother; be he ne'er so vile,*
> *This day shall gentle his condition:*

The philosophy elicited by **Henry V** is explored elsewhere but the poetry glorifies the deeds in the tradition of **Beowulf**.

These great calls to action are by the male of the species only, yet they have dominated our culture and continue to do so as the wars of our own lifetimes are re-enacted on the wide screens that now encircle the globe.

As far as Greek drama goes, in ***Antigone***, Oedipus violated eternal law in marrying his own mother, however unwittingly and Antigone held firm to what she knew to be eternal law when Creon violated it by refusing state sanctioned burial rites for his nephew, her brother and she had to do it herself. These defining actions resulted in unbearable anguish and raised emotions that are universally human and so deep as to be almost beyond endurance. To express these emotions and the intensity of the forward movement of events, heightened language happens.

In Shakespearean drama the action of the play reaches such an intensity that poetry is the only way to express it. Poetry in the course of universal human events is the medium of necessity.

Poetry is able to dispense with connecting words that are so necessary in common usage, in order to highlight the action which is what defines drama that deals with the great universal themes of life and death, human rights and eternal justice.

At the beginning of ***Hamlet***

> *So I have heard and do in part believe it,*
> *But, look, the morn, in russet mantle clad*
> *Walks o'er the dew of yon high eastern hill*
> *Break we our watch up.*

In prose, this may be something like, "I have heard that and I partly believe it. But look it is almost morning. Let's go home" In the poetry, we are alerted to heightened awareness of beauty that elevates our soul to our wondrous connection with the universe, "the morn, in russet mantle clad, walks o'er the dew of yon high eastern hill." Then comes the demand that we pay attention to the necessity of *foreboding* action, "Break we our watch up." The words are juxtaposed in a startling way.

These are traditions inherited by everyone who would aspire to create a work of art using the medium of language. Heightened language is used to express thought that comes from the inner being or spontaneous indignation that is felt when great eternal truths of spiritual harmony are threatened or violated by the progression of human events.

> *High on the camel's hump of Achi Baba*
> *He stood beside a clump of mulberry and oak.*
> *Restlessly the scarlet poppies moved.*
> *The glistening Dardanelles, a silver thread*
> *Arced gently round the golden plains of Troy.*
> *Did this Turk, Mustafa Kemal, know the cause*

For which the valiant Hector fought and died?

The Gallipoli invasion was doomed on moral grounds but the young men who died there, with the death-defying assertion of their own humanity, extracted from the ashes a vision of the human right to live freely and peacefully on their own soil. The land where they died accepted them as native sons.

The poetry in this play is dedicated to that eternal peace where all human beings are native to the earth itself and all human beings belong to one single human family.

Section 2

Frontispiece 1971 publication

For who but those of infinite faith will dare
To question thus the ancient rule of men
And write new covenants with their mortal blood?

Eternal Justice

This play is theatre of a past age and a vision of a future one.

Readers may turn to any scene without necessarily having read those preceding it.

Pal, Nobby, Darkie and Shorty originally belong to the Australia and New Zealand Army Corps and that is how they happen to be called men of Anzac. But they are the eternal soldier who emerges and reemerges feeling always and ultimately betrayed and defeated. The girl, Madeline accompanies them from the beginning and so does the Mad Student. None of the characters age with time and they are joined by the visionary characters Eternal Justice, Justice in Bondage, Liberty and World Commonwealth.

This play marks the distinction between ETERNAL JUSTICE
        and what passes for justice in the laws of men.
This play fuses international and intra-national relevancies among men.
This play redefines woman's role in the government of men.
This play presupposes a brotherhood among men.
This play was conceived in love and born in love.
Nurture it if it pleases you.

Heed me or heed me not beloved,
My debt is paid to the yet unborn
By utterance of the word,
For it is the unborn that will judge me.

Liberty

Back Cover
They are tampering with your inheritance
Not content to lay waste their own age
They plan to mutilate yours

Liberty

GLoBe PLAyHOusE

Shakespeare Society of America

R. Thad Taylor & Jay Uhley, Co-Founders
Clark Branson, Producer.

November 15, 1984

Dear Colleague and Educator,

A 20th Century EVERYMAN,

ANZAC in two long evenings beginning at 7.30p.m.

The GLOBE PLAYHOUSE is honored to present a very special event and a landmark in Los Angeles' theatre history, ANZAC I & II, written by Mary A. Mann and directed by Edward Ludlum.

ANZAC I & II speak directly to all of us who are concerned about the state of our world. In an extraordinarily theatrical way, they deal with issues of war and peace and human rights. ANZAC is particularly relevant for high school and mature elementary school students because the characters stress an idealistic approach to global conflict. The young men and women of ANZAC show us that we as individual human beings can indeed take control of our collective destiny and live in peace.

A N Z A C WAR/PEACE ISSUES & HUMAN RIGHTS is a project of the Center for Public Education in International Affairs, School of International Relations, USC, Los Angeles Ca. 90089-0043 (213) 743-4214. Teaching packets are available to educators as well as excerpts of the script for student use.

As Executive Producer, President and Founder of the Shakespeare Society of America/Globe Playhouse, I am responsible for selecting and scheduling all plays presented and performed under our banner. When I was presented a script for ANZAC, by Mary Mann, I read the entire contents in one evening which I was compelled to do because of the lyric structure of the dialogue and the similarity to Shakespearean verse structure. I indeed praise Dr. Mary Mann for her marvellous method of writing, technique and expression coupled with the tremendous amount of research, dialogue and grueling hours of writing which took years to assemble and organize into the script for presentation to the public.

At the Treaty of Versailles, in ANZAC II, the negotiators appear like models from a wax works museum, unresponsive and non-caring while the dead soldiers wonder what has happened to world peace. In a magnificient scene with the bomb exploding and covering the entire stage in an eerie light, Pal, a young soldier on Gallipoli, now the eternal soldier, accepts personal responsibility and cries out "Is there no vision?"

I would urge you all to see this production at the GLOBE PLAYHOUSE. Here we have a contemporary author aided by an extraordinarily dedicated and enthusiastic cast of over 40 actors, coming to grips in a most remarkable way with the burning issues of our times. I am honored to present this play.

R. Thad Taylor, President

The Story of the Play

1. World War 1 has just been declared. At the meeting of the War Committee in London it is decided to send troops to the Dardanelles in order to reach Russia with munitions and food. The troops to be sent are Australians, New Zealanders and Indians in addition to what British men could be spared from the Western Front.

2. In a small North Queensland town, Charters Towers, we are introduced to a group of young people on a picnic at the weir. Millicent, Pal and Kate, Fred and Jessica, Ilene and Jimmie, Kitty, John Marshall, Iris, Victor and Nobby are all close friends. Darkie, Tommie and Shorty are visiting from the far west. A tropical storm suddenly ends the picnic.

   Returning from the weir, Pal stumbles down a deep incline and in a rock pool there, he sees Madeline, Darkie's sister an aboriginal girl who claims she is a descendant of Eingana the great earth mother. They talk for a few minutes and Pal hurries off to find his sister Millicent and his brother Fred.

3. At home, mother is preparing soup as Fred, Millicent and Pal arrive home from the picnic. Father soon arrives home too to inform everyone that Torley, the owner of the land they have been farming for years, has told them that he might sell.

4. Meanwhile, as war has been declared between England and Germany, Australian boys are asked to enlist and fight for England. Kate's father Captain Campbell comes to Charters Towers to sign the boys up for the war. Fired by a call to duty, all of the young men of the town prepare to join up, even many who were not eighteen, the minimum age.

5. Kate meets with her father as they discuss her future. Iris has been invited too and the two young women emphasizing the differences between how men and women view war, say goodbye to the Captain as he accompanies the men to the war.

6. Pal, torn between his love of the land and the war imperative, stumbles through the bush back to the rock pool. Madeline is waiting for him. She talks to him about the dreamtime and how some people are chosen in their life to transmit and rejuvenate folk legends. Aided by her, Pal sees a vision of Liberty and is told that he will return.

7. Meanwhile Mother and Father have decided that even though they have tried many times to raise the money to buy Torley's farm, this time they would indeed get it. They disposed of all their heirlooms and books and signed all the papers. Eagerly they wait for the boys to come home. Eagerly the boys do come home—to inform their parents they have enlisted!

8. At home, Kate decides to train at the hospital in Charters Towers since no medical school will accept a woman. She comes to live with the family. Jessica is thrown out of her parent's home because she is bearing Fred's child and she too moves in. Mother delightedly announces that she now has three daughters and the boys are expected home before Christmas.

9. The young men who volunteered for the war are sent to Thursday Island for their first training. Here they meet with recruits from Sydney, Enery, Nark, Billo and Danny. They are delighted as they are informed they are going to train in Egypt.

10. The soldiers land on Gallipoli. Fred and Tommie are killed and Shorty and Nobby wounded. Pal is also killed but Liberty appears to him and he rises up and continues his spiritual journey toward the goal for which the men enlisted and laid down their lives, a true understanding of Peace and Liberty.

11. In Charters Towers telegrams are arriving at many households and the family receives two telegrams announcing the deaths of Pal and Fred.

12. Father's hair goes gray overnight and Jessica is on the verge of insanity.

13. The Battle of the Some in France engulfs those Anzacs who survived Gallipoli. Pal leads an attack to silence a pill box. The pill box is silenced, Pal is again killed. Liberty returns to him once more to help him understand how mortals can live in peace. She brings Eternal Justice to him but Death intervenes.

14. Back in Charters Towers, a train arrives bearing wounded. John Marshall returns shell shocked and the young women grieve for the boys they will never see again. Death, laughing, brings in the soldiers who have been killed, but Liberty appears and they exit following her. Pal and Kate cross paths but in different worlds and Kate realizes that they will meet again in the next world.

16. The crazed John Marshall visits Jessica whom he has always loved. In her fever, she thinks it is Fred at first but then as he reveals himself to her and throws water in her face, she realizes it is not Fred, and swoons.

16. Jessica's baby is born but Jessie dies. Mother gives the child to Kate. They call him Young Pal.

17. A group of soldiers on leave in London's East End encounter the Mad Student who flourishes a newspaper informing everyone about the sinking of the Lusitania and tries to espouse the ideas of the sanctity of one's native land and the need for universal Goodwill. Pal enters and meets Madeline, now the eternal woman, appearing here as a Red Cross nurse.

18. At a casualty dressing station in France, the soldiers experience the agony of losing their friends and all living things. The Americans arrive however and Pal, through and beyond the defeat of Gallipoli, is able to communicate some of what he has learned to the Australian and American soldiers gathered there.

1. The Anzacs and Liberty are all present at the Treaty of Versailles where Eternal Justice acts in an ideal but not in a factual capacity. The Australian soldiers send Pal around the world to try to understand the deep seated antagonisms among people.

2. Charters Towers slips downhill becoming almost a ghost town. With few to work the farms, they are sold or auctioned off. The new railroad bypasses the town.

3. Young Pal, now in his teens, presents his mother Kate with a hand made pendant for her birthday.

4. Ilene returns after having left the town on the day the train brought in all the wounded.

5. In Europe, Pal is working as a waiter and Madeline is a factory worker. They meet again amongst the violence of the rise of Nazism.

6. Colonel Campbell visits Kate once more trying to get a commission for Young Pal as the world again drifts toward war.

7. Kate is awarded the MBE for her services to Charters Towers and the outlying areas as Matron of the hospital.

8. Young Pal returns home from the university to spend his last Christmas with his 'mothers' as he enlists in World War II. Kate gives him back the pendant.

9. During the London Blitz, Young Pal meets Kathleen. Sensing his imminent death, he gives the pendant to Kathleen.

10. At Dunkirk, Liberty appears to the cold and demoralized soldiers entreating them to understand her immortal strength. They finally comprehend what she is saying as they are evacuated and saved. Young Pal is killed.

11. Kathleen, bearing Young Pal's child, comes to Charters Towers and returns the pendant to Kate.

12. The Australians are retreating now along the Burma Rad. Pal, still wandering the earth as the Eternal Soldier, again meets Liberty and together they experience the horror of the atomic bomb.

13. In a complete blackout voices relate the story of the holocaust. A tremendous explosion occurs and the projection of the mushroom cloud appears with a huge beast walking across the back of the stage with dead soldiers standing around,.

14. Nuremberg. The bomb backdrop remains but a picture of a shepherd is superimposed with a wire frame and flashing lights. A cast of visionary characters, Eternal Justice and voices together with real people with their nation's name on them, all try to understand the significance of the past events.

15. At Winton, Nobby, Shorty and Darkie who survived the wars, encounter in a dream world, an emanation of the Nuremberg Trials where Eternal Justice and Pal endeavor to clarify responsibility and guilt.

16. The women in Charters Towers, growing old, are persuaded by Ilene to engage in a seance during which time they meet kindred spirits from round the globe as well as Madeline and Young Pal.

17. U.S.A. the 1960s. John Kennedy is elected president and he meets and shakes hands with World Commonwealth who is there with her retinue.

18. There is a presidental address where Kennedy honors Winston Churchill. Pal, still wandering the earth, comes to America and finds Liberty encased in a statue. He holds her torch while she travels through the United States encountering unrest and violence. She chastises the Mad Student for his negligence and celebrates the persistence and stamina of the eternal woman, Madeline.

19. The Valley of the Shadow of Death. In a dreamlike pageant the dead John Kennedy's head is swathed in bandages and he is led up a ladder. Shots ring out and Robert Kennedy falls but the unborn children curl around the feet of Edward Kennedy to prevent him from moving. Men try to raise the Star spangled Banner but they cannot until a big

African man hurls himsel on the pile and the flag is raised to the voice of 'my country tis of thee'.

20. Perth, Australia. There is a colorful backdrop of the moon with men landing on it. A voice in poetry describes its journey as a group of scouts together with Darkie, Shorty and boy scouts debate together as they bring in torches to create a great light as voices are heard from the space rocket that it has been seen and there is great rejoicing.

21. The fiftieth anniversary 1965. There is a pageant representing the death of Winston Churchill, with the voice of General Eisenhower speaking the tribute. This is followed by a soldier debating with a imaginary voice on how to stress goodwill in world affairs and write new covenants for it.

22. Peace on Earth. To commemorate the passing of Winston Churchill commonwealth scholarships are given to children of the world who will participate in the peace. The last child entered declares himself to be the son of Liberty and God.

23. Pal returns to Gallipoli where Eternal Justice, Liberty and Death have been waiting for him for some time. He is given the keys that free mortals' understanding and allow them to experience the Creator's intention for the joyful fulfillment of all things.

24. At an Anzac Day celebration in Charters Towers, Pal arrives looking for the next shepherd. He is finally allowed to die, his spirit is fulfilled in the prevailing of Eternal Justice, his love is eternalized in his reunion with Kate. Madeline is also present. She is a young girl again and talks to Milli an old lady. She and Boy Pal lift up their arms to receive the keys, the covenants, from Pal.

Still in the Dreamtime

Boy Pal is lectured by the old diggers who knew his grandfather. His mother long since returned to England, leaving him in the care of his 'grandmother' Milli. Boy Pal has difficulty in following the old men who speak of honor and freedom with such passion. Nobby, Darkie and Shorty dejectedly prepare to return to the far west when Young Pal looks at them intently. "Wait' he says and enters Milli's house. He comes out holding the keys that Pal has given him. It can now be seen that they contain medals. "Are you talking about these?'. The faces of the old men light up. 'My name is Pal you know. I caught the torch'. The old men joyfully turn and walk away into the sunset. As they walk they appear younger and younger, fading eventually as the young soldiers they were in 1915.

Boy Pal has become interested in the plight of the aborigines. He goes to Townsville. On the outskirts of the town there, there is a large aboriginal community. Boy Pal meets Mindaree a full-blooded aboriginal who challenges him to a debate on the merits of land use—for the white man it is territory—for the aboriginal it is access to trade. Boy Pal is getting the worst of it when Madeline enters. She greets Mindaree affectionately. 'He's my uncle', she says. Mindaree looks at her. 'She takes part in our discussions as if she were a man. She always has. She knows many things though'. Madeline, 'No, no, not more than you, Mindaree'. Mindaree, 'You know more, much more'. Boy Pal. 'What do you know Madeline?' Do you know what we can do about the land?' She nods. 'But we are diametrically opposed to each other'. She shakes her head. Mindaree, 'You have to do it Madeline. You have to'.

Boy Pal meets with the Commonwealth Scholarship committee. He has been posing difficult questions regarding the assimilation and recognition of aboriginals as equals. He is offered a scholarship to America.

Through the dreamtime, he becomes engulfed in what appears to be the eye of the storm of the Vietnam crisis. He drives up into the hills and gazes out across the Pacific yearning for home. In a dream sequence he sees a replay of the scene when his real grandmother, the young and passionate Jessica pleads with Fred to stay on the land and not become a soldier. At that moment he becomes two men. One dons a uniform and goes to Vietnam. The other returns to Australia. Both are angry young men.

Madeline returns to the Rock Pool and pleads with Eingana to release her from her immortality. Eingana warns her that she is in love with half a man only. She tells her she must gather women from all over the world and begin to march. She does this and as they are marching, in the distance two men, one on the right hand side and one on the left hand side, begin to come towards the women. One is uniformed and appears to be Pal. The other is Pal. Suddenly they get closer, a great wall joins them. Thousands of names appear and the women touch them and cry. Boy Pal and Madeline skip off as children again and in her hand she carries the book that the women have written.

The Characters

PAL. A serious young man always filled with wonderment about the land. He is deeply meditative, so much so that others notice it. He appears to be 'different' but in an indefinable way. His idealism is so powerful that, aided by Madeline, he actually envisages full-bodied emanations of Liberty and later Eternal Justice, the latter teaching him how to live on through personal deprivation.

MOTHER. A woman thrilled with the idea of being a pioneer in a new land. Her primitive life style is cherished as she daily sees the results of labor whether it be vegetables sprouting, sheds being roofed, or fences going up. She brought two young children to the country only to have them die when they drank stagnant water. She is always making plans for her three remaining children. In her mind's eye she sees her grandchildren playing in the shade of the trees she is planting.

FATHER. The second son of an Oxford landholder, he is so connected to the soil that when his older brother takes over the family farm, he jumps at an opportunity to emigrate to Australia. With his wife and family, he embarks at Townsville and, moving 75 miles inland, on a bend in the Burdekin river, he finds the place where he can establish his dream farm. He studies the land and experiments with the crops. Over the years he becomes a seedsman and corresponds with people all over the world, importing and exporting seeds. As the township of Charters Towers is emerging he buys a lot on the main street and sells his vegetables and seeds from a shop there. As his two boys are growing up he adds "& sons" to his name on the seed packets.

FRED. The younger son relaxes in the shadow of his intensely dedicated father and his deeply meditative brother Pal. He is care-free and good-natured, enjoying his friends, laughing off the seriousness of his mother—as much a part of his environment as if his family had been living there for thousands of years.

MILLICENT. The daughter, lives her life centered around people. The land is something to be respected and coped with, with its flash floods, sudden downpours, muggy daytime heat and cool evenings. She worships her brothers. With her health a little frail, she has no desire to go riding or even exploring very much, though she does have her flowers and the small animal life around the house. She is very proud of her career-minded friends. She never marries but as her life progresses and her love reaches out, she becomes known as 'Mother Milli'. She goes on to become a very old lady living to see her way of life upheld, enriched in the end by Boy Pal and the life he chooses to live.

KATE. The daughter of an army Colonel career soldier who had served in the Boer war. Her mother died when she was born but her father kept her and raised her. Not knowing a home other than that of the family, she has grown up career-oriented, a true child of her father except that she is a woman and there is something about an army uniform that she tolerates and respects but at the same time despises. She believes intensely that she can become the person she wants to be—a doctor and a healer in a new land where the illnesses are different and much has to be learned about the land and people's tolerance of it.

IRIS. A born teacher, she is an avid reader, aware of any new books that come to town, getting a newspaper sent up from Sydney and delighted when her parents establish the bookshop, selling newspapers and magazines. She attends Blackheath school, graduating at the top of her class, later going to the university and eventually becoming the principal of Blackheath school.

KITTY. The musical one, singing her way out of childhood scrapes, endearing everyone as she learns their favorite songs and performs all over town. When her piano finally arrives, still crated, she has been unable to sleep all night, supervises the dismantling of all the packing material and with tears running down her face sounds out the notes one by one and then remains glued to the keyboard for days as she begins to play by ear, her favorite songs. Later she becomes a music and singing teacher.

ILENE. The beautiful one, gaining insights about people through being beautiful. She is also stylish, turning heads with a single movement of her body. Yet underneath the beauty, there is a deep vulnerability, a keen awareness of the pain in others and the jealousy. When the first trainload brings back the solders maimed and mutilated, she leaves the town not to return for many years

MADELINE. The aboriginal girl with a mysterious father, is a gifted one, a poet who is able to return to the dreamtime, retell what she knows from there and re-create contemporary events so that they too become part of the culture and legends preserved in a living tradition. Even though she may live among average people and find herself in ordinary situations, she always catches the universal thread, is visited by Eingana in her sleeping and understands the continuing relationship between the dreamtime and the nowtime.

YOUNG PAL. A product of the era of peacetime that his father fought for he is happy and well adjusted though lonely in the town as the generation of men who were his father's friends never returned from the war and so he has very few friends of his own age. He enlists in the second war and is killed.

BOY PAL A young man in the sixties, he is much less likely to be swayed by ideals that cut across living an eclectic kind of life. People are his concern, from his great aunt, 'Mother Milli' to the aborigines who are slowly and painfully recovering their dignity. He loves listening to stories which are an endless fascination for him. He is attracted to the aboriginal reverence for the land with as much passion as his forbears were drawn into soldiering.

NOBBY was a close friend of the family. He was wounded on Gallipoli but was later sent to France. He survived the war and lived to be a very old man.

JOHN MARSHALL was very fond of Jessica even though she loved Fred. He was something of a musician and Kitty knew he ought not to be a soldier. She was beginning to love him. He returned shell-shocked and never recovered.

SHORTY, DARKIE and TOMMIE came from Winton. Tommie was under 18 when he enlisted but Darkie was always trying to take care of him. When he was killed and his body splattered all over the dugout on Gallipoli, it was Darkie who had to bury him. Shorty, though wounded on Gallipoli, later fought in France. DARKIE survived the war and lived to be an old man as did Shorty.

Concerning the real people who inspired this epic.

Pal, the ongoing hero, is molded upon Willie Augustus Mann who survived the war after being twice reported killed. He lived a wonderful life and died an old man. Fred, his brother was killed in France aged 18. Millicent, Kate, Kitty, Iris and Ilene did fulfil their lives as recorded in the play. They never married and all lived to old age. John Marshall lived to be an old man almost as described in the play, always the living painful reminder of what might have been. Colonel Frederick William Toll D.S.O., and Bar fought in the Boer War, the Great War and the Second World War. His son was killed on Gallipoli aged 18.

Cast

The War Committee:
Prime Minister (Lloyd George); First Sea Lord; War Secretary (Kitchener); First Lord of the Admiralty:

The Home Scenes:
Mother; Father; Pal; Fred; Millicent; Kate; Ilene; Iris; Kitty; Jessica; Captain/Colonel; Mrs. Dunbar; Young Pal; Nancy; English Kitty (Kathleen); Boy Pal; *Madeline;* Scout 1; Scout II;

Men of Anzac:
Pal; Fred; Jim; Nobby; Shorty; Darkie; Victor; John Marshall; Tommy; Billo; Enery; Nark; Quinn; Officer; Commanding Officer: Razzy; (Fuzzy Wuzzy; Chinese):

Versailles Delegates:
England; U.S.A.; Japan; France; Russia 1; China:

Nuremberg and the Palace of Justice:
Observer; Pole; German; Cockney; Layman; Voice of Martin Luther King; Professor; Policeman; Black Intellectual; Young Man; Panther:

The Dreamtime, Symbolism and Pageant:
Madeline; Eternal Justice; Liberty; Death; World Commonwealth; her retinue; Peace; President Kennedy; Robert Kennedy; Jackie; Figure 1; Second Figure; First Temptor; Second Temptor; Third Temptor; Voice of Bismarck; Mad Student; *Unborn Children;*

Deutchland Uber Alles, Europe
Poet 1; Poet II; Mad Poet; Poet III; Man 1; Man II; Worker 1; Worker II; *Madeline*: Worker III; Tilly; Jew; *Pal;*

The U.S.A.
John Kennedy; Robert Kennedy; Student 1; Student II; Drunk; Black Man; Black Intellectual; Businessman; General;

Epilogue:
Madeline; Boy Pal; *Voice of Eternal Justice:*

Prologue

Ladies and gentlemen,
I ask for your indulgence in this play,
Forgiveness where I have offended,
Lenience where I have erred.

But darkening is the path we walk upon,
And a torch was passed to me
That I have kindled,
And now pass on to you.

So when I speak of men of Anzac
I pray you, take them to your heart
And hold them there,
Till they become you,
Or your brother, or your father,
Or anyone that you have known
Who loves his fellow man.

And when they have become you,
Hold them there,
Until this play is done.

Part 1

Part 1

Cast

Scene 1. A Meeting of the War Committee, January 28, 1915.
Prime Minister (Lloyd George); First Sea Lord; War Secretary (Kitchener); First Lord of the Admiralty:

Scene 2. The Weir—a picnic
Kate; Millicent; Victor; Ilene; Jim; Darkie; Kitty; Tommy; Fred; Jessica; John Marshall; Shorty; Pal; Iris; *Madeline*:

Scene 3. The Home
Pal; Fred; Mother; Millicent; Father:

Scene 4. The Town Hall—August 1914
Captain; Iris; Kate; Pal; Victor; Jessica; Ilene; Jim; Nobby; Shorty; Darkie; Townsperson; Another; Another; John; Kitty:

Scene 5. The Captain's Office
Captain; Kate; Iris:

Scene 6. The Rock Pool
Pal; *Madeline*:

Scene 7. The Purchase of the Farm
Kate; Millicent; Mother; Father; Jessica; Millicent; Pal; Fred:

Scene 8. The Same
Mother; Millicent; Kate; Jessica:

Scene 9. Thursday Island Cable Station
Voices; Jim; Officer; Shorty; Pal; Darkie; Victor; Enery; Billo; Nark; Nobby; John Marshall; Tommy; Commanding Officer; *Kaiser; Crown Prince; Bismark*; Soldier; Stage Manager; *Francis Joseph; William I*; Woman; *Pope*: Voice:

Scene 10. Gallipoli—1915
Quinn; First Voice (Cultured English); Second Voice (Uneducated Australian); Third Voice (Mustafa Kemal—accent); Chorus of Soldiers' Voices; Jim; Nobby; Sergeant's Voice; Darkie;

29

Nark; Enery; Pal; Tommy; Shorty; Razzy; Voice; First Stretcher Bearer; Second Stretcher Bearer:

Scene 11. The Home. The News
Jessica; Mother; Millicent; Father; Kate; Iris; Boy:

Scene 12. The Home—The Next Morning
Father; Iris; Jessica; Millicent; Mother; Kate:

Scene 13. The Somme—1916
Officer; *Pal*; Corporal; Voice; *Death; Liberty; Eternal Justice*; First Stretcher Bearer; Second Stretcher Bearer:

Scene 14. The Return
Mrs. Dunbar; Ilene; Townsperson; Father; Iris; Kitty; Kate; Father; *Jimmie; Victor; Pal; Freddie; Billo; Enery; Nark; Tommie; Death:*

Scene 15. The Same Room—Shell Shock
Mother; Millicent; Iris; Kitty; Townsperson; Jessica; John:

Scene 16. A Little Later—The Birth
Mother; Jessica; Kate; Iris; Father; Aide:

Scene 17. London's East End
Soldier: Waiter; Nurse *(Madeline)*; Radio; *Pal*; Paper-Boy; Mad Student:

Scene 18. Casualty Dressing Station
Soldier; Williams; Darkie; Nobby; Shorty; Orderly; Jenkins: Voice; Freeman; Woman's Voice; Yank; Second Yank; *Pal*; Marine:

Scene 1

A Meeting of the War Committee January 28, 1915.
There is a map of Europe on the wall. There is a round table center stage.

PRIME MINISTER (Lloyd George)
>Our whole civilization is at stake. The fire
>Is lit and either we can quell it now
>Or watch it pass beyond our present control,
>A fiery monster writhing through our lines,
>Tearing our flesh and burning on our minds
>The memories that peace cannot erase.

FIRST SEA LORD
>But we are not aggressors. All our plans
>Are regulated by the enemy;
>We must maintain superiority
>At sea, husbanding our strength, refusing
>To engage in operations that could draw
>Our power away.

WAR SECRETARY (Kitchener)
>And do not talk of men.
>Our armies on the western front are caught
>In the deadly grip of almost equal strength.

FIRST LORD OF THE ADMIRALTY
getting up and going over to the map on the wall
>Exactly. You see our theatre of war.
>There is no strict division here between
>A French or Russian ally, sea or land:
>One war, one conflagration covers all,
>And so must one vision counter all,
>One great manoeuver, one great forward thrust
>Through here, through Hellespont, the Dardanelles,
>And we can cut the Turkish flank in two;
>Constantinople will be ours, and our
>Great ally, Russia, short of munitions, food,
>And all her war exchanges bottled up,

We can reach.
Our spear's thrust if we keep courage up,
Can reach the Danube, drain the German strength
Until a great offensive on the western front
Can overwhelm her utterly.

speaking very slowly

And so avert disasters that no living
Mind can contemplate.

FIRST SEA LORD

And if we fail,
Our supremacy at sea is lost, our fleet,
Attacked by equal strength, will find its grave
Where none can take its place.

FIRST LORD OF THE ADMIRALTY

And if we fail,
We'll envy those young men that died for peace,
Who trusted us with their great hearts to save
The world from the blood that will engulf her;
If we fail, gentlemen . . .

FIRST SEA LORD *slamming his fist on the table*

I am opposed to it. I'll not consent
To jeopardize the Grand Fleet's margin of
Supremacy. No, I will resign . . .

He goes over to the window. The War Secretary follows him. They talk together for a few moments then return.

FIRST LORD OF THE ADMIRALTY

Gentlemen, the ships we'll use to force the Dardanelles,
Are those that would lie rusting in our docks,
Are those that it would he murderous to send
Against the German fleet. Our sea
Supremacy is still maintained, our vision if
This daring enterprise will work, will join
The Balkan states, save Russia from collapse,
And save the lives of countless gallant men
That else will hurl themselves like pawns into
The monster carnage that will gorge unchecked,
Till all the manhood of the world is gone.

PRIME MINISTER

We have discussed this plan and now we must
DECIDE. We can withdraw without great loss—
Lord Kitchener what is your view on this?

WAR SECRETARY

I must concede to Churchill's eloquence.
If it remain a sea thrust and does not
Drain off my army from the Western Front
I'll give what help I can. We have some men,

32

Australians and New Zealanders untried
But trained in Egypt, an Indian Brigade,
And more perhaps as time goes on and as
The need dictates.

PRIME MINISTER

The First Sea Lord?

FIRST SEA LORD

I have opposed this plan but yet I know
That I am outweighed. I pledge you now my full
Support and I will not withdraw but bear
With you in loyal comradeship.

PRIME MINISTER

Then let us join our hands on this and
Trust in our firm resolve.
Come gentlemen

PRIME MINISTER

We are all our brother's keeper
And as strong as the weakest link.

The First Lord of the Admiralty moves from the group and towards the audience as if in something of a trance. The lights dim.

FIRST LORD OF THE ADMIRALTY

And now God speed you vision. God guide
This great offensive, this daring ill-equipped
Attack. And if it succeed, the men
Whose blood we've shed for it, will rest content,
Will feel the joy of children's innocence,
"The silence following great words of peace"
And if we fail, let it not be because
We have gone back on this our solemn pledge,
Our courage faltered under pressures great
That will be brought to bear before this front
Can thrust forward to its goal
And gentlemen,
If for this we fail, may the spirit of the men
Who died in their great love and trust in us,
Haunt ever our souls. And may that part of us
That will most surely die, should this our
Vision fail, still wander ghostly on this earth,
Until our warlike spirits are all destroyed,
Or tamed by some great world catastrophe,
That will with tongue of fire and more
Horrible presaging, cry to the worse
Than plague infested world, that man must live
In peace.

Scene 2

The Weir—a picnic

There's a track winding back,
To an old fashioned shack,
Along the road to Gundagai,

Where the blue gums are blowin'
And the Murrumbidgee's flowin'
Beneath the sunny skies.
Where my daddy and mother are waiting for me,
And the pals of my childhood
Once more I shall see.

Then no more will I roam,
When I'm headed straight for home,
Along the road to Gundagai,

Millicent is laying a tablecloth on the ground. She has a wicker basket next to it and is pulling out rugs. tea, sugar and cakes in tins. A billy is nearby and a few of the boys are collecting sprigs and have set up a device made of sticks to hold the billy over the fire.

KATE
        Do you need a hand Millicent?
MILLICENT
        No, no, everything is ready. It will be a little while before the billy boils. I'll stay
        here and watch the things. That's fine Pal. Thanks. I'll watch it.
Others come running in tossing ball.
VICTOR
        Here, here
MILLICENT
        Watch out Victor. The billy's here.
VICTOR
        Whew! Can those girls run! Milli, Milli where are your swimmers?

34

MILLICENT

> Victor, you know I'm not the swimming kind.

VICTOR

> Aw come on Milli.

MILLICENT

> No, no

VICTOR

> Did you bake things Milli?

MILLICENT

> Yes I did

VICTOR

> O.K. Then save me the very biggest one!

ILENE

> Jim! Watch out Victor. Jim! Over here!

They are playing with a ball and tossing it

JIM

> Oh, Ilene, you are the fastest runner I've ever met
> I couldn't believe a girl could sprint like that.

ILENE

> Aha. You should come down to Torley's gully.
> I race there with Pal and Fred.
> They've got these dingoes they go duck hunting with. Whew!
> Oh, Millicent. Here are my cakes. I hope they're still alright.
> I've been racing the boys. Jim almost caught me.

JIM

> Oh Milli. She's the fastest girl around here. Darkie, hey, Darkie, over here.
> Darkie this is Ilene and Millicent.

DARKIE

> Pal's sister?

JIM

> And Fred's. You met Kate didn't you?

DARKIE

> Yes.

JIM

> Well don't get ideas about Jessica. She only has eyes for Fred.
> And Ilene here of course. Ilene only has eyes for *me*

He slips his arm around her waist

> Darkie comes from the far west.

DARKIE

> Hughendon

JIM

> He goes on over to Townsville. For a dip in the briny eh?
> Isn't that right Darkie?

DARKIE

> Yeah. The ocean's wonderful.
> This time I might go to one of the islands

And get coral from the reef.
I might.

MILLICENT

I've never seen the ocean
I'm sure I would be scared.

DARKIE

Oh, nothing to be scared about

MILLICENT

How long will you be there?

DARKIE

Oh, a short while—maybe not long
My boss can't spare me for long
It's hard to get help in Hughenden.

KITTY

Coming over and looking very interested

It's hard to get help anywhere around these parts.

Pal comes over arm in arm with Kate.

PAL

Well hullo Darkie. I'm glad you could come.
Have you met everyone?
This is Kitty with the golden voice.

KITTY

Oh Pal, why are you always so poetic

KATE *laughing*

Because he is a poet, I guess.
The poet-seedsman, or the seedsman-poet
Which one is it Pal?

PAL

I don't really know. But I do know the billy's boiling.

He lifts the billy off the fire.

Where's the tea Millicent. Is this it?

MILLICENT

Yes Pal

Pal opens up a tin, pours a handful of it out then drops it into the billy and stirs it with a twig.

DARKIE *beckoning to Tommy*

And this is Tommy. he's from Winton.
You wanted to see the world remember.

Tommy is very shy and Millicent gives him some tea

MILLICENT

Here's a lamington

TOMMY

A lamington?
Cripes, thanks.

MILLICENT

Have you left school yet?

TOMMY

>Well sort of, I mean yeah, yeah.
>
>I've left school.

MILLICENT

>Do you like Charters Towers?

TOMMY

>Yeah, yeah, I do. Lamington's good.

MILLICENT *glowing*

>I made it.

TOMMY *nodding and trying hard to be grown up*

>Damn good cook

A group forms around the billy, sipping tea and eating a cake or two. A little to the side Jessie and Fred are together.

FRED

>It's so ideal the life here Jessica,
>
>I feel so strong. As if I'm every boy
>
>That ever loved his sweetheart.
>
>You are my sweetheart Jessie
>
>And I'll love you till the end of time.

JESSICA

>Oh, Freddie.
>
>What is there about you and your brother Pal,
>
>There's something different Freddie.

FRED

>It's not that we are different,
>
>Me and my brother Pal

JESSICA

>Like twin souls you are, Freddie,
>
>Breaking girls' hearts

FRED

>I'11 never break your heart Jessie dear.
>
>But you're right about me and Pal.
>
>When we have children Jessie
>
>If it's alright with you,
>
>Our eldest son—we'll call him Pal

JESSICA

>Why Pal? Why not Fred like you?

FRED

>I'd like to call him Pal
>
>And he'll call his son Fred,
>
>Because you see, we're more than brothers.
>
>I always feel so proud to know him Jessica.
>
>He walks with God, as the saying goes,
>
>And Katie too. Someday I think
>
>Some wonderful thing will happen because of them
>
>And I will be part of it,

And you will be a part of it, you'll see.

JESSICA

Fred, put me down.

FRED

Hold on, Jessie, hold on.

JESSICA

Freddie, Freddie

FRED

Come on, let's join the others.

JESSICA

Come on Freddie, I'll race you

JOHN MARSHALL

I'll race you Jessie. I'll race you

JESSICA

Oh, John Marshall, can't you ever leave me be?

JOHN

Oh Jessie, I'd race you to the ends of the earth!

JESSICA

And what would you do when you came to the edge of the earth?

JOHN

I dunno Jessie, I dunno.

JESSICA

Well, why bother then. Freddie, Freddie?

JOHN *to Kate*

Why is Jessie always so mean to me?

KITTY

It's not so much that she's mean to you John, but she cares for Freddie.

JOHN

I'm leaving, I really am.

Well hullo mate, who are you?

SHORTY

Shorty.

JOHN

Are you one of the blokes from the far west?

SHORTY

Yeah.

JOHN

Can a bloke get work out there?

SHORTY

Cripes. Plenty of work out there.

JOHN

Well I'm leaving.

SHORTY

Fair dinkum?

JOHN

Fair dinkum.

SHORTY *putting his arm around John and taking him out of earshot of the girls*
> Eh, want to hear a yarn?

Shorty and John move away.

PAL
> Do you ever feel that life's too perfect Kate?

KATE
> Yes, sometimes I do but,
> But always in my life there is a pain . . . .
> A sense that I will not fulfill myself
> A sense that I'll be thwarted in my life,
> From doing all the things I want to do
> And not through fault of mine,
> But through some star crossed sensibility,
> That I'm not born a man:

PAL
> Oh, Kate
> My heart sinks deeper every word you speak,
> For I had hoped that someday you and I
> Might see our lives together moving on.

KATE
> Pal, Pal,
> What I spoke said nothing of our love,
> Nothing, nothing,
> We've loved since we were children, you and I.

PAL
> Then I will not fulfill you, oh dear Kate
> You speak such riddles.

KATE
> Of course you will fulfill me with your love,
> And I love you too.
> But would my love ever ask of you
> That you give up one jot of all your dreams?
> Oh no, my love will strengthen every move,
> Will plan and aid you every step you take
> So why my love, deny that strength to me
> In this the thing that I have chosen to do?

PAL
> I love you Kate

IRIS *running in*
> Aha, you two what's all this earnest talk
> On such a day as this?
> The river's overflowing and the falls
> Have never been more turbulent!

JIM
> Hey Iris, come on. Some of these coves can really swim.

39

IRIS

        Wait, wait—
        I want to talk!
        I never talk to anyone except these two
        And even then it's only when they're in the mood
        To discuss more serious matters

PAL

        Such as government?

IRIS

        Don't laugh me down on government my friend,
        Or great philosophers either, we'll need them soon.

KITTY *strolling over*

        Iris, come on,
        John Marshall's going to sell me his guitar,
        He says he's going away.
        Why does he still love Jessie do you think
        Jessie doesn't care a jot for him,
        So why does he stay so enflamed with her?
        I wish someone would love me just like that.

IRIS

        And what would you do then?

KITTY

        I'd love him back with all my heart and soul,
        And have his kids, and care for him.

IRIS

        And give him your mind as well?

KATE

        And never question him if he does wrong?

PAL

        Oh come on you two,
        A lucky man the man that Kitty marries.
        Come let's go swimming.

Pal picks up Kitty and carries her off stage

IRIS

        Marry him Katie
        You are soul mates you two.

KATE

        Yes, we are
        But I have this terrible urge Iris
        To do something with my life.
        When I grow old, I want to say
        I did something with my time on this earth!
        I left this world a better place
        In some small way.
        Oh, why was I not born a man!

IRIS *laughing*

> You, a man
> Oh no, not you, Katie

KATE

> And Pal, Pal has things to do too,
> He has to study the land,
> He has to understand this land,
> He's almost a poet you know.
> I think had he been born
> In another place
> He might have been a poet.

IRIS

> You love each other Kate
> You know you will find a way

KATE

> Yes we will
> We will indeed.

The rain begins to pour down and everyone leaves for home
Pal took a turn in the gully and went down a deep incline. When he got up there was a rock
pool he had never seen before. There were lubras there but he could see only one girl.

PAL

> Madeline?
> It is Madeline isn't it?

Madeline comes out

MADELINE

> Yes, it's Madeline

PAL

> Darkie's sister?

MADELINE *laughing*

> My brother Mindaree—you call him Darkie
> Do you mean Mindaree?

PAL

> You speak English so well I know you are Madeline.

MADELINE

> Yes I am and you are Pal. Pal the peacemaker.
> Pal who would be a 'clever man' if he were with us

PAL

> How do you mean 'clever man'?

MADELINE

> You see things that others do not see.
> You hear things that others do not hear,
> You feel things that others do not feel.
> You should be black like us

There is laughter from the water hole

41

You would be a 'clever man'—a 'medicine man'.

PAL

Madeline how do you know this?

MADELINE

Mindaree tells me. You helped him at the Boolu camp.

PAL

Yes

MADELINE

Mindaree knows

She begins to draw a picture on the ground with her fingers

PAL

What are you drawing?

MADELINE

Eingana the great earth mother—the mother of us all.

PAL

Me too?

MADELINE

Probably. I am trying to find out *she jumps up*

She is the mother of all living things, dingoes, kangaroos,

She is the mother of everything.

PAL

But Madeline where is your real mother?

MADELINE

My earth mother?

MADELINE

My earth mother is with the tribe

PAL

And where do you belong Madeline?

Madeline is quiet. She draws a little more on the ground. She digs her toes into the sand

MADELINE

I move from the Dreamtime to the Nowtime.

In the Dreamtime there is Eingana,

She stays in the middle pool always,

She is my mother's ancestor.

My mother's rangae is far far back in the dreamtime.

She has secrets, many, many secrets.

Someday her secrets will be mine—if I stay with her

But my rangae dreams the water serpent

I sprung from his head and entered my mother's toe over there

And she came back to that same place for my birthing

To give me the double strength from the Dreamtime

PAL

But your real father?

MADELINE

My earth father was the bravest man

That ever trod the ground.

He was one of those who landed
From countries far away
But his skin was darker, not light like most
And his brown eyes blazed their way.
A place called Wales they told me
Was where his tujunga was
And where his spirit will return
When his journey here is over.
It was if he knew our songlines.
He helped our whole tribe to pass through
When the fair man had cut off our passage
And we would have died in the drought,
But he did not come with us himself.

She meditates a little

My mother always told me he was gifted from the Dreamtime
He lived just over there.

PAL

Well that's the land we wanted to buy,
But there's noone living there

MADELINE

But many, many live there and I shall live there too,
When I die and Eingana draws me back,
And I bury my bones in the rock pool.

PAL

I don't understand you Madeline

MADELINE

I have been following you
For the light skinned man is disobeying
The ancient law of our spirit gods.

PAL

What are these ancient 1aws?
And what if they are the laws of your people
And do not apply to us?

MADELINE

Some are the laws of all creatures living,
Mortal, bird and beast and flower,
For ever and ever from the beginning.
When the dreamtime enveloped the earth.
Before the mother of my mother's mother
Swam in the great creek of the orphan gods
She was given the great stone of all fertility
To travel out on the earth.

PAL

But this earth is only one of many,
This is but one continent.
There is another great continent somewhere else,

43

With Europeans all over it
And they have their gods and goddesses too
And they have religions galore.
Christianitv, the one thay taught you—
Well that's what Darkie said—
That the missionaries taught you . . .

MADELINE

The missionaries, the missionaries
My skin is lighter see, not light like yours
But lighter than most of my tribe.
The missionaries were good, kind
And they taught us about one god
Who sent his son to live on the earth
And our Dreamtime loved him and cherished him
And all who spoke of him.
But there was but one son for the missionaries
And no one else would do
But our Dreamtime encompasses the universe
That we must adhere to.

PAL

I don't understand you Madeline
And what am I to do?

MADELINE

You must go home
The others will be waiting.
Pal, don't tell them about the rock pool
Promise?
But come back—come back!

Scene 3

The Home

Pal and Fred come rushing in from the picnic. They look rather bedraggled and splattered with mud.

PAL

        Mother we're back.

FRED

        Mother, mother.

Fred rushes to pick her up, as he is waltzing around

MOTHER

        Aha did the storm put an end to the picnic?

        I thought it would.

        Freddie, Freddie, no picking me up dear please.

        If you want to pick someone up, get Jessica.

        Oh my dears, where have you been?

        And where is Millicent?

PAL

        Well, ah, well we had some fun with the dray.

        We ran it down through Torley's gulley

        And it was muddier than we thought.

        Ah. Ah well, well, I'll go and give Millicent a hand *exit*

MOTHER

        Go clean up quickly Fred.

        Hurry up

Fred leaves as Pal comes in again with Millicent. He carrying the wicker basket and Millicent has a couple of extra things.

MOTHER

        Oh my dears. You are so reckless you children sometimes.

        Who rode the horse? I hope you didn't hurt the dray!

PAL

        Fred rode the horse coming home.

MOTHER

        I knew it. Millicent are you alright?

MILLICENT

> Yes mother, we had fun!

Fred returns

MOTHER

> Off you two and clean up.
> Bring me the soft plums
> I'll cook them.
> And fetch me some water Freddie,
> The tank is overflowing.
> And Freddie, be careful with that horse!

FRED *lilting*

> Mother, Mother. where is another,
> That's so full of worry.

MOTHER

> Be off, you reckless child.
> Oh Millicent, Millicent darling
> Dry these things for me will you?
> Pal. Do take care of the horse dear,
> Your father will be here in a moment.

FATHER *coming in very excited*

> He wants a hundred pounds down,
> He'll take a hundred pounds!
> A hundred pounds and the farm will be ours, ours.
> We'll put an awing by the shed,
> We'll build another bed, put in a stove,
> And we can live out there, we can.

PAL

> How will we raise the hundred pounds!

FATHER

> The buggy, and the horse and dray,
> This house. The piano we might sell.

MILLICENT

> No father, no, not my piano!
> You know how I love that piano.

FATHER

> I only said we might,
> Or we might lump it in with all the rest.
> And borrow on the whole,
> Anyway, the bank will lend us eighty pounds,
> I'll sell some odds and ends,
> The books. I'll sell—
> The dictionary, Shakespeare and the rest,
> There are no books in this town,
> I know someone will buy them
> And read them too I'll bet.
> So how about it, what else to sell?

MOTHER *touching some few silver objects including candle sticks, vases, bowls*
> My grandfather gave me these

FATHER
> Millicent, I'll never ask for those you know it

MOTHER
> Your great grandfather gave me these,
> They came from the old home

She goes over to the bowl of fruit on the table and picks it up
> Sterling silver, hand crafted.
> He knew the family well that made these things
> In the old country. Worcestershire.
> Oh Ben, could the farm really be ours?

FRED
> I thought he said he'd never sell that land
> Whatever made him change his mind?

FATHER
> God knows, god knows.
> But if we don't strike now while the iron is hot,
> We'll never get the chance again. I know old Torley.
> He'll give us just one chance.
> I think he likes you boys. I think he thinks
> We'll make a go of it!

PAL
> I love that farm.
> I never thought that we would ever own . . .
> And if we bought the farm that means
> That we could stay forever . . .
> We could make plans like building things, a house . . .

FRED
> Two houses later on, the farm's enough
> For both of us to raise a family on—
> When there's more grapes and oranges
> For sending into town . . .

PAL
> Someone out there all the time.
> Why we could pay the mortgage back
> From the milk alone . . .
> The paddock, is the paddock in the deal?

FRED
> Is the paddock in the deal?

FATHER
> From Swanson's creek to Torley's western ridge,
> The road to the railroad track, the lot.
> It's all included, every tree, the shed,
> And everything's that on the ground right now.

Mary Anneeta Mann

PAL
        A hundred pounds! And how much every year?
FATHER
        The money down's the worst.
        I grant we'll have to work real hard
        To make the yearly payment.
        But there's three of us and Millicent to boot.
MILLICENT
        Oh father, you know how hard I'll work.
        I have ideas about the shop.
        I'll take orders in for everything you're growing!
        I'll have people lined up and waiting
        Every time the dray comes in.
FATHER
        That's it, my girl. I KNOW you'll sell the stuff,
        Everything, everything. The hospital,
        We'll sell to the hospital.
        Oh, we'll make the payments every year.
        The money down's the worst.
FRED
        But, but we'll never make the money down.
        We can't even fix the dray!
PAL
        The dray's alright. It gets us where we're going,
        Eh Millicent. *laughing*
MILLICENT nods and chuckles
FRED
        We've never been to Townsville,
        We've never seen the sea,
        We've never been anywhere but here.
PAL
        Who wants to go anywhere but here
        The best farm in all the world!
MOTHER
        And if we bought the farm would you two stay
        And work it all your lives and build a house?
        Because for pioneers, the life is very hard.
        You have to live on dreams, my sons, dreams.
        When you are born as you two are
        In a land that's free but young,
        You have to dream ahead, you have to dream,
        Dream of the farm completed and the trees
        All strong and tall and shady
        And the children underneath.
        And the dream will urge you forward to the end
        Of all your days, a shining beacon ever.

48

For us, a dream's behind us of a land
We knew and loved so long ago and left
To start again and struggle far away,
Put down new roots and toil and toil
And this is all I have of my old dream,
A few things of silver and some candlesticks,
But oh, the dreams I dream
When I sit and look at them.

FATHER

This life's not so bad, we have our sons,
And our darling Millicent.

MOTHER

Yes, yes, and we'll share their dream,
And everything that's in the past,
Slips into a haze of painlessness,
For the present is so beautiful,
And the future is so bright!

FATHER

Yes, we must act now
And the price must be paid.
It's the future now,
The future for all of us.
Mother it's time, we're going to the bank.
We're going to the bank. Come on mother. Here's your shawl.
Yes, we're going to the bank
To see what we can do.

MOTHER

Yes, we are. To do what we can see. *THEY EXIT*

The young people laugh

MILLICENT *walking over to the window*

I heard old Torley singing the other day,
My hair stood up on end.
He's going on a journey,
I know he is!

LIGHTS FADE

Scene 4

The Town Hall—August 1914

CAPTAIN

> Britain is at war with Germany.
> On August fourth in violation of
> An international law, Belgium was invaded.
> Now Belgium could have said "I'll let you pass"
> For the Kaiser wanted France;
> But Belgium chose her martyrdom, for friends,
> Belgium was neutral, a little country quite encased
> By great and powerful foes, Germany and France.
> Belgium said "no" and what did Britain do,
> Britain our ancestral home,
> Britain where most of us were born,
> Britain on two scores then declared a war—
> An obligation to honor neutrality,
> An obligation to defend the weak.
> Who of us would want our contracts broken!
> Who of us would trample down the weak?

Iris and Kate are hurrying in a little to the side

IRIS

> But they can't be serious

KATE

> They are serious.
> The word is out all over town
> The days of high excitement of a war!

IRIS

> But it can't last this war.
> And what's it got to do with us?

Pal comes running over to the girls

PAL

> We cannot live a life apart
> And not affected by decisions made
> In any other country on this globe.

50

very earnestly

> I'11 tell you Kate, until this war
>
> My life stretched out before me clear and calm,
>
> Not that it we easy, God knows it wasn't.
>
> We've struggled on that farm since we were kids

IRIS

> Then stay.
>
> Your fight is with the land Pal
>
> Not with men, not other men, not ever!

PAL

> I know it. A man is a man to me.

KATE

> Oh Pal, you've got to be able to kill
>
> To be a soldier

They look over to the box again where the Captain is continuing

CAPTAIN

> And so the call is out for citizens
>
> To aid in this most honorable cause
>
> To enlist young men and fight in this true war
>
> For international peace and governance.
>
> Eighteen's the minimum age and other tests
>
> Of health must first be taken.

PAL

> If universal peace would come of it

VICTOR

> It's honor,

KATE

> Oh Pal, they are only words
>
> Only words that other people speak.

PAL

> Oh Katie, I have to go. I have to go

KATE

> I know. Oh my love, that will become of us?

VICTOR

> It's honor, it's honor for the motherland!

JESSICA

> It's madness: What's England got to do with us?
>
> Your parents left it didn't they to come out here
>
> And fight the beastly jungles of this land,
>
> The droughts, the rain, the old and rotten soil
>
> That yielded up some gold and then made fun
>
> Of those that came to see the gaping holes
>
> While we have fought to live. What's war to you
>
> That's raged on some strange battleground?
>
> Your fight is here in this dirty rotten ground.
>
> It's here!

PAL

> But it's the cause of freedom Jessica
> How can we live secure in this our land
> While others of our blood lay down their lives
> To hold ideals that none can live without!

JESSICA

> Your ideals are here in this land!
> Your children will be born—in this land!
> Your future will be furrowed in this land!

PAL

> That's true Jessie
> But this land has to be safe first.
> We will never be safe, Jessie, never
> As long as any country in the whole world
> Loses its freedom.
> And our children might also die
> In this land, if invaders come.

ILENE *coming in with Jim*

> It's honorable to take care of your family,
> Your parents, your sisters,
> All those who love you
> Oh Jim, don't go, don't go.

JIM

> Ilene, you have so many boys
> Who would swim an ocean for you
> You could have a beau on every corner.

ILENE

> I do have a beau on every corner
> But what will this town do
> If you all go to war?
> Why don't you pick straws or something
> You don't all have to go
> Can't you take turns for instance,
> I'll go and talk to the Captain
> He likes me, I know.

JIM

> Ilene, it's not like that
> It's not like that at all.
> You sign up and you go—for the duration of the war!

NOBBY

> Who wants to he a cold-footer?
> Who wants to promenade the streets alone
> When all his mates are gone to war?

JESSICA

> Don't go
> Don't you understand:

NOBODY go!

IRIS

Then NOBODY can call you cold footer
Because NOBODY else is going!

SHORTY

Ah you don't understand

DARKIE

You really don't. A man's got to go!

JESSICA

You stay here and we'll fight with you
Side by side. We'll fight together
To save and defend THIS LAND!

Much laughter

IRIS

Why do you laugh at a woman
Are women not warriors too?

TOWNSPERSON

Yes we are warriors, go on sonny . . . go to war
And never shirk your duty . . .

ANOTHER

England needs you, begone!

ANOTHER

Will you let your British cousins down?

ANOTHER

England expects that every man will do his duty!

KATE

Wait, wait

IRIS

Wait friends, wait,
We owe allegiances to Britain that is true,
We also owe allegiance to this land
Where all of the younger ones of us were born!
No God however tyrannical
Would take our very all.
How shall the women survive without their men?

There is laughter

TOWNSPERSON

Who wants a cold footer?
Who wants a coward?

ANOTHER

I'd rather send a dozen sons to war
Than have just one be called a dirty coward

JESSICA

We have our babies to be born
You cannot take our men.

FRED

> Jessie dear, please, please Jessie
> I'll be back, Jessie

JESSICA

> You will never come back.
> What I love now will go forever
> Oh Fred, don't go, please don't go

FRED

> You talk in riddles, Jessie,
> First you say I won't come back,
> And then you say I'll come back changed.

John Marshall enters

JOHN

> Oh Jessie, will you read my hand?
> The last thing I shall ever ask of you
> Sweet Jessie.

JESSICA

> Oh John, why are you always so dramatic.
> Give me your hand.
> You will grow old. But there's a jagged line
> No, no, a blurring, what can it mean,
> Oh Fred, I am afraid for all of us.

JOHN

> What is it Jessie, what is it?

JESSICA

> You must not go. You can still draw back!

Kitty has come over to this group

KITTY

> John Marshall, John Marshall, are you going?

JOHN

> Yes Kitty, I am

KITTY

> Oh John, Please don't go, please!
> You're not a soldier, don't you understand?
> You were never born to be a soldier
> You were born to play your guitar John,
> To sing, to be happy, to make others happy.
> You can still turn back
> Don't go John, don't go.

JOHN

> Kitty, Kitty, you really care!

KITTY

> Yes I do John, I do.

FRED

> Jessie, please try to understand, please
> I don't want to go but I must go

JOHN

> It's peace and freedom for everyone

JESSICA

> Can you kill?
> Can you use that thing they call a bayonet
> And run it through the body of a hun!
> I ask you can you kill?

She is screaming now

JOHN

> Jessie, I am ill already.

JESSICA

> You lily livered coward of a man,
> What right have you to go off now to war
> When you can't even wring a chicken's neck,
> Or shoot a dingo preying on your land
> Who do you think you are that you enlist
> To point a gun and shoot your next of kin
> Just because some leader in a far off land has said
> "My man we need you for our country's honor,"
> What's country's honor to the pledge of land
> What's country's honor to a starving farm
> Oh Fred, don't go, don't go.

The band is playing in the distance and more soldiers and friends are entering

PAL

> It won't be long. May be by Xmas even,
> And we'll be home again.

KATE

> Oh war, what monstrous lies you tell your surrogates,

PAL

> But I will come back dear Kate, I will.

KATE

> Oh no, this man I know will not return.
> Pal, I love you too much, I respect you too much
> To try to change your mind—for me
> Our lives go forward step by step
> But both together.
> I will not love you as poor Jessie does
> Who every day will die a little more
> Until when you go down into the grave
> She has gone down before.
> I have my work. And I will love as yet
> I am beloved, a part only, a part.
> I will remember you forever. I'll write
> And I will love you always. Remember that.

PAL

> Oh Kate, someday you'll know how much I love.

> Kate, if I ever say anything in all my life
> That means anything, it is this,
> We will meet again,
> Be it in this world, or the next.

IRIS

> Alright, go fools,
> Innocent chaff for that great war machine
> That churns you up and throws you mangled out.
> What, do you think that you can go to war
> And still not kill? Protect? Oh yes, protect
> But if protection were the issue here
> Then would the world be calling on great skills
> Great skills of government that respect a man
> Not throw his life like fodder to the cows,
> We need more men, fools, fools to give your bodies
> Without one thought on how they plan to use
> The thing your mother raised from infancy
> And gave to you. While with no backward glance
> You throw it all away. Your father's farm
> Does it not have the right to use your strength?

TOWNSPERSON

> The band is coming

PAL

> Oh Iris, please don't speak like that, not now

IRIS

> Oh God, if not now then when—you tell me—ever
> Can noone change your mind?
> Not Jessie's love, not Kate's, not all my womanly anger,
> Can nothing change your mind? It's not too late!

PAL

> Oh Iris some day perhaps someone will understand
> The deep, deep workings of the soul of man
> When he hears the call to duty. You must try
> To understand. And yet I hear the thing
> You tell me. I hear it, but I must go.

DARKIE

> Look it's Campbell's band

The band enters and the men line up as if in a trance. A whistle sounds. They march off stage

Scene 5

The Captain's Office

CAPTAIN

    I asked you here today because you know
    I deeply love you my dear. Your mother died
    In giving birth. She was the bravest soul
    I ever knew with a most discerning mind.
    But my Kate, for that was her name too,
    When I went off to Africa to fight
    The Boer war now they call it. It wasn't then,
    She railed at me. She had the kind of mind
    That I have seen today in you.
    And oh I'm sorry Kate I have not spent
    More time with you as you were growing up,
    But how could I a soldier raise a girl?

KATE

    Oh father, now I wish you had !

CAPTAIN

    Well, I did the best I could
    Sister Margaret at the convent was my friend,
    Your mother's friend. And wise. I trusted her.

KATE

    Oh, it's not just sister Margaret,
    It's accident of birth.

CAPTAIN

    How so?

KATE

    Had I been born a boy would you have sent
    Me to a convent father, would you?

CAPTAIN

    Of course not. You would have stayed with me.

KATE

    And would I be a soldier now?

CAPTAIN

Oh Kate, if you were my son,

KATE

Would I be a soldier now?
Oh hypocrite!

IRIS

Kate, he is your father!

KATE

Yes, my father that I love, oh hypocrite.

CAPTAIN

It's alright Iris. I understand, I do.,
I taught her ever to speak her mind to me,
I understand, I do.
I have a deep foreboding in this war,
Of disaster looming like a heavy cloud
And yet I cannot explain it to myself.
And when today I heard you sounding forth
Among your friends, I felt ashamed to move
And say, "This is my daughter that I love,"
Ashamed because of me, not you and yet
I can't explain it even to myself.
A sense of doom is closing on this war
And it has not begun. And I am here
To draw the young men in., A piper,
A pied piper.

IRIS

To pipe them all to death

CAPTAIN

But yet the cause is just. England has kept
The great powers reconciled by balancing sides
Like dropping measures on a justice scale
But always there has been a sense, that men,
That nations, knew the right from wrong,
But somehow in this trampling over Belgium,
Germany has lost a sense of right and wrong
And tries to justify the act. So clear
A violation that we as soldiers,
Fighting for the peace of nations and sanctity
Of covenants and protection of the weak,
It seems to me will have to go much further
Than just policing violators of a trust.

IRIS

You will do more than kill?

CAPTAIN

Oh Iris, a man that keeps the peace must fight
And sometimes fighting, kill.

But volunteers that keep the peace
Are citizen policemen, nothing more
Not killers but as that's inevitable.

KATE

I think I see. Perhaps I have misjudged you father,

CAPTAIN

Oh how I hope I'll hear you tell me that
When this great war is done.

IRIS

What will change?

CAPTAIN

I wish I knew. I wish I knew.
For what I fear is what you both have said,
That men will die like fodder.
It's men, men, men, they're calling for
As if a life will change a moral code
Because it's sacrificed and offered up
Without an understanding of the cause.
A far better thing it seems to be
To talk to those who planned it, make them see
Every land is sacred and covenants
Are not a scrap of paper to be torn
And tossed upon the wind on some caprice.
But how about your schooling Kate,
What will you do?

KATE

My chance comes by but once
To be a doctor.
When the time has passed for schooling,
It has gone forever.

CAPTAIN

My dear, the hospital's here. Train here.
Stay right here where you have friends,
At least till the war is over
And then perhaps you can try again.
Meantime who knows what you can do
To make this world a better place.
And Iris dear,
I always thought you wanted to be a teacher?

IRIS

I do want to teach
I want to teach things that relate to this world
The activities of this world—

CAPTAIN

My dear, you must learn discipline.
If that's the way you feel

Learn everything the university can teach you,
Just do it.
And then return, like Kate
And teach your daughters to be just like you.

Scene 6

The Rock Pool

Pal is stumbling through the bush shouting incomprehensibly. Madeline is moving from tree to tree watching him. Finally he sits down at the edge and stares into the rock pool

PAL

       Oh, God, speak to me, speak to me
       The clouds are moving across the sky
       The way they're supposed to—
       The trees are still in place
       The rocks—nothing has changed

He picks up a rock and tosses it into the pool

       Yet everything has changed.
       How can a man be tortured like this!
       My country calls yet Jessie's right
       This is my land, my native land
       Why do I have to fight for it?
       Can't those Europeans resolve their differences peaceably?
       One rock tossed in a pool
       And the ripples take everything, everything. *He looks up suddenly*
       Madeline, what are you doing up there?

MADELINE

       Listening to you

PAL

       You are like a siren
       You are so mysterious Madeline,
       I look into your eyes
       And I see a thousand rock pools
       Going back and back and back
       To the very beginning of time.

MADELINE

       Do you see the rainbow serpent
       And my ancient mother Eingana
       Who created everything?

PAL
>No, I see my own soul.

MADELINE
>Then you see the spirit Malinga
>That will not let you die
>I knew it, I knew it
>You live on the thread of the dreamtime.

PAL
>Madeline, I do see something
>It's a woman but she is coming
>Out of the sky!
>This is madness, madness!

MADELINE
>No, Pal, no, listen and look
>You see Malinga?
>You see the spirit Malinga?

PAL
>I don't know the spirit Malinga
>But someone is coming toward me

He grips Madeline's arm
>It's Liberty!

MADELINE
>Liberty?

PAL
>Liberty

MADELINE
>What is Liberty?

PAL
>Freedom! Don't you see her?

MADELINE
>What does she look like?

PAL
>She is tall—well I think she is tall

MADELINE
>What color are her eyes?

PAL
>Brown *Madeline smiles*
>No, blue! No, they are a color
>I have never seen before
>Golden, bronze and everlasting
>Everlasting, she is everlasting
>Oh Madeline, she is beckoning to me.

MADELINE
>It's Malinga
>Protector of the male,
>She has chosen you Pal,

> She will never let you die
> And wherever you go, you will return.

She stares intently at the rock pool

> Pal, is she a serpent?
> It can't be Eingana
> Only women can see Eingana . . . *She turns*
> It is Malinga.
> Oh Pal, where you go, I will go
> You are going to other great continents
> Bigger than this continent
> And I am going too!
> One day, back, back in the dreamtime
> Our ancestors walked a long, long way
> And then the sea came
> And we were cut off
> But we brought with us a secret.
> Eingana, the mother of the orphan gods
> Has it and will not let it go.

PAL

> What are you saying Madeline?

MADELINE

> Liberty, Liberty, is that right?
> I don't know her at all

PAL

> It's freedom Madeline
> Didn't they teach you that at school?

MADELINE

> They taught me words.
> We were free until you came.
> Your people tell us of a word called "freedom"
> Now, there are fences and rooms and this word called "freedom"

PAL

> It's personal freedom

MADELINE

> I am free, I am free.

She begins to dance and Pal joins her

PAL

> But what is your secret Madeline?

MADELINE

> I don't know
> She hasn't given it to me yet
> But she will, she will
> We are going to see the continents, the continents

She twirls around singing and dancing

PAL

> What continents?

MADELINE

       The other continents

PAL

       But how? I'll join the army

       What will you do?

MADELINE

       I don't know. Goodbye Pal

       Goodbye . . . for now . . .

She dives into the rock pool

PAL

       Goodbye Madeline

Scene 7

The Purchase of the Farm

That evening. The home of Pal and Fred's parents. Candlesticks and vases are missing. Kate and Millicent are at the piano.

KATE

        Oh Millicent. what are we going to do?

        How can we tell them?

        How can we?

MILLICENT

        Are you sure Katie? Are you absolutely sure?

        Maybe they just went down there to see what was going on.

        They didn't really believe we'd get the farm.

        We've tried before you know. We couldn't raise the money.

        But this time was different. We had some hope this time.

KATE

        They did Milli. They signed up with all the others.

        We couldn't stop them. We tried Milli.

Millicent turns to the piano and begins to play. Mother comes in and turns to Kate for her approval as the wine glasses are all ready on the table.

KATE

        Oh Mother, it's beautiful.

        You know I could not love you more

        If you had borne and raised me.

        Have you heard from the boys?

MOTHER

        Oh no, they went out very early.

        All this ruckus about the war.

        I hear there was a big commotion

        At Tom Hall this noon. Did you hear anything?

KATE *shifting her position at the piano and coughing in a very embarrassed way*

        Ah, ah, well,

        There was some recruiting I believe. Some men

        I think joined up. But we, we did not stay.

I mean, not Iris, or Jessica or me

MOTHER

Young ladies have no business being there,
But what's it all about? It cannot last,
A war, a war's unthinkable.
We are so far away. I've written home.
Pick some chrysanthemums Milli dear.
That will just be the finishing touch.

Millicent leaves just as Father is entering.

FATHER

Are the boys in yet?

MOTHER

Well it is a surprise my dear.
They won't be rushing home the way they would
If we had told them. Oh Kate
I still cannot believe it. I just can't.
I never thought we'd scrape it all together
Did you?

KATE

No I never did
But the payments will be high?

MOTHER

Oh yes, but that's no matter. Three strong men
And Millicent and me to work the shop
And later on my dear perhaps you'll come
And Jessica that scarry little child
That loves my Fred so madly—
We'll have a lovely family will we not?

FATHER

But what about your schooling Kate, what's happening?

KATE

I can't get in.

FATHER

Is there no hope?

KATE

None. Oh, I'll be a nurse. I'll train somewhere
Like Townsville, Brisbane, then I shall come back.
But there's so much more I could do
If I could become a doctor.
There's so much to be learned about medicine.
Medicine for women—medicine
That concerns itself with land and food from the land
And that's why Pal and I belong together.

FATHER

You two were made for each other my dear.

MOTHER

> Come back and marry Pal dear Kate. There's no need
> To think that you can not still work when children come.
> You'll work, for look at me, there's hardly been a day
> That I've not pulled my weight eh father?
> I've always had the vegetables outside,
> The chickens have been mine, the family meals,
> The shop.

Millicent reenters with chrysanthemums

> Look at those stems. Millicent certainly has a way
> With flowers. I would have carried books you know
> If we'd ever got ahead. The library's poor
> And many's the time I've despaired of things to read.
> The nights are long with only the crickets,
> And the whole town gone to bed.
> But my mother keeps things coming fairly well
> Books and magazines and papers—
> Though nothing about the war—

Jessica enters

> Aha, Jessica,
> Well, why so frazzled child?

Jessica looks at Kate who motions her to be careful

JESSICA

> Oh, nothing really. It's just, it's just
> Some fools are signing up.

MOTHER

> Signing up for what my dear, the war?
> Oh Jessica, our dreams are coming true!

JESSICA

> But what if the war lasts a long, long time
> And Pal and Fred go too?

MOTHER

> Oh they won't, they won't my darling
> Not now we have the farm,
> Now the journey's all worth while, across
> The sea, halfway across a continent,
> A powerful strange land, Australia, isn't it . . .

JESSICA

> It is indeed and it gets in your soul
> And makes you want to hold it forever.

FATHER

> It's a strange, strange call the call of untried land,
> Like some wild beast that must be tamed
> And yet must tame us too for we had plans
> That should have flourished long ago
> If not for stubbornness eluding us

        Like composition of the soil and seeds
        That wouldn't grow. I hope the boys grow keen
        On being seedsmen when they learn this land

MILLICENT

        It's a cruel land sometimes.

PAL and FRED enter

FRED

        Well what's this? It looks like a surprise

He turns to try to put his arms around his mother

        How did you know?

MOTHER

        Know what, we haven't told you yet.

FATHER

        Come fill their glasses and then we'll have a toast!
        To the farm. To the farm for it is ours!

The boys look aghast

PAL

        You bought it?
        How, how did you raise the money?

FATHER

        With every last penny we had.
        Come, drink up. It's only once in a lifetime
        That a man buys a farm. Drink up
        And then we'll sit and plan.
        It'll need every last ounce of energy.
        It'll take everything we have.

PAL

        Oh my God!

FATHER

        Can't believe it ah? I'll tell you neither can I.

FRED

        The candlesticks, the tea set, why everything is gone!

PAL

        The books, the books . . .

MOTHER

        Everything from the past my darling
        But there a future too.
        I never thought that I would feel such joy
        My children around me, my children and land
        Land to put them on to grow and thrive.

PAL

        The payments will be high?

FATHER

        Oh very high, but there'll be three of us.
        I signed everything today. Old Torley's ill.
        We went over to his home, the lawyer came.

We didn't go to town at all.
There is a very quiet moment
      I hear there was a ruckus at Town Hall this noon.
The young people all change positions, cough etc.
      What was it all about? Enlisting men?
      I hear your father was in town too Kate,

KATE
      He's in charge of recruiting. They're recruiting men.

FATHER
      I know they are recruiting, but who of us can go
      With everyone so needed on the land.
      I bet they won't get many from these parts,
      But truth to say I've been so busy of late
      With this important subject well in hand,
      That I've hardly even read the local rag
      About the world's doings, though the war
      Is a sorry business just the same.

FRED *blurting out*
      If you were young, what would you do right now?

FATHER
      You're just eighteen
      You've hardly got a whisker on your chin.

PAL
      What would you do? I'm twenty father.
      England is at war! But they're fighting for freedom
      For the freedom of everyone!

FATHER
      I'd leave the war to those that have the stomach.
      It's a war for honor that is very clear
      And there must be some dozen or more young louts
      That hang around the pubs each day might go
      And do their bit with nothing holding them.
      But all our friends are on the land by now
      Where education's even a touchy thing
      With all the hands so needed on the land.

PAL
      But please father, don't close your eyes to this
      It's freedom, father, it's liberty and justice—

FATHER
      Oh, freedom's at stake most surely.
      I'm only glad that before we gave you birth
      We came out here.

PAL
      How does distance speak to freedom father?

MOTHER
      Oh distance speaks to fear.

Why do we have to bring this subject up right now,
When we all have so much to celebrate
And the tea is almost ready.
Oh I think that I shall never be
Quite as happy as this moment now
Ever in all my life. And yet I should
For we are just beginning on a road—

PAL

Mother, no more, no more, please.

MOTHER

Why Pal what is the matter?
My darling what is wrong?

PAL

I've enlisted mother.

FRED

I have too. I have too.

Scene 8

The same—piano open

MOTHER

> Oh how still and quiet all things are
> When the living sounds have fled. So suddenly,
> What was such a glorious dream has gone,
> All gone, all vanished in a wisp of smoke
> And I am left alone. Oh father, yes
> A good man, a comfort, a partner all my life
> But children, children are something else again.
> Children are life rafts in a turbulent sea,
> Laughing, bobbing, staying all afloat
> Not caring for the waves that lash at them
> Not understanding the peril that they're in.

Millicent coming in with tea

MILLICENT

> Oh mother, you still have me, you still have me

MOTHER

> Millicent, I have thanked God so many times for you.

MILLICENT

> I'll never leave you mother, never.

MOTHER

> Come now child, some young man will come . . .

MILLICENT

> No mother, no young man will come for me,
> Only a soldier would I marry now,
> And they will not return.
> All my young men have gone off together.

There is a knock at the door. Kate is there

> Well Kate, how good to see you. Come on in,
> Is your father gone now too?

Millicent makes Kate some tea

KATE

> Yes. All that would follow him have gone

71

And there arn't many left. Victor even.

MILLICENT

But Victor's not eighteen!

KATE

He lied, he lied. Have you any news of Pal?

they all exchange cards

MOTHER

They both seem happy enough but I wish
They had not joined together.

MILLICENT

Oh Mother, all we can do is pray right now
And Kate, what of you? Will you study here?

KATE

That's what I came to talk about.
My father feels that I should stay here too,
And be among my friends, at least for now.

MOTHER

Well Kate, why don't you come and stay with us,
Pal's room is yours my child. God knows how long
Before the boys will ever return again.
Oh wouldn't that be wonderful?

KATE

I'd love to mother really, yes I would.
But you must let me pay you something for it.
Can you hold till the boys return?

MOTHER

We don't know Kate. We'll try our best you know.
It's not just our boys. It's everyone's that's gone,
No help at all for anyone. No help.

MILLICENT

Mother please don't despair. I'll help
You all I can. I never wanted school.
We can work the shop the way we planned.
We can market food from all the farms around
And send the stuff to Townsville. There's the way.
Mother please don't despair. I cannot bear it.
I loved my brothers so much. I love you too.

She kneels at her mother's feet. There is a loud knock at the door. Kate goes

KATE:

Why Jessie, how are you?

JESSICA

I'm terrible, just terrible.
I wish that I were dead. I want to die.

MOTHER

Why Jessie what on earth's the matter?

JESSICA

>My father turned me out and called me bastard,
>Whore, bitch and more I never even heard before.
>I hate his ugly mind, his wicked leering teeth.
>What right has he to rail at me like that?
>What right has he to try to live my life
>When my Fred has gone and for all I know is on
>Some battleship and out to sea, and all
>My future too. And if he dies I know
>That I shall die.

KATE

>But he won't drown!

JESSICA

>The Indian ocean's reeking with torpedoes,
>And ships are going down like children's toys,
>Thrown in the sea and ill equipped for war.
>Oh whatever gods that rule this crazy world
>I hate you all. What do you know of me?
>I am a woman. I was born to love
>And give you birth, for what I'll never know.
>Destroyers of the good and beautiful
>My Fred is gone. And in my womb I bear
>A child that will outlive you evil ones
>If I don't kill him first. For now I feel
>That life no value has or meaning, none,
>And I am cursed because I bear a son
>Without some idiotic golden ring
>That's supposed to make it legal and me a thing!

MOTHER

>Jessie, Jessie my dear, are you telling us
>That you are bearing Freddie's child?

JESSICA

>I am.

KATE

>Well Jessie . . .

MILLICENT

>Why Jessie . . .

MOTHER

>My darling, did you say just now
>Your father's turned you out?

JESSICA

>Like a dog, like some infected thing he hates.

MOTHER

>Your mother?

JESSICA

>My mother's an appendage.

She's sad, oh yes she's sad but do you know
She never moved an inch when he stood there
And called me all those names I'd never heard,
She didn't stir. She just stood still. Oh God,
Can you imagine being severed from a trunk
And let to fall, without a tear, a step?
She never moved . . .

MOTHER

Oh my dear you must not judge her so.
She has no place to go without your father!

JESSICA

I have no place to go, what's wrong with me?
Why not choose me if choice she had to make?
I want to die.
Oh Freddie, Freddie, where are you?
I'd rather jump into the weir right now
Than ever stand before that man again.

MOTHER

Well Jessie where are your things?

JESSICA *laughing hysterically*

My things, my things?
The little chest my mother gave to me,
It's there by the door. Do you want it? Do you want me?

Millicent rushes to get the chest and bring it in

MOTHER

We want you Jessie.
Come now, have some tea.
Why now I have three daughters, three!

Scene 9

Thursday Island Cable Station

There is a sign on stage. THURSDAY ISLAND CABLE STATION, AUGUST, 1914. There are a few bedraggled soldiers on stage as well as some in brand new uniforms. One is playing a harmonica, **Waltzing Matilda, There's a Long, Long Trail a-winding.** *There is a jungle setting but it is not elaborate.*

VOICES

       All for one and one for all

Nobby, Shorty, Victor, Pal, Jim, Tommy, Billo. Enery, Quinn, Nark come on stage singing,

       Should old acquaintance be forgot,

       And never brought to mind,

       Should old acquaintance be forgot,

       In the days of Auld Lang Syne.

The men are all aware of an officer sauntering by. He importantly clears his throat

JIM

       Now we're in for it.

OFFICER

       Squad—Shun'. Stan' a'tease. Shun. Stan' a'tease.

       Wake up there on the lef'!

       This aint a firin' party for a funeral

       Put some ginger inter it. Now, then—SHUN.

That's better . . . .
Enery. Stand up straight:
There's only one place for yer chest—put it there:
Stick it out, man! STICK IT OUT!
Inflate it or something . . .
Billo, wotcher laughin' at?
Think this is a bloomin' circus, or wot?
STAN' STILL
Squad—right turn! quick march!
Lef' ri', lef' ri', lef' ri',
'Eads up!—'OLD YER EADS UP:
Imagine you can see Aussie UP in the clouds:
YOU ain't swingin yer arms right.
A nice easy swing. Yer ain't shadder sparrin', yer know:
Squad—'alt! STAN' STILL!! NOT A MOOVE!
Yer must stand perfectly still.
I don't care if a bloomin' ostrich bites yer
Yer must STAN' S-T-I-L-L —
Squad! Right turn! Right, not left!
Don't yer know yer lef' 'and from yer right, yet?
Yer'd know alright if yer was asked to produce
Yer lef' 'and for yer pay . . .
Right turn! Wrong again.
Nark, yer 'ad better see the doctor,
Yer must 'ave been given two lef' legs by mistake
Do you want me 'ere bellowing out all day long?

SHORTY *from the rear*

No bloomin' fear

OFFICER

Wot's that? No back chat:
If I 'ear any more back tork like that, inter the
Guard-room yer goes, toot sweet:
Squad: quick march—double
'Eads up—HALT
Wot 'AVE yer done Billo,
Been 'an fell in the mud!
Blimey you blokes is still raw recruits!
Look at yer rifle—
Supposin' yer was to break yer neck
Who'd get into trouble ME, not you
'Ave a bit of consideration for other people:
Orlright—scrape that mud off after . . .
Squad . . . . lef' turn.
Stan' a'tese. Stan'heasy.
Now lads, that'll be all this mornin:
Parade at two-thirty.

Every rifle must be thoroughly cleaned . . .
Squad—shun: Dis-miss:
Turn to yer right when yer dismiss, Enery.
The men break rank, sit down, begin to roll cigarettes, relax

PAL

Well, Darkie, What does your old man say
About the war

DARKIE

Be over by Christmas. he says.
And when I volunteered for Self Defense
It didn't mean I had to go to France.
Eh where did those blighters get their uniforms?

VICTOR

Where did you get your outfits mate?

ENERY

Sydney

SHORTY

Sydney, Cripes.

BILLO *in a new uniform*

Where are you coves from?

PAL

North Queensland.

NARK

What's it like up there?

DARKIE

Like here, hot!

ENERY

Eh, who pinched my chocolate?

VICTOR

I dunno. Can we get uniforms like that?

ENERY

I dunno. I can't find my chocolate
Cadbury's it was.

NOBBY

Well I dunno why I'm going. There's my girl
My girl, she begged me not to go.
And she reads hands you know;
She said she could see some fearful thing
Would happen to me. That I would bring
A sorrow the world has never known
A kind of torment I'd bring back with me
And carry it to my grave. But I'll not die
Across the sea; No hero's death for me.
Yet I shall not die free:

DARKIE

That means that we won't win this war at all.

NOBBY

    She said no one will win.

PAL

    But we must win

VICTOR

    Of course we'll win. Feel that *rolling up his sleeve*
    Hey Nobby, you must bring that girl of yours
    To wish us all goodbye; maybe she'll tell
    What all of us are in for.
    Wish me luck as you wave me goodbye, *singing*
    Cheerio here I go on my way.

NOBBY

    My girl gave me this

PAL

    A packet of seeds

SHORTY

    Cripes

NOBBY

    Custard apple. They won't grow anywhere but here.

JOHN MARSHALL

    Can I have some?

SHORTY

    Me and Victor's got a handkerchief

VICTOR

    We pinched them at the show

He pulls out a large handkerchief

SHORTY

    Mine's blue

NOBBY

    What have you got Pal to protect you against the Hun?

PAL

    Oh, I've got something

SHORTY

    What?

PAL

    It's just a baby owl. I stuffed it when
    I was a kid. My father was so mad
    To think I'd killed an owl, I never could
    Go anywhere without it, as though
    By keeping it, I might make up somehow
    For what I'd done; well now I sometimes feel
    Like that great owl herself who used to sit
    And guard this little thing all day until
    I thought I had outwitted her and used
    My gun to drop in one short moment what
    She ruffled, nursed and cooed to, weeks on end.

SHORTY

    I'd call that a jinx, mate.

VICTOR

    What, to kill an owl?

    If you can't kill an owl you'd better not

    Pick up a bayonet and run it through a hun.

SHORTY

    Cripes. Do you think we'll get as close

    As that? I dunno why I've come.

Looking at Tommy

    Eh, Tommy, Tommy, how old are you?

TOMMY

    How old am I?

    Ah, well, I WROTE eighteen.

BILLO

    You wrote eighteen:

    He wrote eighteen

    Blimey!

    You're nowhere near eighteen mate.

TOMMY

    My mother doesn't know yet.

BILLO

    Silly little bugger.

    What's so flamin'—what's so flamin' attractive

    About signing up for a barmy war?

TOMMY

    I took some wattle

    To protect me from the Hun

BILLO *scornfully*

    Wattle, wattle,

    Who's watching out

    For this silly buggar Tommy?

DARKIE

    His mother thinks

    He's on a trip with me.

BILLO

    Don't envy you

    If anything happens to him.

JIM

    I volunteered for Home Defense and that

    Means hand to hand, but the Hun will have to come

    Before I fight, according to my old man.

PAL

    But it's too late to wait for that!

    The best, the finest things are all cast down

    When man must meet in mortal hand to hand

VICTOR

  Aha. Come on Shorty. Let's have a fight

They wrestle

NOBBY

  Oh, get off me, blokes,—can't you do

  Your fighting over there. All I want is peace.

  Eh Nark, Nark, give us a hand will you

  These buggers are all over me.

  Get off me blokes.

NARK

  Come on break it up, break it up.

  There yer go Nobby

DARKIE

  Oh, this war is nothing Nobby.

  We'll have peace if we all go

  And show the Hun that we mean business too

Victor is flexing his muscles. Shorty and Nark are imitating him. There appears to be some shadow fighting going on in fun

PAL *moving to the front of the stage*

  But we'll not win this war by strength alone

  Without the VISION to anticipate

  Where Fritz will strike and how—

  Where best to use our men

OFFICER

  Attention!

COMMANDING OFFICER *striding in*

  Stand at ease. Stand easy

  You men are now all under my command.

  I want you shaved and tidied up a bit.

  I've requisitioned better outfits

  For the North Queensland men. *looking them up and down*

  I know that you can drill, but discipline

  In everything is what I want from you.

  You're each your brother's keeper through this war;

  Our army is as strong as the weakest link

  And every link's a man. Remember that.

  And remember why we're fighting.

  We're fighting for justice and fair play. *cheers*

  We're fighting for liberty. *more cheers*

  Remember what I said about discipline.

  Good luck gentlemen.

  We'll be shipping out tomorrow. *cheers—he exits*

ENERY

  Ain't no such thing as justice and fair play

  Who took me Cadbury's chocolate?

  Come on, own up.

NARK

>   Eh Enery, is Cadbury's that gooey stuff
>   In the bottom of yer knapsack?

ENERY

>   You just have to put it someplace cold
>   And then it hardens up.
>   You took it, you bloody bastard!

BILLO

>   Well we're still fighting for Liberty Enery
>   Even if there ain't no such thing as Justice
>   Ah, get a load of this tobacco
>   Fair dinkum, it's the best I've ever had

They all get tobacco from Billo and begin to roll cigarettes. Pal ruminates alone

*   *   *

The lights flash on and off again and then there is a black out and silence. When the lights come up again Pal is still at the front of the stage with his hands outstretched to the audience. He turns to face the others who are milling around.

NOBBY

>   Well what's the cause of this 'ere war anyway.

DARKIE

>   That's a good question mate

They start moving towards the front of the stage

>   What do you say, Pal?

PAL

>   Well

SHORTY

>   There's the Kaiser

VICTOR

>   I'll play the Kaiser

He goes to the wings and from the wings upstage the Kaiser appears, the top half of him in his military uniform with a white robe gathered at the waist. One hand is withered. He shouts militantly as he marches across the stage

KAISER

>   Get off the stage and give me room

The soldiers appear to be awed by his presence and jump off the stage; some remain seated on the edge, others go and sit in spare seats in the audience; others sit in the aisles. The Kaiser is obviously enjoying the spotlight which moves with him as he struts across the stage. One of the soldiers shouts

DARKIE

>   I'll play his son the crown prince Frederick

He rushes through the front wings and immediately from the wings upstage, appears Crown Prince Frederick. He is much more slightly built than the Kaiser, wearing a dark royal

81

blue suit with gold braid and cap. He minces on stage completely obsessed with his own importance but in an effeminate way. He takes the spotlight from his father.

CROWN PRINCE *very rhetorically*

>The stars are shining in the heavens tonight,
>
>The orders of honor awarded by dear God
>
>To the house of Hohenzollern for its services.

The spotlight moves back to the Kaiser who puffs out his chest. Meanwhile the Crown Prince moves over in the wings and picks up a globe which he then proceeds to twirl around above his head, tittering ecstatically. The spotlight moves over to him as he picks up the globe and follows him while he is twirling. Then there is a rumbling of drums and German martial music as Bismarck enters in full military and authentic German uniform of 1863. He is carrying a whip, a cat-a-nine-tails with knots at the end of each tail. He cracks the whip expertly and the spotlight moves to him. The Kaiser and the Crown Prince move off stage.

BISMARK

>I'll have a military budget

DARKIE *from the foot of the stage*

>Eh, who's he?

SOLDIER

>I dunno, mate.

PAL

>It's Bismarck

SHORTY

>'Oo?

BISMARCK

>I'll have a military budget.
>
>We must be first in the race for arms.
>
>First, *echoing* first, first, first.

DARKIE

>Eh, yh can't all be the first mate

BISMARCK *very bombastically*

>Everybody needs somebody to love and somebody to hate.

NOBBY

>Eh, I don't hate anybody *Pause*
>
>Except the ser-major.

BISMARCK

>I have my wife to love

As he is speaking a woman centers wearing a long off-white cloak with a hood. Her arms and hands are bare and she crosses them over with her hands on her shoulders. Bismarck continues slowly and deliberately.

>And—Windhorst—to—hate.

At the mention of "Windhorst', he cracks his cat-a-nine-tails and simultaneously a bell rings so that the name is not heard and what the audience hears distinctly are the words 'to-hate'. At the crack of the whip there is some disturbance among the soldiers but the woman advances slowly towards him. Bismark prepares to strike again but the woman is getting very close and the soldiers rush up on stage and try to restrain Bismarck. He yells.

Stage Manager?

The stage manager appears in ordinary working clothes with a pipe in his mouth.

Are we going to have a play or arn't we?

STAGE MANAGER

Hey, get off the stage men,

It's Bismarck's cue.

Your turn comes later.

Bismarck marches to the center of the stage and the spotlight follows him. Francis Joseph of Austria enters. Meanwhile a small table has been placed at the rear of the stage with a jug of water on it. Bismarck leans on this table as Francis Joseph comes up to him. The Kaiser returns with a cloak over his shoulders and becomes his grandfather William I. He appears to be moving toward Francis Joseph who is holding out a gold envelope. Bismarck is now between the two emperors.

FRANCIS JOSEPH

It's an invitation William from all the princes of Germany

BISMARCK

No, No.

He cracks the whip and the paper falls from Francis Joseph's hands, who then steps back, seizes a young man who was standing close to the wings, hauls him desperately on to the stage and stands with a foot on his body while he still looks at Bismarck.

DARKIE *whispering through a microphone*

Eh, who's that?

SHORTY

Serbia

PAL

Piedmont of the Slavs

BISMARCK

The Balkans are no concern of mine

Hungary enters and links arms with Austria and the two men turn to the front of the stage and pull two soldiers on stage. The soldiers struggle a little as Bismarck again cracks his whip, shouts and looks at William I. He takes hold of the jug.

The Balkans are no concern of mine

WILLIAM I *softly as though cowed*

The Balkans are no concern of mine

A bell rings violently as Bismarck snatches the jug from the table and smashes it to the floor breaking out into hysterical sobbing. The soldiers rush up on stage and pick up the pieces of the jug, lead Bismarck off stage and then go back to their places sitting on the edge of the stage and partially in the aisles. In the meantime a Russian has entered upstage left and moved in a little to the center of the stage and a young Turk is standing near the soldiers and looking curiously like them. William is there as is the Kaiser. Austria and Hungary are still linked together and Bosnia and Hercegovenia are still on the floor. A couple of soldiers are still with the woman trying to find a place for her. They stand her in one place then in another. There is dead silence and no other movement as this goes on. Then one calls out from the foot of the stage.

DARKIE

Who is she anyway?

Mary Anneeta Mann

SHORTY

    If you knew who she was
    You would know where to put her.

WOMAN

The voice comes through the microphone and is whispered but is clearly audible.
    I am Liberty, beloved.

NOBBY

    Eh, stage manager?

The stage manager reenters.
    Where do we put Liberty?

STAGE MANAGER

    I don't know

DARKIE

    Where's the director?

SHORTY

    Where's the dramatist?

STAGE MANAGER

    Well we have to go on with the show

Turning to the woman
    Why don't you just stand anywhere
    Till it's your turn.
    You'll get your cue later on.
    Come on now, Alsace-Lorraine?

A soldier runs up

SOLDIER

    I'll play Alsace-Lorraine

The Kaiser strikes with the cat-a-nine-tails and Alsace-Lorraine falls. With the crack of the whip, the bell rings and the woman moves over. She kneels by his side, dropping on his body some red poppies which she has had under her cloak. Then she straightens up, puts a pronged crown on her head, holds a torch high in her right hand, a gold book in her left. She is the Statue of Liberty and steps on to a small platform and is slowly wheeled off the stage. There is the sound of lapping water and a woman's voice comes over the microphone.
    'Give me your tired, your poor,
    Your huddled masses yearning to breathe free,
    The wretched refuse of your teeming shore,
    Send these, the homeless, tempest-tossed to me:
    I lift my lamp beside the golden door'.

The cat-a-nine-tails trails along behind her. Pal jumps up

PAL

    But where do we come in?
    Where do we come in?

The stage manager comes out exasperated.

STAGE MANAGER

    Now look, for the last time,
    You have to wait your cue,
    Everybody gets a turn. It won't be long

But you have to be patient and
You've got to know what you're fighting for.
We can't put you on the stage fighting
If we don't know what you're fighting for
Now can we?

From the wings downstage the Pope enters and walks slowly across the stage looking neither to left nor right. A soldier shouts out at him.

PAL

What are you going to do?

POPE

I pray that the hour of heavenly comfort will come.

A soldier runs down the aisle.

SOLDIER

Man, that's not good enough

He stumbles as he reaches the Pope and pulls at his garment. It falls from his body a crumbled heap of gauze. The Pope stands perfectly still—in flesh-colored tights but only half facing the audience. He is by this time downstage, fairly close to the wings. The soldier stares at the gauze in utter disbelief and incredulity at what he has done. He picks up the gauze and looks at it stupidly, then tears it to shreds in great but mute passion. Another soldier jumps up.

SOLDIER

You can't do that to the pope's garment!

He turns to stop the renting but the garment is already in shreds. He looks around and does not know what to do. He seems to be appealing to the audience as he extends his arms out to them and then back to the Pope. Another soldier runs in with a stool and they sit the old man on it naked. He head is bowed. He remains motionless as they put what bits and pieces over him that they can. The stage manager is again very exasperated.

STAGE MANAGER

Shall we continue?
Austria-Hungry has now annexed Bosnia
Hercegovenia *pointing at them*
Take it from there. Turkey's upset because
Of Russia, and Russia's growling.

The Kaiser takes the spotlight. The stage manager motions to the Kaiser who moves to the center of the stage. He is dragging a tub behind him and the woman re-enters also behind him.

SOLDIER *whispering through the loudspeaker*

Who's the woman now?

SOLDIER

It's Belgium. She's neutral.

Pal jumps on stage again

PAL

What's in the bloody tub?

He puts his hand in and shouts in horror

It's men! It's men!

The lights flash on and off and while they do so, Russia pulls up a tub. France, England and Austria-Hungary do the same. A shot rings out. A voice comes over the microphone.

85

VOICE

        Crown Prince Francis Ferdinand assassinated at Serajevo.

Bells ring, more shots are fired and the militants begin hurling men at each other from their tubs. Some bounce off as if made of rubber, some disintegrate into dust, others burst with brown and green liquid and many burst with red liquid. These shapes of men are about eight inches high and look like little dolls. The lights flash on and off. There is a slight pause as the soldier who first defended the Pope returns. His trousers are torn and there is blood on his arms and legs. He bears a woolen vestment of beautiful cloth but marked with blood and grime. The soldier comes down the center aisle, climbs up on the stage and goes over to the Pope, kneeling by him. He puts the garment on the Pope's shoulders. The Pope rises and the soldier sinks in exhaustion on his stool. The Pope puts his hand on the young man's shoulder and the two remain motionless as the lights begin flashing again. Pal runs in from the rear of the audience shouting

PAL

        Stop, stop . . . stop

Everything dies down and he says stop to the participants and then to his fellow soldiers and then to the audience.

        Stop . . .

        I—want—to—know—

        What—I—am—fighting—for?

Blackout. Then a voice comes over the microphone and two spotlights gradually come up on stage. One is on Pal who is motionless and the other is on the woman who is moving from him towards the wings. Her white cloak is partially thrown off and a glimpse of a red gown can be seen underneath it. This is later shown to be a gown of red poppies.

VOICE

        "The bells of human freedom

        Ring across the sea

        As they have rung a thousand years

        Ringing now for me."

PAL *softly*

        "They woke me from dreaming

        In the dawning of the day.

        The bells of human freedom *exit woman*

        And how could I stay?"

Then as though coming back to reality again he shouts to the audience.

        But that is not freedom.

He turns back to the rest of the stage but everyone is gone. The stage is covered with red poppies. The soldiers have gone too. He stands staring in disbelief then suddenly there is laughter from the wings and all the other soldiers from the beginning of the scene come back as if nothing had happened.

       *   *   *

NOBBY *looking up and coming over*

        Eh, Pal, we've got a song.

        We decided if we're fighting for liberty

We'd better 'ave a song. Come on mates
Let's sing our song

"It's a brown slouch hat with the side turned up
And it means the world to me
It's the symbol of our nation
The land of Liberty.
And the soldiers they wear it
How proudly they bear it
For all the world to see
Just a brown slouch hat
With the side turned up
Headed straight for victory"

DARKIE
Calling to Pal who has not joined them yet

Come on mate.
"Waltzing Matilda, waltzing matilda,
You'll come a waltzing matilda with me
And he sang as he watched and waited
'Till his billy boiled
You'll come a waltzing matilda with me."

Scene 10

Gallipoli—1915

The men are in small boats swaying.
QUINN

> We're coming in closer. We'll take that hill. We'll take it and
> We'll hold it: We'll make them proud of us.

The lights go low.
FIRST VOICE *on tape—cultured English*

> High on the camel's hump of Achi Baba
> He stood beside a clump of mulberry and oak.
> Restlessly the scarlet poppies moved.
> The glistening Dardanelles, a silver thread
> Arced gently round the golden plains of Troy.
> Did this Turk, Mustafa Kemal, know the cause
> For which the valiant Hector fought and died?

The Turks open fire. The men scramble out of the boats and head for the shore
SECOND VOICE *on tape Uneducated Australian*

> Cast off and drift astern 'e says,
> And slowly we drift astern.
> Then crack—crack, zing~zing,
> The surrounding 'ills open fire on us;
> Our oars are splintered
> Boats are sinking fast,
> We scramble out. Some mates are dead,
> Our packs are water-soaked.
> 'Fix bayonets', 'e says,
> And away we scramble up the bloody 'ills.

FIRST VOICE

> They rose up from the sandbanks on the beach,
> The cliff beyond was belching fire and death:
> Fearful and exultant on the sea,
> We leaned and looked, blood racing through our veins.
> Our souls were fighting with those struggling men,
> Their bayonets flashing in the eastern sun.

88

THIRD VOICE *Mustafa Kemal—accent*
>We must hurl the invader back into the sea.
>Not for glory we fight but for our fatherland,
>And rest or comfort now, deprives our country
>Of freedom and peace forever. I do not order
>You to attack. I order you to die!

FIRST VOICE
>Bleeding, persisting, conquering, they threw
>A glittering sheen around them, scintillating
>Like a sea of liquid burnished steel
>Far more alive than the molten sun it mocked,
>Straining, suffering, emanating swathes
>Of terrible searchlight: Haloed around our men
>A cloth of living silver; and we could hear
>"Go on you devils, lads, and give 'em hell!"
>Resistance in the village, also fierce
>At last was overcome. Survivors streamed
>Toward Achi Baba and the olive groves.

SECOND VOICE
>And then we knew we couldn't oust the Turk,
>"Dig in," "dig in,"
>And we dug in all over the flamin' cove.

THIRD VOICE
>The blanket of night has lifted and now to attack.
>"Soldiers, we shall defeat this valiant foe
>And drive him back to the sea. But wait for me.
>Let me get out in front and wave my whip
>And then you all rush forward and assault!"

FIRST VOICE
>Like a river that had burst its banks they leapt
>In an unstemmable tide shouting "allah"
>Exalted and fanatical, those Turks
>Following Mustafa Kemal into hell.

SECOND VOICE—*tragically, slowly, exhaustedly*
>And then we knew we couldn't oust the Turk.
>"Dig in, dig in",
>And we dug in all over Anzac Cove.

FIRST VOICE
>Silhouetted against the invading dawn he stood,
>Victorious on his pinnacle of ruin!

CHORUS OF SOLDIERS' VOICES *slowly, exhaustedly*
>Anzac, Anzac, long live the glorious name,
>Anzac, Anzac, that's where they played the game.
>And when the war is over, and peace again there'll be,
>You'll find that name on the scrolls of fame,

That's A-N-Z-A-C.

DUGOUT 1
The lights go low and come up on a dugout, cut into the side of the hill. Nark has his jacket across his knees searching for fleas etc. Jim is writing a letter, also Nobby.

JIM

"Dear Eileen. When you held me that day at the Town Hall, for the first time I felt you really cared for me.
It's hard for a bloke to know that a girl really cares especially such a popular lass as you are.
Now I feel I really do have something special to fight for.
Don't go out with any cold footers now and someday soon I'll be back to you.
Yours Jimmie"

NOBBY

"Me darling girl. You would be proud of us all. Major Quinn is famous.
Quinn's Post was taken by the Anzacs and Johnny Turk has never been able to get it back.
Poor Quinn was killed however. We all miss him.
He was a Major but he was always one of us.
Thanks for the socks. Can't say silk goes over too well in the mud.
You did say I would return didn't you? Love Nobby".

WIRE GULLEY
SERGEANT'S VOICE

Forward, move forward.

Several men fall into a trench each on top of the other
JOHN MARSHALL begins to shake and scream. A couple of soldiers hold him down while others come up with their guns looking out
DARKIE

They're all dead! My God they're all dead. We can't stay here!
Calm down John, they'll hear us

NARK

Watch out for the snipers. There have to be snipers here.

ENERY

Here we go, come on—this way . . .
Come on. Hurry.

DUGOUT 11
Pal gets up and looks out of his dugout. He catches sight of Tommy stumbling half dazed
PAL

Tommy, in here. Quickly.

TOMMY

I'm lost. I'm lost. I came out for water and I can't find my way back.
They must be sapping somewhere else.
Everybody's dead over there.

PAL
>Here sit down. You can't go out again now. Beachy Bill's too vicious. Here
handing him paper and rummaging for a pencil
>Here, write a letter. They're picking up letters tonight.
>Then, go this way to Darkie. Tell him we're here.
>Tell him we're coming to see him sometime—after dark
>Do it—write your letter then GO!

TOMMY
>"Dear Mum. I love you very much. I have enlisted but don't blame Darkie.
>He tried to stop me but he couldn't. I wrote eighteen.
>I have to see the world. No one will ever make fun of me again for now everyone will know that I am a man.
>Your devoted son, Tommy." *He exits.*

MOMENTARY BLACKOUT

A sign on top reads HOTEL DE BOULIBIF. A sign on one side where the sandbags are propped up, reads NOTICE, TREAD GENTLY, and on the other side a pointer reading, CONSTANTINOPLE—TO THE HAREMS. On the other side to the front of the stage are a number of wooden crosses with graves marked with pebbles around them and a sign at the extreme front side reading DANGER. NIGHT ROAD ONLY. It is fairly dark and along this road, Pal, Shorty and Nobby are making their way the best way they can. There are intermittent flashes of light.

SHORTY

       Watch it, Nobby

NOBBY

       It's these damn pebbles all around the graves.

PAL

       Down

They throw themselves down as a flash of light explodes over their heads

       Come on, we're nearly there.

NOBBY *reading*

HOTEL DE BOULIBIF, that's it. Hurry

They peer into the dugout. There is very poor light inside but some activity is going on. They wait. There is a terrifying yell as Darkie screams and runs outside tripping over the sign TO CONSTANTINOPLE before he stops. He stares up at Pal

DARKIE

       Oh, my God, you look like Pal

NOBBY

       But it is Pal, Darkie. Are you gone crackers or something?

DARKIE *getting up and feeling Pal all over*

       Oh, Pal, I'm sorry. I had a kind of dream.

       I saw you blasted out by Beachy Bill

       And blown to smithereens and it was as if

       I died myself, or part of me, you know.

A short dark figure comes to the edge of the dugout and peers out. It is Razzy, a Maltese

RAZZY

       Darkie, Darkie!

DARKIE

       I'm O.K. Razzy *They all move inside*

RAZZY

       Maybe you want hot water now. I'll go

       And then when I come back you might be done with Tommy eh?

Darkie waves him off and begins to scrape the wall

NOBBY

       Cozy little joint. Reminds me of home.

PAL

       We heard your outfit moved up so we came

       As soon as things eased up a bit. You know

       Victor's got a stripe already and—

       What's that Darkie?

He points to a bundle in the corner from which it looks as though there is an arm sticking out.

SHORTY

       Can't you sit down and talk to a bloke, Darkie?

DARKIE

       I'm nearly done. I'm nearly done.

SHORTY

       Cripes Darkie. What are you scraping?

DARKIE

> Tommy, Tommy. ~ The rest is over there

pointing to the bundle and then sitting down

> Well blokes, I'm glad to see you. I've missed you all.
>
> Tommy's just a kid. A dreamer too,
>
> A child, like Pal, so innocent of what
>
> This war's about. And always talks of peace.
>
> His mother said . . .
>
> For me to take good care of him. She sent
>
> Some wattle in her letter and wrote
>
> The strangest thing.

He fumbles for the letter and finds it. He holds it as though he is reading it but a woman's voice comes over the microphone

VOICE

> Dear Tommy,
>
> The wattle tree we planted on the day
>
> That you were born, has never been
>
> More beautiful. And last night in my dream
>
> I felt the joy of all your childhood years;
>
> I saw you standing in a blaze of light;
>
> A dove was flying toward your open hand
>
> And Tommy dear, you looked so beautiful.
>
> But then I heard the shots and from the sky
>
> A winding sheet was drawn around your head,
>
> And they led you stumbling, Tommy, up to heaven.

Razzy comes to the door, a billy of hot water in one hand.

DARKIE

> Razzy, meet my cobbers. We're all from
>
> The same part of our country. Shorty, Pal
>
> And Nobby here. This is Razzy, mates.

Razzy stumbles, almost upsetting the billy of hot water. Darkie looks at him closely then pours some contents of a bottle into the mugs and then the hot water

DARKIE

> Beachy Bill is pretty wild tonight.
>
> It almost seems as if this whole attack
>
> Is doomed to failure and that we must pay
>
> With all our blood for some great crime that we can never know.

RAZZY

> Did Tommy go to heaven, do you think?

NOBBY

> Oh, sure. He went on wings so strong and broad
>
> That Beachy Bill looked like a cracker night
>
> With Abdul and us all playing games before we went to bed.

RAZZY *taking him seriously*

> I think I'll make some wings.
>
> I want to go to heaven when I die.

SHORTY

      Cripes I'm feeling queer

PAL

      But what I want to know
      Is how you thought that it was me
      All blown to smithereens, why me? why me?

DARKIE

      Because . . .
      As I said before, I feel a jinx;
      I feel we are betrayed, Pal! Our love,
      Held in our open hand extended,
      Whipped by a lash that cuts right through the flesh;
      And all our hopes and dreams exploding
      In Beachy Bill, throw up our ghostly soul
      Whose voice cries out for all the world to hear
      That we have been betrayed!

SHORTY

      But can soul,
      A disembodied spirit, haunt the earth?

RAZZY

      Madre Mia, have mercy on us!

PAL

      Just to adjust a wrong we do not know?

DARKIE

      That's what I feel. That we'll not rest, who die
      In vain on this, our first big battlefield.

NOBBY

      Eh I think we'd better go. The air's all queer.
      You blokes are going crackers.

SHORTY

      Cripes.
      I've got goose pimples crawling down my spine.

NOBBY

      Mind you, I'm willing to forget
      That this 'ere chat ever took place.

DARKIE

      Oh, come on, don't go,
      Razzy'll get some more hot stuff.

Razzy jumps up anxious to be gone, then he pauses at the door

RAZZY

      Do you think I ought to take my wings?

SHORTY

      Go on! *waving him out*

PAL

      But a vision of peace can never die.
      It might just sleep a while, or men forget,

In thoughts of war, what peace is really like.

NOBBY

Come on, let's go . . . It'll soon be dawn

And then we won't he able to.

DARKIE *coming to the edge of the dugout*

It's Beachy Bill exploding in the night,

That's enough to tremble any strong man's mind,

And press a fear deep into his heart,

That's heavier far, and far more terrifying

Than thoughts of just this body's life and death.

PAL

Goodbye Darkie

SHORTY, NOBBY

Goodbye.

In the half light the men walk back until they come to the graves marked with pebbles when there is a blinding flash and than complete darkness on stage. After a couple of seconds a little light comes on and two stretcher bearers are seen walking across the stage

FIRST STRETCHER BEARER

This one's dead. Maltese

SECOND STRETCHER BEARER

This one's alive. And this.

FIRST S.B.

What's this one?

SECOND S.B.

He's got no pulse.

FIRST S.B.

But he's alive.

SECOND S.B.

He's dead.

FIRST S.B.

He looks alive.

SECOND S.B.

He's dead

FIRST S.B.

You sure?

SECOND S.B.

Sure.

Shorty and Nobby are lifted on to the one stretcher and carried away. Razzy gets up stiffly and walks over to the wings. Pal gets up. His face and hands are white. He turns to walk slowly and normally off stage.

Scene 11

The Home. The News

The same house in town 1915.
Millicent is making tea

JESSICA

        The Dardanelles is taking all our men.

        I didn't buy the paper. I couldn't bear—

        I just looked down the lists of killed.

        You know John Marshall's wounded and he's coming home.

        His sister met me in the street and said

        He's shell shocked. I'm not sure what that means.

        Victor's dead you know. He died of wounds.

        Oh God. I'd rather be a man ten times

        Than sit and wait like this and every day

        Another death within your soul. Each day

        A shrivelling up. My heart is filled with stones

        That clank against each other all the time

        And weigh me down like lead so I can't move.

MOTHER

        Darling, it's the child. Remember the child.

Millicent gives her tea

MILLICENT

        Dear Jessie, have you picked a name?

JESSICA

        A name for what, the child, the child, Oh God

        How can I think of life when Freddie's dead?

MOTHER

        Freddie's not dead. Oh darling Jessie please,

        It can't go on much longer Jessie dear

        And he'll come back. John Marshall's coming back.

JESSICA

        John Marshall's crazy, that's what shell shock means,

FATHER *entering*

It's no day to be ploughing on a farm
I met poor Dunbar. Oh it's pitiful.
Oh thank you Millicent. Thank God for daughters *drinking tea*
JESSICA

If you had daughters all instead of sons,
There'd be no war! If you gave women power
There'd be no war.
KATE *entering*

Oh, oh, oh, is everything alright?
Why, everyone is home. I thought I'd be the first.
I got off early.
FATHER

There's much bad news all over.
I met poor Dunbar. He was sitting in the rain.
His lad's been killed. They didn't even know
That he'd joined up. They thought he was in Sydney.
At least we have had time to be prepared . . .
JESSICA

Prepared for what? For Freddie's death?
Shot in the head, the heart, the arm, the leg,
What part of dying can we prepare for now?
John Marshall's gone insane and any day
A telegram will come . . .
He'll knock upon that door and say "for you,"
"We regret: for you" . . . we have killed . . . for you
We have taken him . . . for you . . . We have mangled him.
We have killed him . . . for you." . . . *she is shouting*
Father and Kate restrain her
MOTHER

Jessie, darling Jessie, please, please try
Here take this. Take her upstairs Kate,
Jessie dear, do rest, please, please.
For the sake of the child.
Kate takes her away and returns shortly after
FATHER:

I couldn't work. I couldn't work.
I saw that grey cloud gathering. I know it's going to rain
And I watched it moving forward
Till it covered the sun. And Dunbar came.
The Dardanelles is a death trap Milli dear.
They can't move forward and they can't retreat.
It seems the beach is really very narrow,
And the Turk is on the cliffs.
We're not real sure that both the boys are there
But I think they are, dear Milli, I think they are.

MOTHER

     Then we had better pray that's all.
     Kate, Oh Kate, will Jessie be alright?

KATE

     Sometimes I fear for her mind.
     I don't know what will happen if Fred is killed.
     Jessie is all emotion. There is no way
     That she can ever be reconciled to this.
     There is no argument I haven't used
     Not even hope to live to bear the child !
     If I could find the man that started this
     I'd murder him with my bare hands.

FATHER

     Oh Kate it's something in man's very soul
     That must be better than the next. My dear
     If women like you could tame that roaring hound
     That rears up lusty in the soul of man
     Whenever he feels challenged! If only you could,
     If only, but they would not listen Kate.
     The men that start these wars are womanless . . .

There is a knock at the door. Everyone is startled. Millicent opens the door

IRIS

     Good day
     Why are you all sitting here?
     I knocked on purpose.
     There's been a great attack. And telegrams
     Are speeding everywhere. Are you alright?
     I had to come and see you.

KATE

     I came home early. I got an urge to come.

MILLICENT *going to the window*

     The lightning. It struck the ground. *there is a heavy clap of thunder*
     You can see it! It's hail!

The noise is deafening for a while

FATHER

     The hail won't last. Close all the windows, quick.
     It's hail and then the rain. We need it
     And after that the sun will shine again.
     The sun always shines again.

JESSICA

     I thought I heard the door. I heard a knock.

MOTHER

     No, it was just the thunder and the hail

JESSICA

     I heard a knock. I heard a knock.

IRIS *coming into the room*

No Jessie, no, it wasn't anything.

JESSICA

I heard a knock!

IRIS:

Look, I'll show you Jessie,

She opens the door as a telegram boy stumbles in, drenched. He holds a telegram in his hand. Jessie and Kate look at each other as Father walks over and takes it. He opens it and as he does so, Jessica screams.

JESSICA

It's Fred, It's Fred!

She collapses. The telegraph boy has not gone but is rummaging in his pockets. The wind and rain are blowing through the door. Father looks and motions him to leave.

BOY *finding another telegram*

I had two for you. I had two. *holding the second one out.*

Scene 12

The Home—The Next Morning

FATHER *to Iris*

>Good morning, my dear,
>
>Milli dear, would you mind if I went to the farm today.
>
>I'll come home early but I can't stay here.

She beckons him to go., He turns just as he reaches the front door and then goes out. Millicent rushes sobbing to her mother

IRIS

>Oh Milli, his hair*! It has gone completely gray*

Her mother nods. There is a noise outside the door. Jessica enters, close to her time to deliver, in her night gown, her hair completely dishevelled, hands stretched out

JESSICA

>Is that you Freddie? I thought I heard a noise.
>
>Is that you Freddie? Freddie,
>
>Why women! you're all women!
>
>Oh God, where is my man, where is my man?
>
>Don't touch me. Let me go.
>
>I heard a noise. Freddie was calling me
>
>"Jessie, Jessie." I'm coming, I'm coming Fred,
>
>I cannot live without you.

The reverie is over and she bursts into tears

IRIS

>Have some tea Jessie. Oh feel that baby,
>
>I'm sure it will be a boy.

Millicent starts to brush Jessie's hair

MILLICENT

>Yes it'll be a boy for sure, won't it Jessie.

JESSICA

>A boy, a boy, do you think it'll be a boy

MILLICENT

>Of course, it will be a boy.
>
>It'll be the spitting image . . .

She stops suddenly, drops the brush and runs to the other room
JESSICA

        I feel like a cow. Oh why is it so hot

        Oh Iris my mind.

        My mind is running like a naked thing

        It has gone away from me. Oh Iris

        I can't keep up with it. I follow,

        My arms reach out to hold, but it's gone . . .

        And then I see my Fred upon the sea.

        But just his head and he is floundering

        And then I hear a shot and all his face

        Is covered with blood and the sea becomes blood red

        Blood red. Everything blood red

        And then he sinks and he never rises. I look.

        Why is it that he never surfaces?

She shakes Iris

        Why is it? Tell me why!!

IRIS

        He's dead Jessie. He'll not come back

JESSICA

        They killed him then, the snipers. They killed him.

        I saw that Turk. I saw him high on the cliff.

        He had a long gun and he leaned it on a rock

        He aimed and aimed and waited and I shouted out to him

        Stop, stop . . . .

She shakes Iris

        Why won't he stop? You stop him!

IRIS

        He's dead, Jessie.

JESSICA:

        No, he's not dead. You've got it all mixed up.

        It's me. It's me.

        I'm in quick sand. It's up to here. I'm sinking.

        I can't lift my feet. It will kill the child.

        It's up to my waist.

Iris grips both her wrists and pulls her. It takes all her effort to move her from the spot
IRIS

        He's dead Jessie. Look to the child.

JESSICA

        It was the child they killed.

        I saw you strike his gun Iris. I saw you

        But it still went off and hit me in the belly

        And killed my child. Look, look, it's gone!

She feels her stomach
IRIS:

        The child is alive Jessie. Millicent get Kate

MOTHER *sitting on the couch*

> Jessie do you know how much I love you. Do you?
> Look at me Jessie. Jessie look at me.
> No, no, look at me Jessie. Stay looking at me.
> There are things I have to tell you Jessie.
> Your mind, Jessie, I see it, don't let go
> Hold on to it Jessie. Don't ever let it go,
> And listen Jessie, listen. Freddie is dead
> He's dead Jessie. Hold on. And Pal is dead.
> Don't look away Jessie. Look at me.
> Soon you'll be a mother. Like me. There's something
> I have to tell you Jessie. Listen
> The love a mother bears a child is greater,
> Greater Jessie. Do you hear me?
> Do you hear me Jessie darling do you hear?
> The love for a child is greater than the love
> For a man. It's greater Jessie. Do you hear?
> Your child will live. And you will love him so much

JESSICA:

> Child? Did you say child ? What child?

MOTHER

> Your child. Jessie. The one that's right in here.

JESSIE

> I'll love it? I'll never love again.

MOTHER

> The child Jessie. You'll always love the child.

JESSICA:

> I have no child. What are you talking about?

Kate enters with Iris

MOTHER

> Oh Kate, her mind is going

KATE

> Jessie, do you know me?

JESSICA

> Why of course. You're Kate that sent your Pal to war
> But I held on to Fred. I wouldn't let him go
> I got a rope and tied our bodies up
> And all day long we lay in one embrace.
> But after that something went wrong
> My mind went off alone all naked
> And left my body there,
> And now I'm all mixed up.

KATE

> Jessie. take this and let's go back to bed.
> Iris and I will help you and we'll stay
> And be near you. We'll all take turns. Come on.

They take her through the side door. Kate returns in a few minutes

MILLICENT

> Would you like some more tea, Mother?
>
> The baby will be alright

MOTHER

> But I don't know whether Jessie will.

KATE

> We'll have to keep someone with Jessie all the time.
>
> Oh thanks, Millicent. I'm really done in.

MILLICENT

> What's happening at the hospital?

KATE

> There's hardly a house in town that's left untouched.
>
> There'll never be another Gallipoli.
>
> There doesn't seem to be a single man
>
> That's coming back from there unharmed !
>
> I've got a few days off. Matron is worried
>
> She knows how much . . .
>
> Jessie and I are so different. I wish . . .

MOTHER

> Oh darling, grief is such a crazy animal
>
> It takes all different forms. Yet none can say
>
> Whose love is deeper.
>
> I do not know how we can all survive.
>
> It's only time and effort on our part
>
> To find a way. To make a way, sweet Kate.

Scene 13

The Somme—1916

A sign is up on stage, AMPHITHEATRE OF THE VALLEY OF THE SHADOW OF DEATH.
(The war of attrition). There are a couple of parapets on stage in a half light.
The men are ordered over the top in waves. They are dressed in the uniform of their country
or with their country's name on a T-shirt, England, France, Germany, Russia, Italy, Australia.
There is a whistle then ADVANCE in each of the different languages and the first
line of their national anthem. All go over in formation except the Australians who twist and
turn, shout and blaspheme. After this there is no other sound from the men, only the rat-a-tat
of the machine guns for each wave of men and again at the very end. Then at the front of the
stage an officer walks in, accompanied by Pal who is now a lieutenant.

OFFICER

    We have to silence that pill box.

    We'll never reach our objective.

PAL

    I think it can be taken.

    Give me six men and cover us.

OFFICER

    It's almost certain death

    And we couldn't come back for you.

PAL

    Let me try

OFFICER

    Take whoever you want

CORPORAL *coming up*

    Shall I give the order again sir?

OFFICER

    Cover those men,

    Noone goes over the top again

    Until they reach the pill box.

    God help them. *shouting* Cover them.

There is a rat-tatting and then a tremendous explosion. Pal stumbles in from the stage front
left, bleeding from his stomach and falls on an incline towards the front of the stage. His
voice comes in a whisper over a microphone. The lights are very low

PAL

Now I know what he meant,
That officer that drilled us on Gallipoli.
"You men of Anzac are brave and tough
But your lives belong to your country so take care
Not to throw away recklessly what we have trained,
And depend upon, till all the world is free.
Only when you've paid the price
Can you indulge in camaraderie."

Another jovial voice breaks in on the microphone

VOICE

How many Turks ser-major,
Before my life belongs to me?

Back to Pal's voice as above

PAL

"You will know," he answered solemnly
Hmmmmm.

VOICE *over the microphone*

Oh Lamb of God; that takest away the sins of the world;
Grant us thy peace.
Oh Lamb of God that takest away the sins of the world:
Have mercy upon us.

While this is being spoken, the lights are flashing on and off. Then there is a very soft light on stage. A flute plays 'There's a long, long trail a-winding'. The 'valley' is covered with white and black smoke. A single rifle is fired. There is a short flash of light, long flashes of small lights. A machine gun is firing. Huge long flashes, cannon firing. Tremendous flashes, shells exploding. Then it becomes quiet. Ths vapor is curling around and the colors are murky. Pal is propped up on an incline of ground. He is bleeding profusely from the stomach but there is only a half light on stage. Soon a figure can be distinguished hovering around him. It is Death in a long black gown and a cream colored mask, but Pal appears apprehensive.

The figure comes in eerily laughing but a little way into the stage stops and looks around at the carnage. The laughing stops as DEATH is looking around almost taken aback. She goes to bodies, turns them over, looks at them, comes close to PAL but shudders and steps back each time she tries to approach. She finally starts laughing again.

PAL

I know who you are, and why you're stalking me.
Come, why do you seem to be afraid of me?

DEATH

I have no jurisdiction.

PAL *begins to laugh*

Come, take me. Take me. I'm not afraid to die—

They both begin to laugh together. Then Death stops and goes over to some bodies, moving come of them with her toe

DEATH

But I don't want all these.
Save some for tomorrow.

PAL goes on laughing. She comes over to him but stops short again

DEATH

> It's you I want.

PAL

> Take this body woman. I'm not afraid to die.

DEATH

> Agh

PAL

> You will never have my spirit. Never, never.
> My spirit will live on, ha, ha, ha, ha . . . .

DEATH is gesticulating and Pal goes on laughing. Then she catches sight of someone walking in from the rear of the audience. She has the cream colored cloak and cape over a gown of red poppies

PAL

> But who is that woman? I have seen her before.

DEATH *who dislikes Liberty intensely*

> There are many like her, yet she is only one.

LIBERTY

> I am Liberty beloved
> Do you not know me?

PAL

> You are a woman with incense burning
> You are a nurse to comfort me.
> You are my Kate.
> Are you my Kate?

LIBERTY

> I am Liberty beloved.
> I am coming to set you free,
> But you must learn to know me.

PAL

> I don't understand.

DEATH *spitting it out*

> Look at this woman
> She is IMMORTAL because of YOU

PAL

> I see a shadow on the ground
> Falling as flowers
> Are strewn around

LIBERTY

> Remember my shadow

PAL

> I only know the shadows of my men
> Buried in mud
> Dying for Liberty
> Dying for Justice
> Words, words,

We are all dying for words
That mean nothing.
Wait—
What is happening here?

Liberty is leading the soldiers who have just fallen in the onslaught. Death is following behind. They take a few steps forward and then a few back as if drawn by almost equal forces.

PAL

Why it's my men! It's my own men:

LIBERTY returns

PAL

Who ARE you?

LIBERTY

I am Liberty beloved. Do you still not recognize me?
Were you not dreaming just now beloved?

PAL

Yes I was dreaming and I saw my men
I DID see my men

LIBERTY

Not a sparrow falls to the earth beloved
That the eye of God does not see
Yet many are still born in bondage,
And they too, must be free.

Death is spitting at Liberty and is exhibiting all the signs of jealousy and fury

PAL

But what can we do about it?
Haven't we done enough?
Can we give more than our lives?

LIBERTY

Yes more.

Death is very angry

PAL

More than a life?

LIBERTY

More, much more.

She begins to take off her cape of red poppies

PAL

Don't talk-to-me of flowers
When all I see is blood.

LIBERTY

No drop of blood is ever shed
That does not nurture the flower of love,
And no flower withers beloved
That my shadow does not know.

PAL

But what of those that die unjustly

107

Betrayed as we are now?

There is a long pause

LIBERTY

No man can ever be betrayed
That understands his God

PAL

But who is this one coming,
And moving so urgently,
As if conjured up by my thinking?

Another figure is coming in from the rear of the audience dressed in a white gown

DEATH *springs up and approaches the figure*

He is mortal
You cannot reveal this to him

ETERNAL JUSTICE *to Death*

Stand aside

to Pal

I am Justice Eternal
And I love Liberty

They both begin to move away

PAL

Don't go. I will try harder to understand you!
I will try harder,

DEATH is beginning to laugh again and making herself a nuisance but as Pal speaks these words Liberty and Eternal Justice turn to look at him and begin to come back. Death cowers down

LIBERTY *to Death*

Go from this place
All these are yours.
Take them and GO

DEATH *cowering*

I shall return

LIBERTY *kneeling by Pal*

You must learn to know me.
There is a time to pause
And a time to act.
When the time for action passes
The sacrifice must be made.

PAL

A time to pause and a time to act
But how can I know the difference?

LIBERTY

You must learn to know.
Go seek the cause beloved
And the new world shall be yours.
Nor never let one moment pass
To act for ME

        Vigilance is a joy beloved

        When you learn to know me.

There is a loud explosion and Pal is sent reeling back again

LIBERTY

        Stretcher bearers

        Two stretcher bearers enter

FIRST STRETCHER BEARER

        This one's dead

SECOND S.B.

        He still has a pulse

FIRST S.B.

        No, he's dead.

SECOND S. B.

        Sure?

FIRST S.B.

        I'm not sure.

LIGHTS

Scene 14

The Return

People are milling around. There a few stands set up, one with water and tea and drinks, another bandages and another blankets. Townspeople are going back and forth.

MRS. DUNBAR

       Oh God have mercy, God have mercy. God have mercy

While the other girls are tending the tables and preparations Ilene enters a little dazed or out of this world. She has a huge basket of wildflowers she has just been picking on the way over.

ILENE

       Flowers, I have flowers for everyone.

She gives a flower to Mrs. Dunbar who dashes it to the ground

MRS. DUNBAR

       Oh God have mercy.

TOWNSPERSON

       Can you hear anything?

ILENE

       Here is a flower for you.

Ilene continues walking around with her flowers and a long string of safety pins attached to the basket.

FATHER

       Oh my dearest child flowers, flowers . . .

       I'll have a flower

He looks into Ilene's face then throws his arms around her

ILENE

       Flowers, flowers, here are flowers,

       Do accept the flowers

       Take a flower everyone.

MRS. DUNBAR *to Father*

       Oh why didn't I let them go

       To the weir that day.

       Your boys went

       Everyone had so much fun

       And my boys didn't go

Oh, I'll never forgive myself

FATHER

Oh don't take on so

Really dear, don't think about it

A whistle is heard from afar off—a freight train passes

The girls are working at the first aid stations and at the sound of the whistle the band begins to play

IRIS

Why is the band playing?

KITTY

The band has to be playing

Dear God, fill the sky with music

Music is the only thing in this whole world

That we can do together.

I am utterly terrified

Oh Iris, hold me, held me please

The two girls sway together

Music is always something

You can give yourself to.

KATE

Like a hypodermic needle

To deaden out the pain

When the soul is bleeding inwardly

And will never laugh again . . .

Kitty breaks off from Iris and holds Kate

KITTY

Katie, don't begrudge them,

What else is left to them?

They went for their country's glory

And they're coming back maimed and wounded

And if the band is playing Katie

It's playing for them.

KATE *breaking away*

I know, I know. Let's finish our work here.

The band is playing louder and the excitement is at a high pitch.

KATE *shouting*

We've all got our assignments.

Some families are not here from the west

And all of them have to come and check with us.

I'll have to go. I'll see you later on.

Strobe lights with only one or two men coming in from the train There is the noise of an Australian train clunking to a halt, cheers, the sound of doors opening wild cheers that diminish and diminish to sobs. Possibly the tape of "And the band played Waltzing Matilda" which the band does indeed start to play after a few moments of silence. The movement is that of a flurry to clear the stage as quickly as possible.

111

MRS. DUNBAR *alone*

        Far better that your sons were killed
        Than to return like this. They've sent to us
        The bits and pieces of the war machine
        That can be used no more. Oh Pal, thank God
        Your sons were killed. At least your life is clear.
        You can go on and know that they are dead
        And never will come back. My son's a lump,
        No arms, no legs, he cannot even speak.
        Oh God, what fool could welcome that!
        And Ralph is blinded. Far better he be dead
        Than never see the land he loves so well.
        Oh curses on the governments of man
        That use the flower of youth so treacherously.
        I wish my son had never yet been born
        Than live a vegetable for us to tend
        And pity every day until we die
        When other ruder hands will take him in.
        I'm tempted with my very hand, I am
        To strike him down and bury him myself
        And let the devil take me for the deed.
        Oh thank God that your two boys were killed:

KITTY

        John Marshall, John Marshall:

John Marshall stands in a bedraggled uniform, crouched and staring around as if expecting a bomb to explode over his head. He jumps as if struck as Kitty screams and looks at her completely uncomprehendingly.

        John Marshall, John, John

Kitty holds out her hands to him but he springs back. He starts rubbing his hands together as if trying to clean them. He sees the blankets and grabs one and throws it over his head as if to shield himself from something. Ilene moves over and puts her arms around Kitty and the two girls try to approach him, Ilene holding a flower. He panics and looks for a place to run to as Father and Dunbar take his arms firmly and lead him off stage. The two girls sway together

ILENE

        Where are our boys? Where are our beautiful boys?

IRIS

        Jessie has seen all this for weeks. She has.
        She has described minutely all these things
        That we have seen today. Now, I shall go mad!

FATHER *returning*

        They are taking him to the hospital.
        Oh Kitty my dear, you must put him from your mind forever.
        Death is better. Death is better.
        I didn't think that I would ever live
        Beyond that day. And from that day to this

I have been moving in a dream. A state
Of no existence. No real life at all.
But today something has happened. We are caught
In some great cycle of events that will
If we will but permit it, destroy us all.
I'll go over to the hospital I think.
I feel I need to work among these men
And touch the mutilated bodies. And help
The matron and Kate. Just for today
And get them settled in. And some might know
How Pal and Fred were killed. I'd like to know.
And then dear Iris, you must come to us, Ilene
And Kitty too. We must spend time together.
We must all talk together and open our hearts
And try to understand this monstrous thing
That has engulfed our lives. And try to find
A way that we can yet live on again.
It's better for you I think. Your lives still young
Can yet move again.

KITTY, IRIS, ILENE

No, oh no

ILENE

Never will we see their faces again
Never, never, never
How can I ever walk these streets again?

She tosses out all of her remaining flowers and throws down the basket. Kitty runs over to her and holds her

IRIS

Oh no,
Oh no, because you see we've lost our love
We've lost the men that we might someday marry,
Lost the future and we have no past.

KITTY *still holding Ilene*

I think that I'll go over to your house
The town is closed for everything today.

IRIS

We'll go and see how Jessie is and then
We'll wait for you and Katie to return.

FATHER

Goodbye then. I'll see you later at the house

ILENE

They will never come back, never, never

KITTY

I was drawn to John Marshall—like a magnet
That day at the weir.

113

IRIS

> He will never come back for us Kitty

KITTY

> And I'll not bear his child. I envy Jessie
> For she will have a child
> And had I thought that they would not come back
> I'd have slept with anyone to have a child!

IRIS

> Kitty!

KITTY

> It's true, Iris, it's true
> But now, there's no desire any more.
> I could never lie with any man again
> That had not served his country in its need!

IRIS

> It's need, it's need, it's bloody treacherous need!
> How can you talk about a country's need
> After what we have seen today. The band playing . . .

KITTY

> I made them play "Waltzing Matilda" Iris
> If those men don't think their country needed them
> Oh Iris, what's left? what's left?
> Now John Marshall will haunt me
> All my waking hours

IRIS

> Come on, let's go
> Come on Ilene

ILENE

> You two go. I will be there presently.
> Go on, really, I won't be long

She motions them to leave and they do. She is sitting down on the ground, her body swaying. She pulls a letter out of her pocket and looks at it

> Oh Jimmie, Jimmie, Victor, Pal and Freddie
> And all your friends, Billo, Enery, Nark
> Darkie and Tommie. Nobby where are you now?
> Where are you? Will you never come back?
> Will the streets be empty forever?
> Come back, come back, come back
> Oh Jimmie, Jimmie

The lights flicker or rise and fall. Death enters laughing leading in all the men who have been killed. They walk around the half disassembled tables and wander over the stage with Death still laughing

DEATH

> So this is where you all came from?
> Aha ha, ha, ha.
> So peaceful here, ha, ha, ha

I have ruined a whole town
And I didn't even have to come here
Ha. ha, ha

She calls out all the names that Ilene has just mentioned. They walk stiffly toward her then Liberty also enters and "Glory, Glory Hallelujah". The soldiers follow her

Pal is standing lower stage right as Katie enters from the other side, disheveled but drawn to the place. Death crouches back

KATE *Looking sometimes right at Pal but not seeing him*

    Oh little people
    What have you done . . .
    Oh my beloved,
    What have they done
    To us.

As she is speaking "A Long, Long Trail" is playing in the background. She takes a few steps toward Pal. She pauses

    Oh, how can they know my sorrow
    Who never knew my love.
    How could we let them do it
    Let them part us,
    You and me!
    Shall I ever, shall I ever
    Stand again?
    Yes, oh yes
    The dew is rising
    And I too shall go from here
    As the sun shall wither the flowers
    And the noon day tears.
    I shall go towards your sunset
    I shall wear the flame
    A garland, as a rose in summer
    Your soul on mine again
    Your breath shall span the chasm
    The seasons do not know
    Your love shall be the purpose
    Your eternity, the after glow.

"Nearer My God to Thee" begins to play softly.

LIGHTS

Scene 15

The Same Room—Shell Shock

MOTHER

    How is she darling?

MILLICENT

    She's sleeping soundly Mother. The band has stopped.

    What's that noise. It's a noise like thunder

MOTHER

    Well it could be another storm,

    The sky is dark enough. But listen

    They're playing "Waltzing Matilda". Listen.

MILLICENT

    I think that's much better than the other.

    Oh Mother, I feel that I should go down too.

MOTHER

    Millicent, no. I need you here with me.

    You have to help to fix the evening meal

    I don't want you my darling ever to see

    Those mutilated bodies.

    You were the only one of three of my first children

    To survive the flood.

    The other two were washed away and you

    A babe in arms, just born, I had by me.

    I thought I'd never live through that year either

    Before the boys were born. And then came Pal

    And later, little Fred, a lusty child,

    All gone, all gone, and now there's you and me

    And your dear father, bravest of the brave

knock at the door, Iris and Kitty

MILLICENT

    Oh Iris, Kitty, oh I'm glad you came.

    It's terrible to wait. How did it go?

    Wait, wait. I'll get some tea, sit down.

IRIS
>Don't worry about it Millicent

MILLICENT
>No, no, don't speak,. It's alright, really it is.
>Really it is. Mother and I've been cooking
>We're expecting lots of people tonight
>The train's coming in from the west with families.
>Is the hospital quite full? Where's father?

IRIS:
>He's taking it quite well.

MILLICENT
>Who did you see?

MOTHER
>Millicent darling you can see they're very tired

KITTY *taking her hand*
>Lots of people were out there Millicent,
>The band was playing

MILLICENT
>Yes, we heard.

KITTY
>Oh Milli, I wish that I'd not gone
>I wish that I had stayed right here with you

IRIS
>The hospital's very full. How's Jessie?
>I think I'll go and just look in on her

knock at the door

TOWNSPERSON
>The hospital needs some help. Kate sent me here
>To see if Iris had got back from town
>And could come and give a hand. Just for a while.

IRIS
>I'm coming. Just let me check on Jessica.

MILLICENT
>What's happened at the hospital?

TOWNSPERSON
>The ward's are overcrowded. The men are sick
>They should have stayed in Townsville for a rest.
>But they were all full up and so they sent them on.
>They've got to get them settled before the families come.
>The relatives are much worse than the men.
>The men are sitting calmly very still
>And families throwing tantrums and going into fits
>I'd never work at a hospital if it was the last place on
>god's earth!

IRIS
>Come on, let's go. Don't worry. I won't be long.

another knock

TOWNSPERSON

> Can anyone help at the hospital, anyone who can?
> Some loonies have got loose. They're harmless.
> We need help bad.

MOTHER

> Millicent you stay. Don't disobey me dear
> You keep watch over Jessica for us

Mother and Kitty exit. Millicent sits very still. After a few minutes of absolute silence

MILLICENT

> I can't, I can't stay here.

She looks in on Jessica

> She's sleeping. I have to go. *exit*

A few moments after she has gone there is a face at the window, a rattle at the catch and John Marshall crawls in, bedraggled and quite insane. He goes to the table and begins to eat ravenously, knocking over cups and things. There is a rustle at the side door. Jessica enters in a long gown as if in a trance, her hands outstretched

JESSICA

> I feel much better. I think I felt a pain
> But the baby's very still. I had a sharp pain,
> Millicent, Mother, I think I'll just sit here
> My eyes are not accustomed to the light,
> The room's so dark up there. I dreamt I heard
> A band playing. Was it playing for my baby?
> I dreamt there was a train all full of babies
> Babies without arms or feet. It was horrible
> And then I woke and faces came to me
> Faces that I heard but could not recognize.
> What's that? Is that you Fred?

JOHN

> Oh Jessie, don't you know me?
> I killed them all for you
> I killed them all Jessie with my bayonet
> Look at my hands, Jessie, see how red they are!

JESSIE

> Your hands? Is that you Fred?

JOHN

> Yes, Jessie. It's Fred, look, look, it's Fred
> Look Jessie at my hands, the ring,
> I brought it back for you. My hands Jessie.

JESSICA

> The ring, is that the ring I gave you Fred,
> But they said that it was gone. It was not there!

JOHN

> It's mine,
> I took it off his finger. I took it off.

I knew you always meant to give it me
You always loved me Jessica

JESSICA

Yes, yes, I loved you Fred, I always did

JOHN

And you gave me your body Jessica

JESSICA

Yes, yes

JOHN

And I gave you mine

He takes his clothes off partially. She stares at him vacantly

Jessica, I love you, I love you *rhythmically*

Jessica I love you will you please be mine?

abruptly

I'm hungry Jessie

his hands are shaking

Why did you do it Jessica?

JESSICA

Do what my darling *coming over to him*

Give me back my ring Fred, my darling

I knew that you'd come back to me

he jumps back like a cat and then throws a glass of water in her face

JESSICA

John Marshall! John Marshall! *She swoons*

Marshall exits naked through the window

Scene 16

A Little Later—The Birth

Mother and Millicent re-enter
MOTHER

        John Marshall's running naked through the streets

        As crazy as a crazed mind could ever be

Seeing Jessica

        Go get Katie quick. Get a doctor

She cradles Jessica in her arms

        Oh Jessica, hold on my darling, please hold on.

        What luck I brought this with me, Jessica

She puts something to Jessica's nose

        Jessica, Jessica, oh Jessica, wake up.

        The baby will be born real soon you'll see

        Oh Jessica wake up, please, please

Jessica murmurs something incoherently. Iris enters

        Her mind is gone, her mind is gone, Oh Iris

        Put water on. Get sheets

        I can hold her. Hurry, I've sent for Kate

        Oh hurry, Iris, hurry

Kate enters with a hospital aide and Kitty and Millicent

        Oh Kate, her mind is gone, quite gone,

        I can't get her to rally.

They lift Jessica and take her to the room off stage
KATE

        Kitty you work with me.

        Millicent, you keep the water boiling.

        Here *to the aide* Go take this to Matron Kelly

        Hurry *giving the aide a piece of paper*

        Mother get clean clothes, I might need you.

IRIS:

        The doctor?

KATE

        He cannot come

Kitty and Kate go into the other room

MOTHER
> We have to wait now and my thoughts
> Keep racing to the hospital.

IRIS *Father enters*
> I'm glad I went. I'm glad I went.
> Oh God, if I ever thought a child
> That I should ever bring into this world
> Should be so mutilated, cast aside
> I would rather that my body to the grave
> Go sterile.
> For though I live to be a hundred years
> Never will I understand why men
> Would do this to each other.
> Don't tell me they obeyed an order,
> Don't tell me that. From now on in my life
> There's only one thing shall engross my mind,
> Thou shalt not kill, nor maim nor mutilate
> And this engendered in the hearts of man
> From shore to shore in countries round the world
> Would render quite invalid, governments
> That for some gain or God knows whatever for,
> Should order thus their men to kill each other.

FATHER
> Oh my dear child that you were a man
> And could shout until the heavens themselves could hear
> But who would listen to a woman's voice
> Crying like a fragile weed the pain
> That we all feel. Oh Iris, my two sons
> Are dead. Swift deaths the both of them I hear
> And how we grieved, all of us, as though that end
> Were the utmost grief to bear in all the world
> I tell you it is not. Dead they are
> And God knows how we'll live through all the years
> Without them.
> I cannot now imagine how we will.
> I cannot see beyond a few more years
> But yet if choose I must, I'd choose their deaths
> Than watch then suffer agonies of pain
> Far greater than the physical. Bereft
> Of limbs, of sight, of hearing, all the things
> That make a man a man. Oh mother

The hospital aide briefly appears with a bag and goes into the other room
> How is it with Jessica? A woman's woman
> A woman she is the same as we are men
> Who give up utterly to the passion in hand
> While you dear Iris and my darling Kate

And all the women like you in this world
So secure, serene, are yet the only hope
To lead us out of this great maze we're in.
Millicent, my only child come here
And let me stroke your hair the way I did
When you were such a little girl, my joy
Oh Millicent what is your future now?

MILLICENT

I'll take care of you and Mother, Father dear
And do not think that I shall be deprived
For we have loved and lost together
And that's a bond that none will overcome
I'll not have children though. No children.
For I could never mate with anyone
That had not known my brothers when they were young.
And I am glad I went dear father too,
To the hospital. For at the hospital today
I buried my dead brothers and that life
That we all thought would last us to the end of time.
And now a new life lies ahead for us
Oh father! *she bursts into tears*

IRIS

I can't stand it any longer, I'm going in.

MOTHER

Wait, wait, Iris. it's so quiet in there
I've been praying while you've all been talking
Praying for the child and Jessica
But though I can't imagine agony
Greater than what we've already seen this day
It's too quiet in there.

There is dead silence then the cry of a baby is heard. No one speaks. Soon the nursing aide brings out the child. Mother takes it. Kitty and Kate appear at the door and look ready to collapse

FATHER

Jessica? *they shake their heads*

Kate sits down dejectedly on the couch, her eyes looking up at everyone in turn

AIDE

No one could have saved her.
You're lucky you have the child

MOTHER *taking it*

A boy is it?

She walks slowly and shows it to everyone again and then goes to Kate

My darling Kate, it is yours, yours . . .

She puts the child in Kate's arms

LIGHTS

Scene 17

London's East End

There is a bar on one side of the stage and a big black man is the waiter. On the other side there are tables. The street is at the rear of the stage and there is a door leading to it. Professional soldiers enter singing, in a tipsy way,

> Take me back to dear old Blighty
>
> Put me on a train to London town.
>
> Take me over there
>
> Drop me anywhere
>
> Liverpool, Leeds or Birmingham
>
> But I don't care.
>
> I should like to see my best girl
>
> Cuddling up against me soon she'll be
>
> Oh oity diddly oity
>
> Carry be back to Blighty
>
> Blighty is the place for me.

A soldier stumbles in

SOLDIER

> War won't be over for a long time now

WAITER

> No

SOLDIER

> I might even become a general

WAITER

> You might, or you right keel over
>
> Take a seat lad. Take a seat

SOLDIER

> Where were you born mate?

WAITER

> I dunno.

SOLDIER

> I mean what country do you come from?

WAITER

>Doesn't matter. Don't do me no good

SOLDIER

>Well I can see it's not much use trying to talk to you

WAITER

>Well what you want me to say, man
>You go out and you kill each other
>Just because youse born in different countries.
>It don't make sense to me.
>I ain't never killed nobody
>And nobody's gonna make me kill
>Till I knows the reason why.

SOLDIER

>That so, that so.

He is still nodding and nearly falling off his stool when a Red Cross nurse enters from the wings, walks in front of the café, peering in, then enters. She looks at the soldier rather sadly. All eyes are riveted on her as she looks at the soldier then sits at the bar next to him. Then talking to the nurse and pointing tipsily to the waiter the soldier continues,

>He ain't never killed nobody.

WAITER

>What's for you Miss

NURSE

>Shandy.
>Well couldn't it be a wonderful world
>If we didn't have this war?

The waiter has gone over to a little radio he has near the drinks. There is little music then a voice is heard.

RADIO

>This is 7pm. Greenwich mean time.
>Stand by for the news.
>Special war report.

There is a lot of static and the lights go on and off as Pal enters from the wings, walks across the front of the café peering in, then enters and is about to go over to the tables but sees the nurse and sits on the other side of her near the center stage. He is wearing white slacks with an army coat. He looks as though he is on leave for medical reasons. His face and hands are very white. He takes his seat, whispers what he wants to the waiter who has come up to him and then the static stops and the broad ast begins.

RADIO

>The great Cunard Liner Lusitania was torpedoed by a German submarine off the south coast of Ireland yesterday afternoon and sunk. She was on a voyage from New York to Liverpool and was within a few hours steaming from her home port.
>
>An experienced observer who witnessed the opening of the recent combined operations in the Dardanelles tells me that it is impossible to praise too highly the spirit of the allied troops. The Turks, according to French officers are brave but, outside the trenches, unskillful fighters.

Mr. Lloyd George presided at the fifty second anniversary dinner of the Newspaper Press Fund, held last night at the Whitehall Rooms. Mr. Lloyd George proceeded, "The question is repeatedly asked, how long will the war last? This question was put to Abraham Lincoln in another war full of trials, vicissitudes and moments of depression and his answer was 'We accepted this war for a worthy object and this war will end when it is attained.'" There were cheers from the audience. He added, "What is our supreme object? The Freedom of Europe." More cheers.

Lord Kitchener has issued an appeal for 300,000 more men. The new conditions of enlistment are: age, 19-40, height, minimum 5'2", chest, minimum 33 ½. God save the King.,

The Liberal Government has been blamed for the acute shortage of shells both on the western front and in the Dardanelles. Trouble in the admiralty also. Lord Fisher has resigned leaving Mr. Churchill with full responsibility for the daring Gallipoli campaign. It is rumored that the Prime Minister will attempt to form a coalition government.

Three other people enter during the broadcast and sit at the table to the rear of the stage. The soldier has moved closer to the nurse and is making passes at her. But she is obviously very tired and somewhat repulsed by his uniform and bearing. Instead she shows a little curiosity toward the man on the other side of her with his rather bedraggled and mixed appearance. As the broadcast ends he motions slightly with his head towards one of the tables and she nods. They get up and go over to a table where they sit together. The soldier is fuming and is taking it as a personal affront but does not quite know what to do in his condition so he just changes seats at the bar, orders more drinks and glares over at the table.

Outside of the cafe a paper boy is hollering

PAPER-BOY

Paper, paper, read all about it. Lusitania torpedoed.

Lusitania torpedoed. Extra, read all about it.

The Mad Student rushes in with a paper in his hands reading. He is well dressed in civvies but his tie is loud and crooked and he wears a hat from the brim of which numerous flowers are wildly dangling.

MAD STUDENT

The Lusitania was torpedoed by a German submarine off the south coast of Ireland and sunk. Sunk, sunk, that is going to bring America into the war

He goes on reading avidly at the bar

PAL

Have you been at the front?

She nods

On leave?

She nods again

How Long?

MADELINE

One week

PAL

How much longer?

MADELINE

Three days

You?

PAL *in an otherworldly way*

I was killed at Gallipoli *smiling*

Madeline?

She nods

I thought so.

MAD STUDENT. *looking up from the paper, surveying the scene at the cafe and deciding to liven the place up a bit*

Pack up your troubles in your old kitbag,

And smile, smile, smile,

The soldier looks up, Pal and Madeline look over at him momentarily as the waiter comes and puts a candle on their table

MADELINE

Funny isn't it

How the words of a silly song

Can reach your heart

And a loving gesture

Bring comfort to your soul.

He nods

Will this war never end?

The Mad Student still needs attention so he slaps his fist down on the bar and shouts

MAD STUDENT

The war's going to last for fifty years!

MADELINE

Fifty years

PAL

Nineteen sixty five

MADELINE

Will we be alive then?

PAL

Our spirit will.

MAD STUDENT *jumping up again from the other table*

It is a categorical imperative to hold sacred

One's native land,

And to defend it against attack!

MADELINE *She takes off her nurse's cap. There is a beginning transformation on her face*

What is our spirit?

PAL

The spirit of those who died for peace.

Noone can kill that spirit,

Noone

MADELINE *partly as the Red Cross Nurse*

I hope you're right. *then as Madeline nodding*

I know you're right!

MAD STUDENT

> In a conflict of two categorical imperatives, a hierarchy of values must be established which is acceptable to all mankind.

The soldier has decided to get into the action. He gets up, goes over to the Mad Student and looks him up and down and then goes over to Pal

SOLDIER

> Well who are you anyway?

PAL

> A man. I'm a man!

SOLDIER

> Well I'm a ruddy soldier.

coming over to the bar and repeating

> A man. What's a man when it comes to war

turning to the waiter

> Do you want to know how many Turks I killed?

WAITER *turning on the radio*

> No, ah don't

RADIO

> And now for our commentary on the news. First a special report from our news correspondent in New York.
>
> President Wilson gave a gathering of 4,000 naturalized Americans the first intimation of the course the U.S. would presumably pursue as a result of the loss of the Americans on the 'Lusitania'. 'America', said the President, 'must have its consciousness that on all sides, it touches elbows and hearts with all the nations of mankind. The example of America must be a special example. It must be an example not merely of peace because she will not fight but because peace is a healing and elevating influence in the world and strife is not. There is such a thing as a man being too proud to fight. There is such a thing as being so right that it does not need to convince others by force that it is right." These remarks called forth a tumult of applause.
>
> The coalition government is attempting to form a cabinet. The Liberal rank and file are looking about for a scapegoat. All day yesterday they were furiously raging against Mr. Churchill. They look upon him as the author of all their party's ills. Has he not brought the government down by adventures? The news that Mr. Churchill is leaving the Admiralty has been received with a feeling of relief in the service, both afloat and ashore.
>
> Private circles however, quote Mr. Lloyd George as remarking emphatically that failure in the Dardanelles is due not to Mr. Churchill's vision but to the faltering courage of those ministers who have gone back on their solemn pledge to support the expedition. Failure to provide timely naval and military reinforcements is turning what could have been a most brilliant feat in the interest of world peace, into the most unique tragedy in recorded history. All this unofficially from Mr. Lloyd George. Mr. Churchill himself is pale and ghostly. It is clear that something

in him has died. The thought of the carnage weighs heavily on his conscience and if he ever emerges again, it could be as a warrior.

While this broadcast has been going on the soldier has spied the goldfish bowl with a single fish swimming in it. He has taken it up and is glaring from the bowl to the nurse though it is important that he is not too conspicuous until the broadcast is switched off. Then there is silence as he steps forward on the stage. Suddenly he thrusts his hand into the bowl and grabs the fish, sending the bowl sliding along the counter. Then he viciously bites off the head of the fish.

SOLDIER

> That'll teach you to splash
> While I'm here looking at 'yh.

He spits out the fish

MAD STUDENT

> Now look what you've done, you blockhead

picking up the bowl

> What are you going to do now
> In a world without beauty.

SOLDIER

Very reminiscent of Bismarck's position when he breaks the jug-picks up the bowl and smashes it on the floor.

PAL

> He was on Gallipoli too

She nods

> His star is rising
> And mine is on the wane.
> I looked out over Imbros
> On the morning of the day
> And I knew that I would die there.
> And we were fighting for Liberty,
> For freedom of all the world,
> A vision shaping the destinies
> Of every nation on this earth.
> Not victory on placards
> And headlines in the news,
> But freedom and equality—
> The right of men to choose
> The way of their own manhood,
> And it was for that we landed
> And fought on Gallipoli

More noise at the back of the stage

MAD STUDENT

> Any man with a grand and abstract vision has the ethical responsibility to anchor
> it to the ground.

This time the soldier does march over to him

SOLDIER
>Eh man
>
>I don't know what you're blasting off about
>
>But you don't make sense to me

MAD STUDENT *unperturbed*
>That's because
>
>You are the anchor and I am the vision.

With a sweeping gesture and bow of dismissal, he sits down at his own table and ignores the soldier

PAL *very quietly to Madeline*
>And I am the thread between.

SOLDIER *scratching his head*
>I am the anchor
>
>Eh *to the waiter*
>
>Do you know what he's blasting off about?

MADELINE *helping the soldier sit down again but speaking to Pal*
>If we all had goodwill would we still have war?

MAD STUDENT
>Ah, she has it! She has it*! he dances*
>
>She has it!
>
>There is only one TRUE categorical imperative
>
>And that is GOODWILL.
>
>She has it, she has it!

He grabs hold of the soldier and tries to dance with him. Madeline moves back to Pal

MADELINE
>It is goodwill isn't it?

PAL
>Yes. but why are we so lonely?

MADELINE
>There are worse things than loneliness.

PAL
>Then you are still searching too?

MADELINE
>Yes

PAL
>We shall meet again.

MADELINE
>Yes

LIGHTS as a flute or harmonica is playing 'It's a long way to Tipperary' followed by 'There's a Long Long Trail'

Scene 18

Casualty Dressing Station

There is a bit of an awning on stage with a red cross on the top of it and men are wandering around limping and bandaged. At the front of the stage four men squat on the ground playing cards—Pal, Nobby, Darkie and Shorty. There are several gas masks around. A soldier stumbles in bare footed, his trousers torn off, a gas mask on and dragging a haversack behind him. He sees the red cross and takes off his gas mask and without talking to anyone, hastens to open up his sack. He takes out a cat and putting it gently on the ground, he lies down with the cat next to his cheek.

SOLDIER

> I'm sorry, Tipperary. You shouldn't have hidden them. If you hadn't have hidden them, I would have found them in time and thrown them in the bag with you. But they were dead. Don't you see. When I found them they were dead. Don't be mad at me Tipperary please. *He strokes the cat.* I'll find you a big Tom. *He begins coughing violently.* As soon as I can. You'll have some more kittens, real soon you'll see, Tipperary. Beautiful kittens, just like you. He continues to cough violently, covering his throat and mouth with his hands. *They become covered with blood. He draws the cat close to his face and it too is covered with blood. He lies still. One of the others comes and turns him over, listening to his chest.*

WLLLlAMS

> He's dead

Darkie comes over very angrily

DARKIE

> So's the bloody cat *picking it up*

NOBBY *very calmly*

> Bloody's the word mate

Darkie glares at him and hurls the cat out through the wings. It hits another soldier in a similar condition to the one that had just entered

SOLDIER

> Eh, oh, you killed Tipperary. She was our mascot.
>
> We had her for days. She had two kittens *then seeing his mate.*
>
> Eh. they killed Tipperary. Why didn't you stop them?

the others come up to him and talk very gently
DARKIE
> He's dead, mate
NOBBY
> Come and get some tea
SHORTY
> Want a fag?
SOLDIER *he shakes his head at each soldier in turn*
> Is he dead?
DARKIE
> Yes mate
SOLDIER
> Is he really dead?
SHORTY
> Dead as a maggot, mate.
SOLDIER
> Oh, he's dead
He turns and looks at the body in disbelief
> Are yh really dead?
He falls on the dead man and shakes him up and down
> Yh not dead, yh not dead! not dead, not dead, dead.
The voice fades away as the men lead him backstage. Darkie picks up the cat and furiously hurls it through the wings, this time successfully. An orderly comes out of the awning with letters in his hand and a couple of packages.
SHORTY
> Eh, mail!
ORDERLY
> McCullough
A soldier takes his letter
ORDERLY
> Jenkins
JENKINS
> Here, mate
ORDERLY
> Martin
JENKINS
> He's gone west, mate
ORDERLY
> Grey!
JENKINS
> Ditto
ORDERLY
> Stiles
JENKINS
> Ditto

ORDERLY

      How do you know?

JENKINS

      They were all in my company mate

They are interrupted by a soldier coming in from the wings carrying his mate on his back. He eases him down gently. He is obviously exhausted. The Orderly goes over to the man on the ground, looks at him, puts his ear to his heart.

ORDERLY

      He's dead, mate

SOLDIER

      Nah, he's O.K.

ORDERLY

      He's dead, mate

The soldier has been calmly walking over to the men playing cards. He stops. He looks at the Orderly.

SOLDIER

      They blasted his leg, that's all. He couldn't walk.

ORDERLY

      He's been hit in the head, mate

SOLDIER *going over in disbelief*

      They blasted his leg, that's all

He looks at the man on the ground. He half kneels and looks as though he is going to burst into tears. Then suddenly he straightens up

SOLDIER

      Well, you rotten bloody bastard!

      I carry you over half of no-man's land

      And you bloody well kick the bucket.

      What kind of a bloody cobber are you anyway?

He turns to the others

      When's the bloody armistice?

      We had a pact him and me

      Not to get blasted till the bloody armistice.

      Give us a hand, mate.

One of the others gives him his cards and he goes on with the game

DARKIE

      We'll be boiling the billy, later.

      We got some tea from home.

VOICE SHOUTING

      G-A-S *Then, a little later*

ALL-CLEAR

The orderly continues to distribute the mail

ORDERLY

      Freeman

FREEMAN

      Here

He gets a parcel and a letter. There are all kinds of exclamations about the letter which is highly perfumed. He settles himself down with his back to a stump and turns the letter over and over in his hands

DARKIE

> Well man, you've done nothing but talk about your girl for a week and now you hear from her, you don't even open the letter.

Freeman makes a barely perceptible movement. He finally opens the letter and everyone quiets down and looks at him expectantly. A girl's affected voice comes over the microphone.

VOICE

> "Dearie. Be sure to keep your hat on at all times. The doctor was telling me the other day he could hardly sit on the veranda of Sheperd's in the middle of the day. Iced drinks and heavy meals are dangerous Doc says" *Freeman throws the letter down and picks up the parcel.*

He takes out hair oil, twenty five cigars, a cigarholder, a pair of pyjamas. There is another letter inside the parcel. He reads it and again the girl's voice comes over the microphone

VOICE

> "Darling. Keep these in your tent. It must be a fag getting the oil you liked so much. I suppose you have to walk some distance from the firing line to the nearest shops. Don't think me forward in sending the pyjamas—I know fellows do wear them. Please don't get shot dear".

DARKIE

> The yanks are coming.

In the distance is heard 'Over There'

SHORTY

> It's about time, fellas

FREEMAN

> Well, better late than never. Here

he gives them the cigars

SOLDIER

> Eh, you going to win the war for us Yanks?

YANK

> Of course we will, if we can fight like you guys

DARKIE

> Hey, will you coves be here for a while, we've got some tea from home
> And we're just about to boil the billy.

YANK

> Yeh, is this NO MAN'S LAND?

DARKIE *waving his hand*

> Out there's no-man's land!

YANK

> Hey, have you seen Alsace-Lorraine?

SECOND YANK

> It's a lake, isn't it?

SHORTY

> Cripes, I dunno

PAL

    It's a piece of land

YANK

    Oh, a piece of land

then pulling himself together

    Well, we're fighting for liberty

SHORTY

    But you have to have faith in your government

    That they're not taking you for a ride.

YANK

    What do you mean by that?

DARKIE

    Nothing, really. It's just that well, we were on Gallipoli

    And we had no business being there, because it's somebody else's land.

YANK

    What did you do then?

DARKIE

    Oh man,

    Nothing was more beautiful on Gallipoli,

    Than the day that we walked off—

    Unilaterally.

YANK

    You mean without a treaty?

DARKIE

    We just up and left

YANK

    Evacuated?

DARKIE

    Yes

YANK

    But that's surrender, man

DARKIE *vehemently*

    We never surrendered

YANK

    But that's defeat,

    To evacuate unilaterally.

DARKIE

    Well, what if it is

PAL *coming over*

    We were defeated, but yet we won

YANK

    How do you figure that?

PAL

    We were defeated

    In that we did not gain our objective

DARKIE

       But we won out as men

YANK

       How do you figure that?

DARKIE

       We proved that we were fighters
       And something to be reckoned with

SHORTY

       And we were fighting for liberty

YANK *laughing*

       You don't make sense.
       You were fighting for liberty
       But you didn't gain your objective
       And so you lost.

PAL

       But we were at cross-purposes.
       You see. We were on Gallipoli
       And we had no business being there,
       Because it's somebody else's land,
       And so we left.

DARKIE

       The government took us for a ride.
       But we came out victorious
       Because we proved that we were men.

YANK

       But it's bad news for a government
       Ever to admit defeat.

SHORTY

       The government gets over it
       Quicker than we did
       Who got blasted by Beachy Bill.

YANK

       A man can be defeated
       But a government, never.
       A government can never surrender,
       To lose face, is something awful.

The lights go down on the following speech and Pal moves downstage a little

PAL

       The stronger is the nation,
       The more that it can yield.
       Face-saving man, is only for the weak.
       The strong man, when he has his values straight,
       Holds Liberty before him like a light
       And never is afraid to give or yield
       What he has gained, for what he knows is right.
       And never is a nation justified

To tread upon another's sovereign soil.

The lights go up again. There is a slight pause

DARKIE

Hey, come on, let's have our sing song,
The billy's boiling.

The men bring in their mugs and the tea is poured from the billy

SHORTY

The English boys came over the top parlez-vous,
The English boys came over-the top, parlez-vous,
The English boys came over the top
Because they wanted the war to stop
Inky pinky, parlez-vous.
The Scotty boys came over the top parlez-vous,
The Scotty boys came over the top parlez-vous,
The Scotty boys came over the top
Because they heard a penny drop
Inky pinky, parlez-vous.
The Yankee boys came over the top parlez-vous,
The Yankee boys came over the top parlez-vous,
The Yankee boys came over the top
Because they saw a curly mop,
Inky pinky, parlez-vous.
The Aussie boys came over the top parlez-vous,
The Aussie boys came over the top parlez-vous,
The Aussie boys came over the top
Because they heard a bottle pop
Inky pinky, parlez-vous.

MARINE

From the halls of Montezuma
To the shores of Tripoli etc..

LIGHTS

END OF PART 1

137

Part 2

Cast

Scene I. Versailles 1919
Pal; *Liberty*; Darkie; Marine; Stage Manager; *World Commonwealth*; *Eternal Justice*; England; U.S.A.; Japan; France; Russia 1; Shorty; Soldier; *Jim; Tommy*; Germany; Chorus; Another Voice; *Victor; Fred*; Nobby; China; America Voice; Chorus; French Voice; Wilson:

Scene 2. The Sale of the Farm
Father; Mother; Millicent; Iris; Kate; Kitty; Mrs. Dunbar:

Scene 3. The Gift
Young Pal; Nancy; Millicent; Mother; Ilene; Kate; Iris; Kitty:

Scene 4. Later that Evening
Ilene; Millicent; Iris; Kitty; Kate:

Scene 5. Beer Garden, Europe
Poet 1; Poet II; Mad Poet; Poet III; Man 1; Man II; Mad Student; Worker 1; *Madeline*; Worker II; Worker III; Tilly; Jew; *Pal*:

Scene 6. The Colonel Comes.—Charters Towers
Colonel; Kate; Mother:

Scene 7. Daughter of the British Empire
Iris; Mother; Millicent; Kitty; Kate; Ilene:

Scene 8. Christmas 1939
Millicent; Young Pal; Kitty; Ilene; Iris; Kate:

Scene 9. The London Blitz
Young Pal; Kitty (Kathleen):

Scene 10. Dunkirk
Liberty; Peace; Soldier 1; Soldier II; Soldier III; Voice; Soldier IV; Civilian; Chorus; Young Pal:

Scene 11. The Pendant's Return
Kate; Millicent; Kitty; Iris; Ilene; Young Woman (Kathleen);

Scene 12. The Burma Road
Soldier 1; *Pal*; Soldier II; Nobby; Fuzzy Wuzzy; Soldier III; Chinese Soldiers:

Scene 13. Deutschland Uber Alles
Voice; Voice—Cultured Abstract; Voice—Distant; Voice—Cultured with an accent; Voice—Observer; Voice—Poet; Voice—Scientific; Voice—Statesman; Voice—Observer; Voice—Cockney; *Liberty*; *Pal*; Man; Others:

Scene 14. NUREMBURG
Voice; *Eternal Justice*; *World Commonwealth; her retinue;* Justice in Bondage; Voice—Distant; Voice; Member; Observer; Pole; German; Cockney; Layman:

Scene 15. The Clubhouse—On Nuremberg
Darkie; Nobby; Shorty; Chorus*; Pal; Eternal Justice*; Justice in Bondage; *Enery; Fred; Death; Liberty; Tommy; Jim; Victor; Soldier1; Soldier II; Billo; Nark; Anonymous Soldier*; Attendant:

Scene 16. The Seance—The Palace of Justice
Kate; Millicent; Iris; Kitty; Ilene; *Madeline; Eternal Justice; Liberty*; Voice of Martin Luther King; Professor; Voice of Millicent; Voice of African American; Another Voice; Voice of *Madeline;* Policeman; John Marshall; Mad Student; Black Intellectual; Young Man; Panther; *Young Pal*:

Scene 17. U.S.A., The 1960s
John Kennedy; Voice of Kennedy; Voice*; World Commonwealth; Soldiers:*

Scene 18. A Guest of the Nation, U.S.A. 1963
World Commonwealth; her retinue; President Kennedy; Student 1; Student II; *Madeline; Figure 1; Second Figure*; Drunk; Black Man; *First Temptor; Second Temptor; Third Temptor*; Voice; Voice of Bismarck; *Liberty;* Child's Voice; Voices; Child; Pal's Voice; *Pal;* Mad Student; Black Intellectual; Businessman; General; *Death;* Robert Kennedy:

Scene 19. The Valley of the Shadow of Death, U.S.A. 1963
Voice; John Kennedy; Robert Kennedy*;* Jackie; Edward Kennedy: Young girl; Young man*; Unborn Children*; Stage Hand; Several men; Big African American Man; African American Woman's Voice:

Scene 20. Perth, Australia
Voice; Darkie; Shorty; Voice One; Voice Two; *Pal*; Scout One; Scout Two; Voices:

Scene 21. The Fiftieth Anniversary, 1965, The Earth
Voice; *Girls of different races; Winston Churchill*; General Eisenhower's Voice; Soldier; *Eternal Justice; Liberty*; Woman's Voice:

Scene 22. Peace on Earth
Official; Child; Mad Student; *Pal; World Commonwealth; her retinue:*

Scene 23. Gallipoli Revisited
Liberty; Voice on tape; Father's Voice on tape; Pal; Eternal Justice; Death; Soldiers' Chorus:

Scene 24. ANZAC DAY, Charters Towers
Darkie; Shorty; Nobby; Boy Pal; Millicent*; Liberty; Dead Soldiers*; Ilene; Kitty; Iris; *Pal; Mother; Father; Eternal Justice; Madeline*; Kate:

Epilogue
Madeline: Boy Pal; *Voice of Eternal Justice:*

Scene 1

Versailles 1919

A few soldiers come on stage exactly as they did at the beginning of the play, except that there are uniforms from England, Russia, Australia, India, Canada, a marine and a soldier from the U.S., France, Germany, Italy, Poland. Their uniforms are worn and the men are a little tired but very excited. There is a large oblong table in the center of the stage and the men are setting the places for all the treaty signers. They pick up place names from the downstage part of the table, read out the names of the country and put it in the place. The name of every country that participated in the war, called out but finally chairs are drawn up from L. to R. England, Japan, Germany, China. Justice in Bondage is at the downstage end of the table and there is another small table next to his place. Then continuing around the table there is France, the U.S. and Russia. The head of the table is vacant but the chair there is better than any of the others and is raised a little. The soldiers are reading an instruction sheet. While they are busy about this, Liberty enters with her gown of red poppies and her cream colored cloak. She look at the proceedings then a soldier notices.

PAL

>I seem to remember you. Who are you?

LIBERTY

>I am Liberty, beloved.

DARKIE

>That's right. It's Liberty that will sit at the head of the table

She shakes her head

MARINE *reading the instructions*

>No, it's Eternal Justice

Then turning to the woman

>But there's got to be a place for you.

>That's the whole reason why we fought.

Panic grips the soldiers as they all search for her place.

PAL

>This is preposterous. There's got to be a place for Liberty. Stage manager, stage manager . . . stage manager . . . ?

STAGE MANAGER

He comes in with his pipe in his mouth

>You're not supposed to interrupt the show like this.

145

PAL

> But there's no place for Liberty

The stage manager looks at his notes

STAGE MANAGER

> I know there's no place SET. But she's in this scene I'm sure.

He flicks over the pages.

> I know she's in this scene but I can't find her cue.

> Look, all the others are here

He turns to Liberty

> Why don't you just stand here and wait for your cue.

He looks around the stage

> Where's the perambulator?

Someone wheels in the perambulator stage right, and a huge hobby-horse is wheeled in stage left with a young girl sitting on it, dressed as a bride. It is World Commonwealth. She is very still with her hands behind her back. It is clear after a while that they are tied. The soldiers are in a frenzy of excitement as they step back, surveying their work at the table. The nations enter in order of their total war casualties, namely

	Dead	Wounded	Total
Russia	1,700,000	4,950,000	6,650,000
Germany	1,718,000	4,350,000	6,068,000
France	1,385,000	3,000,000	4,385,000
British Empire	874,000	2,536,000	3,400,000
U.S.A.	124,000	232,000	356,000
Japan	300	900	1,200
. . . .	. .	. .	. .
WORLD	8,164,000	20,204,000	23,368,000

A couple of bars of their national anthems are played as they enter. They are all dressed identically in white silk with the flags of their countries sewn across their backs and across their breasts but two men center for Russia. They all take their places and stand still. Justice in Bondage enters with a lot of paraphernalia. He looks like a judge and enters as does a member of the Supreme Court. He comes sedately from the rear of the audience and walks slowly down the aisle followed by a couple of attendants who carry his scales and weights etc. He looks at the table. The soldiers automatically cringe and step back. There is a moment of terrible expectation as he is about to go to the head of the table but something stops him and he takes his place instead at the lower end down stage. The solders relax again. Then the lights on stage grow dim and the light is focused on the stairs which are first seen in the Gallipoli scene as Razzy goes up them and which have had a little light as various soldiers group all through the war, but this is the first time the light goes slowly upwards to show a platform above, which is lined with soldiers and they are all looking down on the proceedings below. As this has been going on, an organ has begun to play very softly but now it becomes distinct

> *Nearer my God to Thee*
> *Nearer to Thee*
> *Even though it be a cross*

That raiseth Thee.

The light fades and returns to the lower stage. The soldiers are gone and where they stood the floor is covered with red poppies and Liberty is standing there with her cloak thrown back over one shoulder. She is picking up a couple of poppies and adding them to her gown which is made of them. At the head of the table on the platform a man is standing dressed exactly as everyone else except that he has no flag but his costume is all white. It is Eternal Justice.

ETERNAL JUSTICE

> In the beginning was the language
> And the language was with God
> And the language was God.
> I declare this meeting open.

They all take their places except that the Russians turn their chair away from the table and sit on it dejectedly looking at their feet. After the shuffling subsides, Eternal Justice hits the gavel. Immediately England, the U.S.A., Japan and France rise and begin reciting in their own languages.

ENGLAND

> I can see peace coming now—not a peace which will

U.S.A.

> What we demand in this war is that the world be

JAPAN

> We desire a declaration of race equality which will

FRANCE

> Justice is not inert, it does not submit to injustice

ENGLAND

> be the beginning of war; not a peace which will be an

U.S.A.

> made fit and safe to live in and that it be made safe

JAPAN

> place us fully on a level with all Europeans in any

FRANCE

> What it demands first when it has been violated, are

ENGLAND

> endless preparation for strife and bloodshed; but a

U.S.A.

> for every peace-loving nation which, like our own,

JAPAN

> diplomatic negotiation of the future.

FRANCE

> restitution and reparation for the people and individ-

ENGLAND

> real peace

U.S.A.

> Wishes to live its own free life, determine its own

FRANCE

> uals who have been despoiled or maltreated.

U.S.A.

> institutions, be assured of justice and fair dealing by the other peoples of the world, as against force and aggression.

While this has been going on World Commonwealth has been rocking wildly on the hobby horse which she cannot control. As the U.S. is ending his speech, Liberty moves over to her and frees her wrists. She jumps off the hobby horse and runs in panic across the stage. She shakes the perambulator and then looks helplessly at it. Suddenly Pal comes running in from the wings looking rather bedraggled. He trips as soon as he comes on stage and goes sprawling but he gets up and comes over to World Commonwealth. He takes her hands and looks at her. Then he moves to the perambulator and takes out a bundle and gives it to World Commonwealth. She holds it close to her as if it is a baby. Then Pal helps her to unwind the cloth. It is a beautiful illuminated globe. She puts it in his hands and he moves over to Eternal Justice who nods and he puts the globe in the center of the table then steps backwards. World Commonwealth moves back to the hobby horse and puts her hand on it. Liberty goes over to Eternal Justice and sits at his feet. She has long hair and Eternal Justice lifts it across his knees and caresses it. England, the U.S., Japan and France have meanwhile decided on an order and the deliver their speeches again, beginning with Japan, then France then the U.S., then England

JAPAN

> We desire a declaration of race quality which will place us fully on a level with all Europeans in any diplomatic negotiation of the future.

FRANCE

> Justice is not inert, it does not submit to injustice. What it demands first when it has been violated, are restitution and reparation for the people and individuals who have been despoiled or maltreated.

U.S.A.

> What we demand in this way is that the world be made fit and safe to live in and that it be made safe for every peace-loving nation which, like our own, wishes to live its own free life, determine its own institutions, be assured of justice and fair dealing by the other peoples of the world, as against force and aggression.

ENGLAND

> I can see peace coming now—not a peace which will be the beginning of war; not a peace which will be an endless preparation for strife and bloodshed; but a real peace.

Eternal Justice strikes the gavel and the proceedings begin.

All of the countries that participated in the war are here as well as the dead soldiers. ETERNAL JUSTICE, LIBERTY and JUSTICE IN BONDAGE make appearances. The dead soldiers read from scripts handed to them.

ETERNAL JUSTICE

> In the beginning was the language

> And the language was with God
> And the language was God.
> I declare this meeting open
> At the Palace of Versailles
> In the Hall of Mirrors

FRANCE *Accompanied by the French National Anthem*
> Justice is not inert, it does not submit to injustice.
> What it demands first when it has been violated, is
> Restitution and reparation for the people and individuals
> Who have been despoiled or maltreated.

RUSSIA 1
> The peace negotiations are at an end.
> The governments of Germany and Austria
> Possess countries and peoples vanquished by force of arms.
> To this authority the Russian people,
> Workmen and peasants, could not give acquiescence.
> We could not sign a peace that brings with it
> Sadness, oppression, suffering
> To millions of working men and peasant stock.
> We will not and we must not continue war
> With Germans and with Austrians—
> Workmen and peasants like ourselves.
> Landlords and capitalists made this peace
> And we are not signing their peace.

SHORTY *jumping up amid shouts and jeers etc.*
> Yes, proletariats of the world unite,
> A vulture is a vulture in any language.

SOLDIER
> Good for you, Russia
> The American worker joins with you
> And all the workers of the world.

JIM
> Sit down will you, Russia pulled out early

TOMMY
> All the Germans that were fighting Russians
> Came and massacred US on the western front.

ETERNAL JUSTICE *Gavel*
> Of the twenty eight million casualties
> In this war to end all wars,
> Six million casualties
> Were suffered by Germany.
> Germany.

CHORUS *of England, France and the U.S.*
> The allies interpret the terms of peace.

ETERNAL JUSTICE *Gavel*
> Considering the price of humankind,

Germany

GERMANY

Our war aims from the beginning were defense of the Fatherland, the maintenance of our territorial integrity, and the freedom of our economic development. Our warfare, even where it must be aggressive in action, is defensive in aim.

ANOTHER VOICE *After some ruckus and blaspheming*

The huge "super guns" used by us in the bombardment of Paris were one of our chief triumphs of the war. Had they been completed at an earlier stage, they might well have proved the decisive factor in forcing a peace upon our foes.

ETERNAL JUSTICE *Gavel*

GERMANY *In a very subdued and passionate voice*

May I with your permission respond,
When the victors have expressed themselves.

PAL

I would like to hear him speak!
Men don't fight without a belief in
What they are fighting for.
What were the Germans really fighting for?
The soldier, the human being?

JIM

Look here, their guns were powerful
And they killed us
What more do we need to know?

PAL

We need to know why!
If we don't know why it will happen again!

VICTOR

It will never happen again.

PAL

What makes you so sure?

JIM

This war happen again?

MANY VOICES

Never, never, never, never . . .

ETERNAL JUSTICE *Gavel and turning to Germany*

Granted.
Of the twenty eight million casualties
In this war to end all wars
Four and a half million casualties
Were suffered by France.
France.

FRANCE

There is no need of further information,
Or special inquiries into origins

150

Of this drama which has shaken all this world.
The trap, premeditated, is now revealed
And the truth is bathed in blood. Imperial archives
Can never hold within their iron walls
This abominable plot of a so-called master race
To crush all nations beneath its iron heel.

More clapping and ruckus

ETERNAL JUSTICE *Gavel*

FRANCE *Continuing*

Yet not just for ourselves but for all men,
We felt that we were fighting in this war;
And we could feel a kind of vision here,
Something immortal, some new kind of peace,
Some new ideal of justice perhaps it was,
And Liberty held sacred by all men,
In their pursuit of national happiness
And concord among the nations of this world.

ETERNAL JUSTICE

Of the twenty eight million casualties
In this war to end all wars,
Three and a half million casualties
Were suffered by the British Empire.
Britain.

ENGLAND *Accompanied by the national anthem*

Without a certainty of punishment
There's no security in any land.
There's no protection for life or property
In states where criminals are given more power
Than the law itself.
And the law of nations is no exception here.
We must vindicate this law or else
The peace of all the world is at the mercy
Of any nation whose professors stand
And teach—assiduously—men to believe
That crime is not wrong as long as it will lead
To enrichment of that to which they owe
Allegiance, be it country, doctrine, cult.

SHORTY *amid ruckus*

What do we owe allegiance to?

FRED

Let's go home. We owe allegiance to our homes and families.

PAL

We owe allegiance to Liberty and Justice.
That's what we're here for.

NOBBY

That's what WE want. But this 'ere Peace Conference is supposed to make

JIM

    Well I wish they would bloody well get on with it. All this Yiking. I want the truth.

SHORTY

    Come on, let's have the Truth. What's going on here

ETERNAL JUSTICE *Gavel*

ENGLAND *continuing*

    In the history of the world, there have emerged
    Criminal states, many times, and here is one.
    And criminal states will always rear their heads
    Until rewards of international crime
    Become too precarious to profit from
    And punishment becomes too sure
    To mar its any apparent attractiveness.

DARKIE *amid ruckus*

    Punishment, punishment,
    Why do they always talk about punishment.
    Streuth, let's get this bloody thing underway.
    Gawd blimey you peace blokes
    Needed to sink in the mire at the Somme.

NOBBY

    We've had our punishment.
    The Germans and us, all the soldiers.

SHORTY

    We're punished enough
    Let's get on with this flamin' peace thing.

ETERNAL JUSTICE *Gavel*

ENGLAND *Continuing*

    Yet I can see a real peace shining now,
    Not just preparations to repeat
    The strife and blood shed that has drenched the world,
    No more racing to pick up our arms
    With arrow, sword, and gun and tank and bomb,
    With missile and counter missile and who knows
    What yet ingenious thing we may invent
    To splatter the blood of men.
    Our world is old and never has known peace,
    Rocking and swaying like a decrepit ship
    That battles with the sea; while all around,
    Children with flowers deck their bark canoes
    And cry out for their right to happiness.

Much applause and the men dance around with Liberty

ETERNAL JUSTICE

    Of the twenty eight million casualties
    In this war to end all wars,

A half a million casualties
Were suffered by the United States of America.
The United States of America.

U.S.A. *accompanied by the national anthem*

We must cry out against these human wrongs,
That cut to the roots of all our sacred rights.
Each generation rises with the sun,
And it is our sacred covenant
To fade so imperceptibly from sight
That warmth with warmth is mingled in our sons.
There must be peace without a victory.
Peace forced, leaves bitterness of memory
That serves as quicksand for our children's feet.
Only the great can show a mercy keen,
Can humbly yield to what has greater claim
In the chronicles of everlastingness.

much applause

ETERNAL JUSTICE

And now there are some other matters here.
That touch upon a nation's sacred right
To hold and withhold it's people's sovereign soil
From intervention of a foreign power.

shouting followed by the gavel

CHINA

Germany obtained in eighteen ninety nine,
A forced lease of Ciachow Bay, Shantung.
A free port was created at Tsingtao,
Until Japan, at war with Germany,
Captured Shantung, and held it to this time.
And now our Chinese delegation claims
That lease is not possession, and Shantung
Must now revert to China where it belonged
Before the foreign intervention there.

ETERNAL JUSTICE *Gavel*

The territory belongs to China

ETERNAL JUSTICE *Gavel*

JAPAN *Jumping up*

Japan must have control of Yangtze mines,
Our whole industrial complex will break down.

ETERNAL JUSTICE *Gavel*

The territory belongs to China

U.S.A.

But wait. My country too divides on this.
It may not ratify my power to sign,
And I have promised others secretly,
To uphold Japan in this her fixed intent.

NOBBY

Come off it Wilson.

FRED

What about your fourteen points Wilson,
The first of your fourteen points

SHORTY

Open covenants of Peace—no secret treaties.

PAL

The territory belongs to China
Just as Gallipoli belonged to Turkey

ETERNAL JUSTICE *Gavel*

The territory belongs to China

JAPAN *amid boos and ruckus*

Japan will not sign. We will hold out for this.

ETERNAL JUSTICE

A cornerstone of this our solemn peace,
Is that no foreign annexations ever
Can still be forced upon our weaker states.
No intervention for whatever cause,
Can justify a nation setting foot
On any other country's sovereign soil.

CHEERS and applause

AMERICAN VOICE

The senate won't ratify that.

JIM

Wilson is still in his crib when it comes to European politics.

FRED

The League of Nations. What about the League of Nations?

TOMMY

We want President Wilson's League of Nations!

MANY VOICES

We want the League of Nations!

AMERICAN VOICE

The senate will not ratify the League of Nations.
The Monroe doctrine keeps American politics separate from European politics.

DARKIE

To hell with the Monroe Doctrine

FRENCH VOICE

The magnitude of it, the majesty of it.
We must have President Wilson's League of Nations!

AMERICAN VOICE

The United States assumes no obligations towards independence of other countries.
America will not ratify joining the League of Nations

Boos, applause, much ruckus

The Senate won't ratify that.

PAL *Running after China*

      Don't go. You can't leave now.

CHINA

      I can't stay

PAL

      But there will be no peace if China is excluded!

CHINA

      Tell that to those who break the faith.

PAL

      But you must stand your ground!

CHINA

      I cannot stand my ground. I am outweighed.

PAL *Looking back to the delegates*

      You cannot let him leave

The U.S. and Japan turn their backs and the other delegates either ignore Pal or express ineffectuality.

PAL

      But we can never be free

      If trust is violated

      What am I to do?

      You must have good will!

He spins around and faces first the U.S. and then Japan. They ignore him and he ends up kneeling by Eternal Justice.

ETERNAL JUSTICE

      The territory belongs to China.

The U.S. and Japan salute each other.

FRANCE

      Let us continue with our negotiations, gentlemen.

      Let us continue

ETERNAL JUSTICE *Gavel*

      Before we continue gentlemen,

      Let us pause,

      Let us reflect in this, a moment

      Snatched out of our collective destiny,

      Silence please.

A different light plays on stage

      Now let us in our hearts turn to Justice

      The meaning of an International Court of Justice

      The meaning of Eternal Justice

      The meaning of Goodwill

      The meaning of Liberty,

      For it is these grand ideals imbedded in the hearts of men

      That will in the chronicles of time

      Lead us with certain steps

      To that essential peace,

      Our civilization's only chance of continuity.

Reflect gentlemen please.

Lights back to normal

NOBBY

Gawd blimey what is eternal justice anyway.

PAL

Well we know what goodwill is. We know we must have goodwill on the part of all countries, all peoples.

FRED

We must have justice

DARKIE

We are fighting for Liberty

PAL

We understand Liberty. She is with us. But the rest are still only words if we all don't agree on what they MEAN.

SHORTY

You find out what they mean.

TOMMY

Go to Europe

NOBBY

Go to America

JIM

Go to hell

DARKIE

They are the ones that can't agree on what bloody terms they want.

JIM

Let's go home. These buggers will be quarrelling to the end of time.

FRED

Let's go back to Aussie. At least life is nice and simple there. When a bloke says something he means it.

NOBBY

Fair dinkum. It's the only way to go. To say what you mean.

PAL

I will go to Europe. I will find out. I will. I will.

I will travel the whole world.

Much jumping up and down and ruckus

DARKIE

Eh let's get on with this peace thing. We want to go home.

ETERNAL JUSTICE *Gavel*

WILSON

These laws are null and void. They do not show

How we can resolve these problems of the world.

ETERNAL JUSTICE

A different light plays on stage.

And yet they do. Let Germany repay

In goods and chattels and material things,

Whatever Germany has. Let every man

Erase, as does the setting sun,
His vengeance from the sky!
the lights return to normal.
And now gentlemen, may God be in your hearts,
As all the world is listening for your voice,
And will abide by what you here decide.
For the laws that you write down this day can guide
Your children and their children through the seas,
To that new world the vision of which, you feel,
At this brief moment in your destiny.
Law makers, all.
Break not the faith of those that died for you.
VOICES
Peace, Liberty Justice.
The soldiers march behind Liberty but Pal stands next to Eternal Justice. Death weaves in and out laughing.
PAL
How can I know you?
ETERNAL JUSTICE
Seek me with patience around the globe
I DO PREVAIL. I DO PREVAIL.

Pal and the men march out singing an international song

Scene 2

The Sale of the Farm

The same room. 10 years later

FATHER

    It's done. Sold to the highest bidder.

    It doesn't seem like a dozen years

    Does it? Nothing's changed. Thank God for daughters.

    A grand and beautiful dream all gone, all gone.

MOTHER

    It could have been much worse.

    Did Dunbar lose out in the end on his?

    It's worse than if he'd never bought the place.

    His wife is ill and the vegetable lives on.

MILLICENT

    Oh please don't speak like that of George.

FATHER

    George. He's not a human being Millicent,

    His mother feeds him, bathes him, oh my god

    How foolish women are that cling to life

    When all is dead except the breath alone!

MOTHER

    I'm only glad my dear

    I didn't have to make that choice myself,

    For who knows what I might have done, who knows?

    Oh poor dear broken woman. She couldn't cut

    The past so cleanly as was done for us.

    But never judge her for her terrible choice.

    What will they do?

FATHER

    Try to find a place nearby

    Where they can live. Oh what a wicked waste

    To see a man at fifty so destroyed,

    And forced to find some menial job in town.

Far better had he gone off with his sons
And perished with them on Gallipoli,
Than live to face an old age such as his
Away from friends and all the memories
That filled his early years with so much joy!

Iris, Kate and Kitty all arrive

My dear ones have you come to visit us?
Or did my Millicent invite you here
On just this day of all days in our lives?

IRIS

On just this day we decided that we would come
Since we all came the day you bought the farm.

MOTHER

Who would have thought those twelve years would have gone
The way they did.

FATHER

Well we did not lose. I'll tell you that.
We could have done.

MOTHER

But what a price for you to pay my love
Twelve years of work that no man should have done.

FATHER

Oh no, don't speak like that my dear,
There was no choice. The mortgage was so high
We could have lost this house as well you know.
It was something we went into all together.
Where is young Pal tonight?

MOTHER

Oh he went off like a lark today
Singing and swinging boots and haversac!
Tonight's a camping trip out at the weir
And his whole class is going with their tents
And bikes. He was so excited.

There is a knock at the door. Millicent opens it

MILLICENT

Why Mrs. Dunbar
Come in and sit down!
Would you like some tea?

MRS DUNBAR

Yes Milli, I would.
They took him today, my boy.

MOTHER

We know, we know
What will you do now?

MRS. DUNBAR

I thought I would talk to Katie

        She'll be the next Matron
        At the hospital.
        Perhaps we could be the janitors
Turning to Iris
        Or work in the linen room
        At St. Gabriels.
        Thank God for the schools!
        Young Pal's at All Souls isn't he?
        Do you know the headmaster there?
IRIS *running over to her*
        I'll see what I can do
KATE
        I'll try too
        Where will you be?
MRS DUNBAR
        Where will we be?
        That's a good question
The clock begins to strike
        Oh, the pub is closing.
        I don't know where we'll be.
Looking up at the young women
        Why do you stay in a ghost town?
        Why?
        I have to go. I'll come back soon.
        My boy is gone, gone.
EXIT
IRIS
        It would not be a ghost town
        Had they lived.
MILLLCENT
        There would have been so much of everything
        To take on into Townsville.
        The new railroad would never have passed us by.
FATHER
        A ghost town she calls it
        Oh Milli, what happened to our dream?
        Where did it all go?
MOTHER
        Last night while I was reading
        With all the town asleep
        It seemed Pal came to me
        "Mother", he said "Hold on,
        I'm learning things, I am"
FATHER
        Oh that I could see his face
        Once more before I died!

The young one, he is yours
But my two boys
Brought laughter into every gully,
And joy to every storm.

He goes over to the rocking chair and sits down.

MILLICENT

Father, father.

She stands behind him with her hands on his shoulders and they both appear to be looking up at the same thing.

IRIS

We stayed because we chose to stay!

KITTY

We stayed because we had to stay!
John Marshall's shack was on the Dunbar farm
What will he do now?

She looks at Iris. Iris shakes her head.

KATE *determinedly*

Well, think of young Pal. Such a studious boy
I hope someday that he will be inclined
To study further. Even in Sydney perhaps,
At the University. And if the farm
Were still the mainstay here it might be hard
For him to choose his own career even though
We all would tell him to. The young cannot
Be burdened with the pain of those before.
We must remember that and we must do
Ourselves, what we must do. Not live through him.
We have to hold what things we can together.
We fought for the railroad with everything we had.
Who can do more than that? We lost and now
The farm is gone that held such memories,
But we'll make a future just the same.
We can't admit defeat. We still have young Pal,
His foot into the future for us all.
We all have work, good work, you'll be headmistress Iris
And someday if I'm lucky, I'll be matron here.
Kitty you have your music and the children
And Millicent your love.

The lights fade leaving the spot on Father with Millicent still standing behind him. His face becomes illuminated with joy!

Scene 3

The Gift

The same. Six years later

YOUNG PAL

    Come on Nancy. It's my mother's birthday,
    There's going to be a soiree here tonight.
    One of my mother's evenings with her friends.
    I swear since my grandfather died last year
    There's nothing but women ever come in here.
    Women's conversations are so weird,
    I think they're on a pacificist kick this time.
    I know I shouldn't talk to you like this
    Because you're a girl and you probably feel the same,
    But do you know that you're the only kid
    That's in my class at school that comes from here!
    Everybody else is from the west
    And boarders at the school and they go home
    For all the holidays and then I'm left—
    No one to play with. Gee I'm glad you come
    For tutoring in math. I wish you could
    Come over for some French. I need some help.
    I'm terrible at languages and yet
    I've got to have it for my scholarship.

NANCY

    Well then go ask your mother and she'll ask
    The headmistress at my school and I'll come.
    I need some help myself. A language is tough
    With no one to practice on.

YOUNG PAL

    And tell me when we'll ever use our French
    After all the studying is done.

NANCY

> Oh well, if we went overseas we would

MILLICENT *entering*

> Oh Pal you're home. Why hullo Nancy dear,
> Will you stay and join us later on?
> Oh what a lovely evening
> We're going to have tonight. Do stay. And Pal
> I got the birthday paper that you asked me for
> The prettiest in the shop.

YOUNG PAL

> Thanks Millicent *to Nancy*
> Come on. I'll show you my stamp collection *they exit*

Knock at the door. Enter a very smartly dressed woman

MILLICENT

> Ilene. Ilene, oh let me look at you.
> Oh what a surprise for Katie this will be.
> Tonight we're having a party for her birthday
> Oh what luck of lucks that you should come.
> We expected an ogre. Not someone so young,
> And certainly not you. Oh Ilene dear
> How wonderful that you should come back home,
> You've been away so long. Mother, mother

MOTHER

> Why it's Ilene. Don't tell me you're the matron?
> And now you'll stay forever, won't you dear?

ILENE

> Yes. I expect I will

MOTHER

> Oh darling, how often
> We've talked of you. Come sit by me awhile
> And tell me how things are with you my dear,
> You never found another?

ILENE

> No never

MOTHER

> You are still beautiful. The years wear well
> On wholesomeness my dear. How strong you were.

ILENE

> You were all strong too.

MOTHER

> But tell me of yourself my dear.

ILENE

> There's nothing much to tell. I went to school
> I wanted to be a doctor too but couldn't,
> And when my youth was gone, I turned to the old . . .

163

Enter Kate, Kitty and Iris

KATE

        Well who's that? Ilene? Oh what a day you've picked

IRIS

        Oh thank God you've come back home

MILLICENT

        A toast to friendship first with our own wine

        We've got such a party planned tonight, a goose

        And all the trimmings, and such a thing to talk on,

IRIS

        Pacifism

KATE

        Later, later

ILENE

        And I can't tell you how it feels

        To be back here again and see you all

        As if I'd never left you all those years.

        I didn't write. I couldn't, though I knew

        That someday I would have to come again

        And make my peace with all the shades of men

        That wander through these streets even now

        And speak at every corner. Oh how did you stay?

        How did you all hang on and keep this life

        Together? I envied you your courage,

        And I knew that someday I too would come back . . .

        What happened to Jessica? Did she have the child?

MOTHER

        Pal? Pal?

He comes racing in with Nancy, a gift in his hands

        Pal dear. This is Ilene, a friend of your mother's

YOUNG PAL

        How do you do? Ilene this is my friend Nancy.

ILENE

        Oh hullo Nancy.

YOUNG PAL

        Excuse us. It's my mother's birthday and we planned something.

They put Kate in the center of the room and skip around her singing "Happy Birthday"

KATE

        Stop, stop children. I'm dizzy.

YOUNG PAL

        Dear mother. this is for you.

She opens the small package.

        The opal was found by Hughie's dad and the gold

        Was found by me. Rick tied them both together

        And Hughie made the chain. And mother dear

        I hope you'll wear it always in memory of me.

KATE

      My darling boy, I will

Ilene points to him and mother nods.

ILENE

      And Jessica?

PAL

      Oh I'm surrounded by mothers.

Giving Kitty a bear hug

      And someday if I have a daughter maybe
      I'll call her Jessica. But right now,
      My mother's Kate, the matron of the hospital,
      The best mother in all the world, my Kate.
      The others are my mother Millicent,
      My mother Kitty and my mother Iris.
      It's great to have a lot of mothers
      And a grand mother as well.

KITTY

      He gets away with murder. I teach him music
      He calls us all our first names, even Kate.

PAL

      What's wrong with that? Hm. I smell goose.
      Hey Nancy. Let's see what mother Millicent's been doing. *Exit*

MOTHER

      My dear I cannot tell you the joy he is
      We spoil him rotten all of us but no harm.

KATE

      He's doing very well at school. He's obedient,

IRIS

      Most of the time

ILENE

      And Jessica?

KATE

      She died the very moment we walked in.
      We were lucky to save the child.
      We made some resolutions years ago,
      Like ways and means to hold on to our lives,
      And make them meaningful in spite of all.

IRIS

      And one thing we have always tried to do
      Is comfort each other when we needed help,
      Move up in our professions to the top
      That is permitted women, and have our soirees.

KATE

      Evenings that we would come and be together
      And discuss a topic that we planned before

And read about and thought about before.
Tonight it's pacifism.

IRIS:

In earlier talks
We tossed around the idea of patriotism
And what it really means, for it's a shame
If countries do not hold up true ideals,
And true ideals it seems are global issues,
If the devastation that befell us all,
Is to be rendered quite impossible.

MILLICENT

Dinner is served

Bringing in the birthday cake

Scene 4

Later that Evening

ILENE

    Oh Millicent I had almost forgotten
    How wonderful your cooking is.

MILLICENT

    Well it's my specialty.
    We grow our own vegetables,
    We have our own chickens, fruit from the shop,
    It's natural that I should learn to cook.
    But really I do love it all the same.
    I know everyone's favorite dish
    And we go with what's in season.

ILENE

    I cannot express what contentment I feel tonight
    To be with you. I've been running all my life,
    Trying to fill the void with other things
    Not made up of the substance of that life,
    And when I opened that door tonight I knew
    That I had made the right decision to return,
    As if by taking in the thing I fear
    I would overcome it utterly.
    And someday will I come to peace of mind
    And fully accept the tragedy
    As just a drought, a long and cruel drought
    But a part of life as surely as the hail and rain.

IRIS

    Yes, that is what we've done with our soirees,
    It is as though we imagined there was strength
    Somewhere in the global universe,
    To build anew an ideal world or life

KITTY

    Because when lovers are killed, it's women who suffer.

KATE

> When sons are killed, its women who suffer.

IRIS

> It's men who say that France and Germany suffered
> What's France or Germany to us?
> What's England or Australia to them
> Who lost their sons and lovers in the war?
> They only know the loss and so do we,
> And so we're natural friends for ever and ever,
> For someday we know the time will come for women,
> Life givers and life preservers ever yet,
> To rise up in the friendship of their strength
> And shout for all the world to hear, halt !
> Kind sirs do pardon us but we must speak.
> Killings are not the answer, never were!
> And they, all pompous in their robes of state
> Will look benignly down and say "dear child
> Its not for you to fret affairs of state.
> Best leave it to us men who've studied law,
> And balance of power.
> Why, you have never even been to school
> While we've been fighting wars and winning them,
> (One side or the other) from time immemorial"

Everyone laughs

KATE

> And at some moment all the quiet ones
> That have suffered from this time immemorial
> Will suddenly flare up spontaneously
> And overthrow the martial law of men.

ILENE

> Oh my God! You're revolutionaries!
> I knew when we were young that you were free,
> Your minds uncluttered by the niceties
> That Victorian women in a social age
> Gave energy to and lost sight of their rights—
> But never did I expect to find you here,
> In Charters Towers, almost a ghost town,
> Plotting the overthrow of governments,
> Dissolving national boundaries in a sea
> Of oh, dare we call it thus—humanity?

laughter

IRIS

> This is just beginning, and it's not
> Just here and now.
> As we speak here, so women around the world
> Are speaking or are thinking to themselves

As daily they live out lives destroyed by men,
Mutilated, barren, stubborn lives
That can't surrender quite the nurturing force
That must preserve us all.

KITTY

So here we are
Playing our little part as other women,
Keeping alive the better part of us
When all the rest is dead. One child we have
Among the five of us. No manly voices
Laughing.
No heavy footsteps ever walk our floors.
No voice we have in city politics
Or governments of state or federal.
We fought to have the railroad come through here
But who was there to listen. All for greed
And expedience of the moment, men act upon
Without a care for those that follow after,
The legacy, the future, for all the world.

IRIS

Let's get more wine
You won't believe it but we still have wine
Made from the grapes the boys grew on the farm.
Their father was the bravest of the brave,
And killed himself with work
Just to keep the farm alive and pay
The mortgage down each year.
Then the railroad goes right by and does not stop,
A death knell to the town so decimated
And then he sold. And do you know Ilene
He was a pacifist before he died.

KATE

I was glad he sold because you see
I never was sure the farm was best for Pal.
The age old pattern of this father to son
Among the common people of the land
Has kept them subjugated to survive,
And at the mercy of the soulless ones,
Who order them in name of government
To give their all to this great foreign thing
Called liberty or freedom or the peace
When what they end up with, is worse than death.

ILENE

So you hope that young Pal might think on this
And make a different choice when he must choose?

169

Mary Anneeta Mann

KATE

> I hope he'll give some thought to government,
> Though pacifism may yet come hard for him,
> With such a heritage of martial men
> Still stirring in his blood.

KITTY

> And though we try
> To teach him music and the gentler things,
> He plays with boys that play with soldier toys,
> With guns and sabers uppermost in their minds,
> And not because they're naturally inclined
> To all the martial arts but just because
> Some ex war hero with a martial strain,
> Has opened up a factory for toys
> And made them all into soldiers just like him.
> And young boys listening to their fathers talk,
> Will imitate and plead with mothers too,
> To buy them guns. And so they are all ready
> When the wheel of fortune turns again to war!

IRIS

> But look how we are talking
> And the rest of the town asleep.
> Come, dear friend I'll walk you to your house
> Goodnight, goodnight. Katie, Happy Birthday once again. *They exit.*

MILLICENT *Comes over and puts her arm around Kate*

> Oh Katie, when we lost Pal and Fred and Jessica
> I thought my life was coming to an end.
> I didn't think I could go on living,
> I wanted to jump into the weir or shoot myself.
> I didn't think I could handle all the pain
> I really didn't. But then you were there.
> You came with your quiet strength
> And I discovered a wonderful thing.
> I love you more Katie than if you were my sister.
> I know I love you more
> Because all through the years when I look at you
> My heart smiles and I'm glad that you are here
> And I know it wouldn't be like that
> If you were my sister
> Because I would expect you to be there
> Do you understand me?

170

KATE

        I do Millicent, I do.

MILLICENT

        Listen to the crickets

Kate pulls at some blades of grass at her feet. There is a long pause.

KATE

        When the wheel of fortune turns again to war.

        My father's coming. What does it mean?

Scene 5

Beer Garden, Europe

Dada paintings are being brought in and hung everywhere. The Mad Student enters with flowers in his hat and dangling down his back. There are other poets with him fishing in their pockets for scraps of paper. They are dressed in rags.

POET I *reading and declaiming*

We renounce a language devastated and ravaged by journalism.

We must preserve for poetry its most sanctified domain.

POET II

We are still living under the reign of logic. Boundaries have been assigned even to experience. In the guise of civilization, we have succeeded in dismissing from our minds, anything that could be regarded as superstition or myth.

MAD POET *jumping up*

Abolish logic. Dada, abolition of memory; Dada, abolition of prophets; Dada, abolition of the future; Dada, absolute and unquestionable faith in every god that is the immediate product of spontaneity:

POET III

I'm running toward happiness.

I'm burning in the eyes of passing days

I swallow jewels,

I sing in courtyards.

The Mad Student and the three poets then declaim all their lines in unison for a few moments.

Meanwhile three men stroll in, middle class and rather comfortably dressed. They sit down looking very disdainfully at the poets who immediately begin to hover around them.

MAN I

Sirs, kind sirs, would you leave us alone please

The poets retreat a little.

These men are cruel. They are cruel instinctively and without effort. They are cruel with a scientific refinement that almost amounts to genius.

MAN II

The Germans

The poets, very much relieved that they are not being discussed, return to their hovering. They speak to each other.

POET I

The conversation is lagging isn't it.

POET II

Very lagging.

MAN II

Is it all the Germans do you think
Or just the extreme militarists that go into the army?

POET III

Very lagging isn't it.

POET I

Naturally, isn't it.

POET II

Obviously isn't it

MAN II

There's a mechanical mathematics about the army,
A certain kind of precision
That appeals to a certain kind of mind.
A logical mechanical mind.

POET III

Very lagging isn't it.

MAN III

A precise algebraical mind.

POET II

Obviously, isn't it

MAN III

A dictionary of straight lines
In precise formation,
A rational logical line.

POET I

Very lagging isn't it.

MAN II *getting a bit frustrated*

Gentlemen would you leave us alone please?

MAD STUDENT

Could not dreams as well be applied to the solution for life's fundamental problems?
One night before falling asleep, I became aware of a most bizarre sentence, separate
from the sound of any voice—a sentence I might say which KNOCKED AT THE
WINDOW!

POET I

The poet works. the poet works!

POETS 1, II and III and the Mad Student *Fishing out pieces of paper*

The poet works, the poet works, the poet works . . .

*They fade down a little as they become engrossed in a group of men who come stumbling in
quarreling violently. Three men push each other in an effort to get next to the single girl and
talk to her. The poets move excitedly to their original table, fishing pieces of paper out of
their pockets and reading poetry to each other. The Mad Student stays hovering around as
PAL enters carrying a knapsack and still in his old army uniform although rather bedraggled*

173

by this. He had been coming closer as the men were speaking. He comes over and points to the empty chair as if asking permission to sit there. The men nod although not very impressed with his attire.

PAL

> You are not listening to each other.

MAN I

> Why should we listen to each other?

PAL

> Because you are men!

The three man laugh, looking Pal up and down

MAN I I

> Yes, yes, we are men, but what are they?

PAL

> They are men too.

MAN III *derisively*

> Oh, they are?

They laugh and look over at the poets

PAL

> You were talking about an army. What do you mean?

MAN I

> The German army is being mobilized. The youth are signing up.

PAL

> But why?

MAN II

> It's simple. When in doubt, return to order.

They begin to get up as if bored with the conversation. Pal follows.

PAL

> But what about goodwill? What about goodwill?

workers enter.

WORKER I

sitting next to Madeline while the others get chairs

> Madeline, you're the only one in the whole shop who refuses to join the union. Don't you have any pity for us? Just think of the things we could do for everybody if we had a whole union shop.

MADELINE

> I am not joining the union.

WORKER II

> Madeline, look, look, look

WORKER III

throwing his hands up in the air in the air

> That's what you get for emancipating women!

The girl glares at him

WORKER II

> Madeline, look, if you join us we can push that much harder for shorter hours, more pay, longer vacations.

MADELINE

Yes, and lazier workers, sneaking off to sleep when you should be working: cutting down on working hard for fear you might do more than somebody else. you all act as if you hate work. Every time a new rule comes out, you try your best to get around it, to try to find loopholes in it, everything rather than obey it. And yet do you want to go and make a new rule yourself? Oh, no, not you. When Mr. Wilson called for volunteers the other day to help him draft the new work load for the machine shop, did anybody offer? That machine's doing the work of five men. Was anybody fired? No. They were all trained on something else. And who benefits? Every body. That new workload can be done in six hours and you know it. You won't help draft anything new yet you complain about every workload that Mr. Wilson puts up on that board. And if it's the union that makes your head so addled that you don't know how well off you really are, than I don't want any part of it. Thank you, no.

WORKER I

Whew! That was quite a mouthful, Madeline

WORKER II

Where have you been hiding all those evil thoughts about us all the time? I knew you were Mr. Wilson's favorite, but I didn't know he's brainwashed you to that extent.

MADELINE jumping up

I am not brainwashed! You are the ones that are brainwashed. I happen to like working. I happen to like my job and if you don't like yours, why don't you quit. But I'll tell you something man, it bugs the hell out of me when I stack up all that work in front of me and really have fun doing it and then the others come over and say, "Go slow Madeline, go slow—you make it so hard on us." And yesterday I got so mad I jumped up and shouted "Look you've got the union to protect you so go and cry to the union and leave me alone."

The men begin nodding their heads. She steps back. Than she speaks slowly

That's why you're here.

One of them pulls an application form out of his pocket. She stares at it. There is absolute silence. Then Madeline throws back her head and bursts into a peal of laughter which is still good-natured. The men are in complete confusion.

What's not black, is white. Gee you're funny.

She laughs again, not hysterically, but openly and freely. But then she realizes that the others are not comprehending at all.

Well I can see you're all upset.

There must be a way out of this dilemma.

They all come close again

I'll tell you something. I'd like to join but you have to alter come conditions. Look, I happen to work a little harder than the person next to me. Is that my fault? You've already fixed it so I can't get paid any more than anybody else with your mathematical computations about sliding scales and seniority and all those union figures you keep pestering me with *Waving a hand in the air* But what I do is the expression of my spirit, and you can't regulate my spirit, man.

WORKER III

> Look. I told you, you can't talk to Madeline. It's no use trying to talk to Madeline.

MADELINE

> Look, you know very well if I joined and made it a union shop then you would be the boss instead of Her Mueller. Why should I swap bosses when I have more freedom now than I would have with you. If you let me work at my own pace and have extra time to myself to do my own thing in, without everybody staring at me, then I'll join your union.

WORKER I

> We can't do that. You know how jealous everybody is. If we do it for one we have to do it for all.

MADELINE

> Well then, I can't join, can I!

WORKER II

> You haven't heard the end of this Madeline.
>
> The union will live on Madeline.

They go off and Madeline sits dejectedly fingering her glass of beer. The Mad Student comes over to her

MAD STUDENT

> You should be proud. You beat them.

MADELINE

> No. What they don't know is that I was offered the job of supervisor too. And I wouldn't take it.

MAD STUDENT

> Why not?

MADELINE

> I belong with them

MAD STUDENT

> Well why don't you join their union'

MADELINE

> I want to join. Do you think I enjoy being left out in the cold?

A couple of girls waft in, smoking cigarettes in long holders with bands around their heads and garters on their legs. They are looking at the paintings and eyeing the Mad Student at the same time. He begins to describe the paintings.

MAD STUDENT

> In this world, machinery becomes human, people become things, things dissolve into nature and everything becomes petrified in a mechanical universe.

MADELINE *jumping up*

> Oh, no, no, no

The girls stare at her in amazement

TILLY

> But my dear, what are you so excited about. It's only a painting.

MADELINE

> You're right, you're right.

she sits down

TILLY

Where did you pick her up?

MAD STUDENT

Oh, she just chanced by. Now note this, ladies. The aim of this painter is to combine the spontaneous with the planned, to wrest order from the chaos without sacrificing freedom.

The unconscious is the all powerful.

TILLY

But a woman is so weak. Is man the unconscious that he is so—POWERFUL!

MAD STUDENT

As a matter of fact, my dear lady. it is the woman's role that is the unconscious.

MADELINE

NO, no, no,

MAD STUDENT

Tangerine and white from Spain

I'm killing myself Madeleine

Haven't I met you somewhere before?

Your name is Madeleine isn't it?

In some earlier reincarnation perhaps?

In the dark night of the soul maybe?

Where have we met Madeline?

Oh well, no matter.

However Madeline, I do wish you would let me demonstrate these paintings in peace.

MADELINE

But I cannot, if you don't tell the truth!

MAD STUDENT

Gather around ladies. Here is someone who has the truth.

MADELINE *she is very embarrassed*

Woman is freedom.

TILLY

A woman is the most unfree thing in the whole world.

Her man commands her very soul.

MADELINE

Not mine.

MAD STUDENT

Well Madeline, if woman is freedom, pray tell me what is order?

MADELINE

Order is a union. Order is an army. Order is a NAZI.

MAD STUDENT

Careful, careful, expediency cannot be denied!

MADELINE

I don't have to be careful. Careful for what? Careful that my friends don't beat me up for not joining a union?

She steps back in horror as a Jew with his cap and beard stumbles in through the wings. The workers enter from the other side.

177

Look at that, look at that! Can't you see where you are headed?
the Jew stops walking and stands still

Don't you pity him? *they all nod*
Well then DO something. DO something!

MAD STUDENT

Madeline what can we do? I am a student. Nobody pays any attention to me. Not even my professors!
he looks so comical that everybody laughs, even the Jew

MADELINE

What about goodwill? Huh, what about goodwill?

MAD STUDENT *in revelation*

Aha that is where we have met before. We have met in the categorical imperative of goodwill.

MADELINE

Well then DO something.
She moves toward the Mad Student. He acts quite insanely not unlike John Marshall and ends up in the arms of his poet friends who try to calm and quiet him while Madeline making a gesture to acknowledge the hopelessness of trying to work with him, returns to the workers

DO SOMETHING *They all step back*
she goes over to the Jew

Who did it?

JEW

The brown shirts

MADELINE

Why?
He laughs a little pitifully and points to his cap and his beard. She turns back to the workers. Pal has reentered quietly backstage with an armful of flowers for the tables.

MADELINE

Is that a sufficient reason to beat a man up?

WORKER I

Madeline you don't understand

MADELINE

No, I don't understand, and I don't want to understand and I never will understand.

JEW *coming over to bar and talking gently*

Look, this is a man's business and you had better not get mixed up in it.

MADELINE

You fool, you fool. Go and walk with them.
she points to the workers.

You all belong together.
she speaks slowly and deliberately as she backs away from them all

And-I-will-never-join-your-union, and I will not quit either, so take it from there.
Martial music plays, as brown shirts enter and shoot everyone. The music goes on playing. Pal comes out from the back room and stares in horror.

Scene 6

The Colonel Comes
Charters Towers

COLONEL

      Good evening my dear
      It is so good to see you once again
      And nothing's changed except the young one's gone.
      Where is he now?

KATE:

> In medical school. It's a long six year stretch

COLONEL

> Where is he? What year?

KATE

> Third year medicine, and three to go

COLONEL

> It's a pity he didn't stay with government

KATE

> I thought so too at first. But now I don't
> Regret his choice.

COLONEL

> But why? I thought you were
> So anxious that he go in to government.

KATE

> The time's not right. They would have broken his heart.
> He's manly. There's no doubt of that you know,
> But yet he's gentle, surrounded by only us, his mothers.

COLONEL

> Hm. Well of course

KATE

> He sees things as they are, we taught him that.
> And he's not interested in politics
> That seek immediate ends, not long term goals—
> And something turned him off.

COLONEL *coughing*

> Well I've come a long, long way to see you.

KATE

> Something is troubling you. What is it?

COLONEL

> Kate, in spite of all our differences
> I love you more than anything in this world.
> The last time that I came and we had words
> I went back so dejected I couldn't write.
> But now I've come again and must speak
> And tell you what I know.
> Oh dear Kate it's probably too late
> For you or me or anyone in this world
> To avert what's written in the sky even now,
> Another war.

MOTHER

> Another war? another war?

COLONEL

> Oh there have been rumblings for a long, long time.
> There were rumblings when I came one time before.
> But is the boy a pacificist Kate? Is he?

180

KATE

> He's not a boy father, he's a man
> He's twenty three years old and old enough
> To make his own decisions whatever comes.
> He's lived three years longer than my Pal
> And five years longer than his father did.
> All this already. What shall we ask of him?
> Pal will you now be a pacifist?
> A conscientious objector to a war
> For which all glory will be strung out in the sky—
> Lines and lines of banners, medals too,
> To lure the young men on?
> Oh father, we have lived these twenty years
> A life apart.
> We've watched men err again and yet again.
> We've watched the League of Nations grow not strong
> But weak and weaker as the years passed.
> We've watched things happen. Germany withdraw,
> Japan withdraw.
> And though we do not know what Jewish means
> Because no Jews have ever come up here,
> We do know that there's human dignity
> That's being violated even now,
> While so-called strong men look and turn their heads,
> Too weak or too afraid to speak their minds.
> Oh yes, I do believe in Pacifism
> But Pacifism with international law!
> And as for Pal, he's twenty three years old,
> He'll make his own choice when the moment comes.

COLONEL

> But do you think that he'll go to a war,
> Because dear Kate it will be worse much worse.

KATE

> Your mind and mine remember the last war.
> Each generation writes its own memory.
> How could I tell him and to what avail?

COLONEL

> If he had graduated maybe I could
> Get a commission for him. It would help.
> Or he could be a medic. They're much safer.

KATE

> Oh father, Colonel Campbell, don't talk
> Of how to save his life. That's sheer expedience.
> Far rather would I here debate with you
> The possibility of some form of peace
> Before the world's committed to a war

That people do not want in my country !
Far rather should we talk of cancerous growth,
A little corporal rearing his ugly head
With others watching on—there's a difference
I've found and I think Pal has found it too.
The time for action passes, pacific action,
When evil could have been contained by good.
Then comes the sacrifice. No other choice.
This is a different war. This is a war
Of good and evil yet no one will win.
Great sacrifices once again of men,
Great sorrow once again for women
And Pal my son, my lovely human being
What will become of him?

Scene 7

Daughter of the British Empire

Millicent and Kitty at the piano, mother in the rocking chair. A knock

IRIS

      Is Kate home yet?

MOTHER

      Oh she's like a soul divided Iris,

      On the one hand, the greatest honor

      And on the other, the greatest defeat

MILLICENT

      Oh mother don't say it like that

MOTHER

      Well it's how she feels.

      Daughter of the British Empire

      Why an honor such as that for Kate,

      Our Kate, our darling strong and brilliant girl!

she bursts into tears

KITTY

      Oh I'm so proud of you.

As Kate enters

KATE

      What's the matter?

MOTHER

      Oh Kate my darling *hugging her*

MILLICENT

      Congratulations. I got some wine from the old farm

      We still have one bottle left you know Kate

      From the very old stock. We could use that you know.

KATE

      Oh no, absolutely not. That's to be saved

      For Pal's wedding whenever it may be.

MILLICENT

      Let's open it Kate

KATE

No, no, it's for Pal's wedding.

MILLICENT

Well, fill up everyone

IRIS

To Dame Katie

KITTY

D.B.E.,
Daughter of the British Empire, Kate
It has been worth the effort hasn't it?
I used to question that philosophy
So long ago. For every blow received,
Root down into your inner soul and add
One grain the more of love, or encouragement
To others. And that is what you've done dear Kate

KATE

Oh, come on now Kitty
But I know some people from the west had written—

IRIS

Kate,
If you had been a doctor
Could you really have done much more?

KATE

Oh yes, much more. The times I've had to wait
And hand the instruments when in my heart
I knew I could have done it all myself.
And sometimes watch a life go by because
I could not act. And this achievement here
Has come, a recognition for which I'm proud
But one within the boundaries of my life
The boundaries that have been forced on me.
But still it is a great honor isn't it?

MILLICENT

How was the reception Katie?

KATE

How was the reception Iris?

IRIS

Oh the mayor was there and made a speech,
And Doctor Riley from the hospital.

MOTHER

Oh this wine is awfully good!

IRIS

And people came in from the west, so many
Hundreds of miles they traveled some of them
Just to share with Kate her golden day.

MILLICENT

Hear, hear, Katie!

KATE

It was wonderful. I'll never forget it,
And Pal so proud sitting next to me
And his finals right upon him, dear child.
He wouldn't take a penny for the fare.

IRIS

Ilene went with him to the station. They left
Early. What a great kid!

KITTY

Katie, did you talk at all?

KATE

No, no, we didn't. He wouldn't. He just refused.
"Mother," he said, "This is your day today
This is your day and not a cloud
Shall darken it. I'll be home," he said, "for Xmas
When the exams are all over, and then we'll talk,
But not today."

KITTY

I wonder what that means?

MOTHER

It's just as if a cloud passed over the sun
And even though we've been prepared so long
I'm not prepared at all.

MILLICENT

It's not
As distant as it was before somehow,
It's very close. Not just because of Pal
But because our own minds have been tuned to it
Through all our evenings, all our soirees. Oh God,
What shall we do? How can we live through this?

there is a voice heard, singing and Ilene knocks at the door and enters

ILENE

Well, I saw him off
And he'll be back right after Xmas.
Oh, what a handsome young man he is.
You know, when he was sitting next to me and talking
He was so mature, so wise and his face was so radiant,
I wanted to throw my arms around him,
And kiss him passionately.

she throws herself into a chair and begins to smoke. Millicent rushes to get her an ashtray.

IRIS

Ilene

KATE

Well, Ilene

185

ILENE
>Oh, don't be concerned. Don't really.
>I was just telling you how I felt.
>It's not as though I would act on it,
>Or anything like that,
>But the urge was there, just the same.

she looks around at the flabbergasted group
>Is that a sin? I am still young aren't I?

MILLICENT
>Well, no, it's not a sin—to feel—

IRIS
>You could be his mother you know

ILENE
>Well that's exactly what I was thinking,
>A young mother though!
>While all the time I was feeling
>As though I would like to be his lover—
>I mean—just momentarily—
>You understand—don't you?

KATE
>Well, I think I do but I must say I am a little surprised.

ILENE
>I was surprised too.
>I mean women are not supposed to—

IRIS
>Well now, I don't know about that—
>I mean, it's our Pal and he's our child
>And we can't consider Pal
>But what if it had been someone else?
>Have a cigarette

ILENE *very excited*
>Well that's what I mean
>The culture—we aren't taught
>How to handle anything like that are we?

KATE
>No we aren't.
>And we often used to talk when we were younger
>About why we never found other men,
>Younger men, when all our boys were gone.

MILLICENT
>We never really wanted to try, did we.

KITTY
>Some women love only once.

ILENE
>But life is to be enjoyed,
>Now really isn't it—I mean as best we can

IRIS

    Whatever you say. What did she say?

KITTY

    Well, we certainly enjoyed it when we were young

MILLICENT *laughing*

    Oh Ilene, you do bring a ripple of happiness
    And lightheartedness into the household,
    Doesn't she though?
    Just don't think about our Pal, O.K.?

MOTHER

    This wine is so lovely!

KITTY

    I believe I'll have a cigarette!

IRIS

    Tell me when you were in Sydney though
    Weren't there other men Ilene,
    Didn't you ever find anyone else?

KITTY

    I think if I had been in a bigger town
    I might have tried all kinds of affairs,
    I might have—I don't really know.

ILENE

    Oh yes, lighthearted affairs
    Waltzing around, trying this, trying that,
    Always cross sectionally—you know what I mean ?
    Never longitudinally.

KATE

    You mean you could never put down roots again?

ILENE

    No, my childhood was here, my man was here,
    You are here, my roots are here.
    Now, this is what we must do
    On our next soiree we must discuss LOVE
    No, no, no objections
    We are going to discuss love.
    L'amore, l'amore. That's all there is to it!

MOTHER

    My cup is brimming over.
    I've had my Millicent,
    My companion all my life it seems.
    I've had you all, my daughters too,
    And now young Pal, the sparkle of my aging years.
    What is there more to life than fading
    In the joy and love of youth?
    And Pal is always with me. "Mother, mother,
    There's more to life than dying", and his face is all aglow.

Scene 8

Christmas 1939

The same with decorations, candles on the table, open piano
MILLICENT

      It's been three months since war has been declared

      Perhaps he will not go. Oh God,

      I never prayed for anything before

      As I pray now for safety of that boy

      That we all call our son.

Young Pal enters—perhaps played by the same actor as played his father Fred before
YOUNG PAL

      Merry Xmas Millicent. Well now

      I've never seen you so dressed up. What's this?

MILLICENT

      I bought it just for you. You're such a grown man

      You make us all feel young again dear Pal

YOUNG PAL

      You're always young to me dear Millicent,

      You're barely in your forties all of you,

      You have so much ahead.

MILLICENT

      So much of what?

YOUNG PAL

      So much of friendship, love and deep compassion.

      Millicent, remember that.

      You should not play it down the way you do

      Because my dear it it so important.

      Whatever happens to me in my life

      I know my roots are set in pure gold!

MILLICENT

      Oh Pal, my darling boy *crying*

YOUNG PAL

      Come now. The others are coming

Kitty enters and Millicent goes to the piano

Oh my, another all dressed up to kill!

KITTY

Well, you'll he surprised all evening then.
Every single one of us went out
And bought a dress. The last evening dress we'll buy
Until the war is over.

YOUNG PAL

Oh what a lucky man.
I'll be dancing with my beauties all night long.
I'll never let you go, never. Always,
I'll remember you dear Kitty, the music lessons,
The love and care. Music has always been
So much of the life here. And thanks to you,
I've shared it. Piano lessons, violin,
Remember when I won that prize?
And you accompanied me? You've filled my life
To overflowing. I've had more love right here
Than most men have their whole life through

A ring at the door. Iris and Ilene enter. Kitty and Millicent play the piano

PAL

Most honored ladies. Welcome.

ILENE

Down on your knees. I knight you Sir Pal!

YOUNG PAL

Will you reserve a dance for me tonight?
Was ever man so lucky. I can't believe
That I could ever have deserved
Such elegant companions as you are.

ILENE

Now don't get a swelled head young man, remember
These evening gowns are the last that we will buy
Till the war is over pray God it won't be long.

IRIS

Certainly not long enough for anyone
To interrupt their schooling in mid-stream

Kate is at the side door

YOUNG PAL

Go back and put it on
I made her promise me she'd wear it.

IRIS

As I was saying, I certainly would stay
In school if I were halfway through right now!

Kate enters wearing the DBE. The two at the piano play up her entrance

KATE

Merry Xmas

189

OTHERS

>Merry Xmas, we wish you a Merry Xmas

YOUNG PAL

>Let's open up the wine, my wedding wine,

There is some protest

>No, no, no protest, not from anyone
>And here is why. Someday maybe I'll marry
>But I shall never feel in all my life
>The way I feel tonight. Just here with you.
>I've had more love than any man alive.
>You've all been mothers, every one of you
>And this is our night. To all of us.

KATE

>From us to you.

YOUNG PAL

>Now everyone sit down.
>I have some news. Sit down Millicent.
>I know that you have all been wondering
>Just what I plan to do about the war.
>And now I have decided. I will enlist.
>All of you are women of Anzac,
>And none of you has ever married,
>Not only because your men were killed,
>But because you held on to their memory,
>And now I stand for them. I really think
>That freedom is in much more jeopardy
>Than what it was in nineteen fifteen.
>And even though I do not have to go
>Since there's no conscription and not likely to be,
>I can't forget my father and his friends
>And what they died for on Gallipoli.
>What they died for once again is threatened
>And I must go.

MILLICENT

>Oh Pal

YOUNG PAL

>But I cannot kill
>And so I'll be a medic. Not quite a doctor.
>I only wish I'd started from the first
>I'd be a doctor now. But anyway
>I'll go to France.

IRIS

>When will you leave?

YOUNG PAL

>This is my goodbye. I go from here.
>But there's much more I want to talk about

Tonight. Much more. It's about your soirees.
You must keep up your evenings and make notes,
Women everywhere. I realized when
I lived away from you how much I missed
The long, long evenings spent on world affairs.
It's only depth of suffering makes clear
The urgency of a world community.
Last night I dreamed of all the men you lost,
Lying in a land they did not know,
And I am going now to France. Who knows
What shall become of me? What difference,
That I shall be in France or Germany?
The world's divisions now are all wrong.
The only division, and that a hazy one,
Must lie dividing good and evil.
You must write down these things. In Germany,
Women think like you. France, Turkey.
I pray you all my mothers and God knows
When we shall meet if ever in this world—
Use well this time of inactivity
That you all have before your worth is known.
Write down the things that all the world must know
Before we can build up again from ashes.
And you my mother *Taking Kate aside*
Hold on to all your strength for it is mine.
I could not go feeling the way I do,
Without your life before me and what you've done.

KATE

I know you have to go. I knew you would.
Here. Take this. I've treasured it ten years.
I've never been without it, not a day.

She gives him the opal and gold pendant then turning
Come now everyone, let's have something
At the piano. One thing we all have learned,
Is to take what's coming.

ILENE

And even though we'd never tell him so
We're all so proud of him aren't we?

KITTY

We bought you a fountain pen so you can write,
And never forget us.

MILLICENT

We're lucky he has no girl.

IRIS

How do you know he has no girl?

YOUNG PAL

       Sometimes I wish I had—a wife even—
       I am the only one of all those men
       And who will follow me?

ILENE

       Oh, you'll come back, of course you will,
       And have a dozen kids.

YOUNG PAL

       The woman gives
       You children that's what I want to say.
       The woman is the life force. Oh God *aside*
       How can I survive this night?

MILLICENT

       More wine, more wine, let's drink ourselves drunk—
       I've never been drunk before and I never shall again.

YOUNG PAL

       No, no, no, no drunks. Let's kiss and let's begone
       Each to our separate things. Remember,
       Don't ever let me down in this world. Or the next.
       Goodnight sweet ladies, goodnight . . .

The women stand around the piano and begin singing in broken voices "Joy to the World"

Scene 9

The London Blitz

YOUNG PAL
>So your name is Kitty
>That's a special name for me.

KITTY
>I'm terrified when the bombs start falling.
>I can't go home again

YOUNG PAL
>Were they all killed Kitty?

KITTY
>Yes

YOUNG PAL
>Don't you have anyone?

KITTY
>No

YOUNG PAL
>Well young Kitty
>I'm not going to let you be sad for long.
>Think of us walking in Hyde Park
>Arm in arm.
>If this were peace time Kitty
>I'd be courting you,
>You know that?

KITTY
>But I love you Pal
>And I might never see you again.
>What if I never see you again?

YOUNG PAL
>Kitty my sweet, don't talk like that.

KITTY
>But I must.
>You feel it too. You feel it too,

Don't you!

YOUNG PAL

Yes, yes.
Oh Kitty, there are five women
In Australia
That raised me, only me,
And I shall not return
I know it.

KITTY

Isn't there something you can do?
Go AWOL, get sick, or something'
Miss the train?

YOUNG PAL

I can't

KITTY

Why not?

YOUNG PAL

Because of my father, and my father's friends.

KITTY

If you know you are going to be killed
You can't go.
There's got to be something you can do.

YOUNG PAL

About going back to the front?
There's nothing I can do about that.
I had a chance once to slip through the net.
I was studying government. Iris wanted that,
And she was right.

KITTY

Well what happened?

YOUNG PAL

I got discouraged in government.
I changed my major.
I might have been an officer,
If not for that.

a bomb explodes nearby

Oh Katie, Millicent,
My mothers are all floating around me
Did I tell you about my mothers
And their new evening gowns?

KITTY

Yes Pal, you did.
I love you Pal.

YOUNG PAL

Oh Kitty, I want so much to make love to you
But you'll have a baby,

194

You will you know
And I want that with all my heart
God help me.
But you are alone Kitty
You are alone.
What would you do if I never came back?

KITTY

I would have something to love and to live for
In this rotten ugly world.
I would have one night with you
To last me to the end of time.

YOUNG PAL

But a baby, a baby,
What would you do
If you had a baby?

KITTY

I want your baby.
I would have something of you forever,
Something to remind me always,
That there can still be some joy in this world,
Still some hope.

YOUNG PAL

Kitty, I have to leave at dawn.
Here, take this.
If I do not return,
Take it to my mother.
Promise me Kitty.
It will be a long journey
But promise me.

KITTY

I promise.

Bombs dropping

LIGHTS

Scene 10

Dunkirk

Memorial Day, May 30, 1940. It is dark. Bombs are exploding in the distance lighting up the sky, and near at hand making a dull thud as they hit the soft sand, or splashing as they hit the water. Upstage is a makeshift pier behind which the small craft are arriving to pick up the exhausted soldiers. In front of this is water and on the extreme right is a beach where the soldiers are waiting to walk or wade out to the pier and on to the craft. A fog is rolling across from the wings, stage left. In the center of the stage on a half submerged wreck of a small craft which shows some movement, although the water is comparatively calm, two women are sitting. One is sitting up straight and steadying herself. It is Liberty wearing her gown of red poppies with her cream colored cape over her shoulders. Although the fog is moving from stage left, there is also some wind blowing from higher up stage right and her hair is loose and is caught in it as well as part of her cape. The lower part of her body is submerged in the fog. Next to her and dressed in a see-through white loose flowing chiffon gown, is a very young girl. She has a veil attached to her head and could be a bride. Veil and gown are drenched and she is struggling to keep her head above the water. Liberty is secured and can pay attention to the soldiers on the shore, but the girl is not. She is nearly drowning, rising and falling all the time. Liberty is still aware of her and helps her when she can. The drowning girl is Peace and bears a very close resemblance to the other bride, World Commonwealth

SOLDIER I *on the shore*
>Oh, we're in for it this time, buster.

SOLDIER II
>We'll never get out of here. We'll get pushed right into the perishing sea.

SOLDIER III
>It's pitch dark, Eh, what's that out there?

SOLDIER II
>It's the dawn. It's nearly daylight.

SOLDIER III
>Something's moving out there. Eh you, who are you?

The light comes up very gradually to reveal the silhouette of the girls, the pier and the soldiers but it never comes up to full strength in this scene

LIBERTY

    I am Liberty beloved

SOLDIER 1

    Well, what the hell are you doing here?

SOLDIER II

    Eh, you can't talk to a woman like that!

SOLDIER 1

    Liberty my bloody foot. We're all doomed and she knows it!

SOLDIER III

    What are you doing here?

LIBERTY

    I came to be with you

SOLDIER I

    Do you think we will get out of here?

LIBERTY

    Body or Soul beloved?

SOLDIER I

    Body, you bitch.

    Who gives a damn about our ruddy soul.

    My father fought in the war to end all wars,

    Till a bloody maniac sets the world on fire

    And here I am.

    What's liberty to me?

SOLDIER II

    You can't blame her

LIBERTY

    Let him speak

A few bombs drop very close. There is a dull thud in the sand nearby and a splash in the water

SOLDIER III

He is looking intensely at the derelict craft.

    Come on. Come ashore. Get down.

He wades in and pulls the girl up and rocks her in his arms like a baby. It is getting a little lighter. A voice is heard from the pier.

CIVILIAN

    Eh grab that rope,

    I can take five men, two strong ones.

After this the men are being ferried away continually throughout the rest of the scene. The various skippers are dressed as if on a Sunday picnic, a fisherman or sea-patrol men or men off the street.

SOLDIER III

    Is Liberty in peace time different from Liberty in war?

LIBERTY

    I am forever and always the same beloved

    Though many times you do not see,

    And when you see, sometimes you do not know.

SOLDIER IV

I am afraid to look at you

LIBERTY

Why are you afraid beloved?

SOLDIER IV

It is easier, if I look at you

And I do not know that you are Liberty.

I do not have to say, even to myself,

That there is something that I have to guard.

LIBERTY

But I am in everyperson.

SOLDIER IV

I know, but I don't see you everywhere,

In everywoman, only when you stand

Before me as you're standing now.

LIBERTY

Why do you fear to gaze

At the concrete and see the ideal?

VOICE

I can take five more.

SOLDIER IV

It makes life too difficult. It makes me feel responsibility

And if there is one thing I hate, it's responsibility.

LIBERTY

Why?

SOLDIER III

How can I accept responsibility for the twentieth century?

I will go mad!

A bomb explodes nearby

The burden is too great for anyone to bear

LIBERTY

Guilt is a burden,

But not responsibility.

SOLDIER II

To be responsible is to be guilty

LIBERTY

No beloved

SOLDIER I

I tell you it is, it is

LIBERTY

When responsibility precedes the action, it averts the guilt.

SOLDIER IV

But it is too late. Hitler is upon us.

There is a lot of commotion

CIVILIAN

I can take ten men and it is the maiden voyage of ANTIGONE BRITANNIA

The men file out on the pier

LIBERTY

> Each generation rises with the sun
> To take this earth and hold it is their hands,
> And wipe it clean if it is dripping blood,
> And spill their blood if it has been betrayed.

SOLDIER III

> But where do you come in?

LIBERTY

> I am the choice beloved

SOLDIER II

> You are free will then?

LIBERTY

> Every man is born free:
> I am his soul's choice, beloved.

SOLDIER I

> But every man is not born free,
> Some men are born slaves. They are not free.

LIBERTY

> Why do you fear to see
> The ideal in the concrete?
> Look at me.

SOLDIER IV

> I am looking at you

LIBERTY

> The concrete is the bombs exploding,
> The ideal is the thought of me.
> Beloved, do you know me?

She is shouting at the end to be heard over the roar of sounds overhead, and artillery fire and bombs.

CHORUS

> Yes, yes, you are Liberty
> And you are free

CIVILIAN

ANTIGONE BRITTANIA calling. I'm back for more men. The trawlers are in real close, fellows. Hurry up, we'll get you all back home!

YOUNG PAL

> Hullo, you can't stay here
> Aren't you coming with us?

LIBERTY

> It's not necessary.

YOUNG PAL

> My name is Pal.
> I've always been fond of Liberty.

LIBERTY

> I know.

Liberty in wartime
Is the spirit of men,
Something they have in their hearts forever
And hold on to without end.
And faith is given by the universe,
Nature's equilibrium.
For every voice that is silenced,
A new one shall be heard.
And every field falling fallow,
Shall await its turn to produce.
Europe is guilty. Yet her children shall be free.

She is moving off the stage a little Go now, to England, and remember me.
The new world shall be ours, beloved
Remember me.

Scene 11

The Pendant's Return

The same almost one year later. The lid of the piano is down. Millicent crosses in her night gown, exits and returns with the morning paper, makes tea, and reads the paper.

KATE *entering*

      Not dressed Millicent?

MILLICENT

      Oh, I hadn't noticed. I'm sorry Katie.

KATE

      What news?

MILLICENT

      There is no news anymore Katie.

KATE

      Come on now, what is happening?

MILLICENT

      Nothing, nothing is happening,

      Death upon death upon death, that's nothing,

      Death is nothing Katie

KATE

      But we have to go on living Millicent,

      Remember your promise

MILLICENT

      I remember nothing Katie, nothing *bursting into tears*

KATE

      Oh Millicent you must you really must,

      Please don't make it any harder Millicent,

      I have to go to the hospital Milli

MILLICENT

      Oh Katie, Katie

      How have we deserved this Katie, how? *holding her*

KATE

      We haven't Millie, we haven't.

A knock then Kitty enters at the front door

      Oh thank God you're here. I have to go

I'll come home early if I can tonight.
Kitty and Millicent cry together
MILLICENT

 I can't survive it Kitty. This time I can't.
 I'm somehow paralyzed. I can't get up.
 I can't put on my clothes.
 It was my blood, Kitty. The only blood I had.
 My own, the blood of my two brothers. Why did he go?
 It's been weeks now hasn't it.

KITTY

 Months, many months
 But you will survive my darling. I know you will
 You will because you must. And think of us,
 This house is home for all of us Millie.
 Dear Katie has been here ever since the war,
 And that's how long we've all been coming here,
 How can we go on without you Millicent?
 But you are tired.

MILLICENT

 I'm very tired Kitty.
 I could not sleep last night. Not a wink.
 Dear Mum was coming to me in my dreams,
 And telling me to make the bed upstairs,
 To open up the door and change the sheets.
 But Kitty I can't go back into that room.
 But Mum was so insistent and Pal appeared
 But he was a little boy and on each side
 Dear Pal my brother and his father stood,
 And they were smiling as though they were so happy
 And mocking me in all my misery.
 Oh Kitty I had rather not be born
 Than suffer so the loss of my loved ones.
 My life has been too sheltered Kitty dear
 And my whole life just spent in loving them
 So hopelessly, so passionately and never
 Any grip on what the fates have done.
 I tell you Kitty, one ought not live like this
 No one should live like that. You have your work
 Your music and the children. Something to do.

KITTY

 Oh Milli, Milli,

MILLICENT:

 All through the years you told me
 "Millicent, you have your love,"
 As if "love" was the answer,
 As if in loving you I would find the faith,

> The courage, to know that my life was worthwhile.
> I tell you Kitty, love is not enough

KITTY

> But Milli, it is you, you—
> You are the one thing permanent—

MILLICENT

> No, there is no God to let me suffer so.
> You took my brothers. and their friends,
> Yet still I trusted you,
> And then you took the child.
> My arms are yearning, yearning to hold—
> You have forsaken us, you have! you have!
> There is no justice in this world, none.
> How much pain can one human being endure?

KITTY

> Millicent, now come on up to bed
> I'll come and sit with you.
> We'll talk a little. Then you'll go to sleep
> Everyone is coming here tonight
> Remember . . . *They exit*

Kate softly lets herself in with a letter and a package just a little later

KATE

> Oh Kitty is still here *making some tea*
> I had to come home. I had to get away
> Ha what's this?

She sweeps the rest of the paper off the table. She opens the package. It is all of Young Pal's things. She goes through them feverishly

> It's not here. The pendant is not here.
> Dog tag, pen, colors, the wallet,
> Not a word! Oh not a word! The same,
> Quite the same. Ignominious retreat
> Yet glorious. Gallipoli, Dunkirk!
> I can't go on. I really can't. This time I CAN'T!

She sits still on the couch for a long time

> I came home with a premonition so strange,
> That Pal was needing me.
> Oh terrors of the dead that die so young!

There is a faint knock

IRIS

> Oh Kate. You here too? How are you dear?

Looking around

> What's all this?

KATE

> It just arrived. A train
> Came in today. I wonder how anyone
> Can ride that train and live and the express

So streamlined, beautiful, just whizzing by
And never stopping.
Will Ilene be here tonight?

IRIS

Yes she will
I think she's coming early to help,
Where's Millicent? Is Kitty with her still?

She sits on the other end of the couch both silent

KATE

I can't go on Iris. I can't.
When we were young with lives ahead of us,
It was much easier though we didn't know,
That anything could be worse.

IRIS

Death is so final.

KATE

Yes it is.

IRIS

I wonder had he never been born?

KATE

Oh no,
He looked like Fred. he never looked like Pal
But Pal he was in his eternal soul,
And that is why I can't survive it now.
I felt we snatched him from the jaws of death,
And held him, all of us. And he would live,
Because of our refusal to give in
When life in death was all we could expect.
We held him all of us, we gave him all
The life force that our bodies ever had
And now, not even the pendant. Not a word
The silence is what I cannot understand . . .

IRIS

And yet he said goodbye to us
Oh Kate, as clear, as clear he said goodbye
It was as if he knew that Xmas night!

KATE

I wanted more, no, no, I expected more.
A long silence, Kitty enters

KITTY

Oh why has this day been so terrible?

IRIS

It may be that a train came in today.

KATE

There were many soldiers on it but nothing like
That first train that came back from Gallipoli,

205

>   Perhaps it's the train.
A knock Kitty opens the door to Ilene
ILENE
>   How are you darling?
Looking around
>   Well what a melancholy group you are,
>   You're worse than my own dears at Eventide.
>   Whatever's the matter? What's all this?

KITTY
>   Oh we'd better put all this away
>   Before Millicent comes down.

KATE
>   No leave them there,
IRIS
>   For now.
These two don't stir an inch
ILENE
>   Shall I make some tea?
Kitty sits on a chair, Ilene another one. The kettle whistles, Kate without stirring
KATE
>   The tea
CHORUS OF THREE:
>   The tea
ILENE
>   A little tea always livens the spirit.
She goes out to turn off the kettle
KATE
>   The tea, goddamit it, the tea.
>   Put all this stuff away. Pick up that paper.
>   Go—get—Millicent
Looking in the icebox
>   There's no food here. Absolutely none.
>   You two go get some food. And Kitty,
>   Go get Millicent and make her dress!
>   Go!
They all exit quickly—when they are gone she sits down again on the couch—a faint knock at the door—she rises puzzled
YOUNG WOMAN *(May be the same actress as Jessica), pregnant almost to delivery with a small suitcase*
>   Are you Kate Campbell?
KATE
>   I am.
The young woman collapses in her arms. Kate takes her to the couch, fans her and gives her some water, revives her.
>   My dear, my dear, your baby's almost due.

YOUNG WOMAN

     Yes it is.

     I came on the train today. I had to walk.

KATE

     Rest, rest, don't talk!

YOUNG WOMAN

     I must, I must. I have to give you this.

She takes off her neck the opal and gold pendant and gives it to Kate.

Scene 12

The Burma Road

April 25, 1942. The jungle. The men are all dressed in jungle green. A group of men are sitting down at the front of the stage. Pal is there and also Nobby Every couple of minutes a couple of Fuzzy Wuzzies—distinguishing features, black skin with Fuzzy hair and very white teeth—bring in a stretcher with a wounded man on it or they lead in a couple of less critically wounded men.

SOLDIER I

Do you think the Chinese will be able to reach us in time?

PAL

Some might make it

SOLDIER II

What's the bloody river called?

SOLDIER I

The Irrawaddy Nothing like ours. All overgrown with vines

Suddenly there is a piercing scream from backstage. Nobby jumps up

NOBBY

I can't stand it. I'll go mad! *He claps his hands to his ears*

SOLDIER II

I'm going out

Pal holds him

PAL

You know you can't. We've lost Thompson already. If we don't keep a few of us alive we'll never be able to lead the retreat even if the Chinese do break through.

Scream

NOBBY

Retreat, retreat, retreat. I have been retreating all my life. Will my life never end? We retreated from Gallipoli. We retreated from Dunkirk, Singapore—impregnable Singapore. Did someone say something about victims? It seems to me that we have been victims for a long, long, time.

There is another tortured scream. The men are completely disoriented until it subsides

PAL

This is probably a good time to talk about the difference between the destroyer and the victim.

208

NOBBY

> One destroys and one is destroyed.

PAL

> And yet, not so. The destroyer only takes
> What is already grown up and left unguarded.
> Complete extermination seems to be
> His very goal which then defeats itself,
> As parasite that grows upon a tree
> Dies and withers when the tree is dead.

NOBBY

> Well then the question seems to turn upon
> Just how to stop the beast or parasite
> Before the thing of beauty is destroyed.

There is another scream

> I'm going mad. I'm going mad . . .
> I cannot stand that screaming,
> Oh God have mercy.

The men are completely disorganized. Two Fuzzy Wuzzies bring in a stretcher

FUZZY WUZZY

> This man very bad

Pal grips the Fuzzy Wuzzy's arm

PAL

> Is there is way to rescue him?

FUZZY WUZZY

> Only God can rescue
> But every man can try.
> I got trail coming. Many men.
> Chinese. Chinese coming too. You'll see.
> But you don't go after him.

Motioning to the direction of the screaming

> Many men need you for retreat.
> Burma Road must be abandoned
> White man cannot live in jungle.
> White man foolish man.

PAL

> How do you mean that?

FUZZY WUZZY

> White man so beautiful head,
> So beautiful inventions,
> So child in what he hates.
> He hates a nose that is not made just so,
> He hates a hair that fuzzy wuzzy grows.
> He hates a skin that is both black and white

Showing his hands with black above and the palms white

> He hates to hear the scream of dying man,
> Yet he will not oppose the torture till too late.

He returns to the jungle

PAL

> Yet he will not oppose the torture till too late

Another scream and the men are again disoriented

> It's never too late. Men, men,
> Sit down, sit down in a circle.
> We've got to work this out before we all go mad.

They sit down in a circle

> It's quite clear we can't just sit here
> And let them torture him.
> We have either got to convince ourselves
> Beyond a shadow of a doubt
> That there is nothing that we can do,
> Or else we've got to do something.

SOLDIER I

> I never liked the man
> In fact, I hated him,
> And yet that makes it more than horrible:
> Because I do not know the reason why
> I won't fling myself out there to save him.

PAL

> It cannot be a question of love or hate

SOLDIER I

> But it is. It is.
> Man, I would go out there to save you
> I know it. Then why will I not go for him?

PAL

> It cannot be a question of love or hate

SOLDIER II

> I think we should try again

SOLDIER I

> Thompson tried, and Thompson's dead

NOBBY

> But that's a man out there, that's a man

another scream

PAL *distraught*

> O.K. Let's try to be reasonable
> Are we all agreed that we have to try again,
> Not just for his sake but for our own;
> Because if we don't try now
> Then we'll carry this uncertainty
> Forever in our hearts
> Should we have tried again?
> Wasn't there something we could have done?

SOLDIER II

> And the guilt would be there forever

PAL

>Whereas if we try . . . if we do everything that is humanly possible to do, then whether we succeed or not, we will know in our hearts that we are not guilty.

SOLDIER III

>I think we could hoist a dummy
>To draw off their fire over there.

SOLDIER II

>And then one of us try from the other side to cut him down.

There is silence as they all look out and the Fuzzy Wuzzy enters silently from the other side leading in four wounded men

PAL

>Yet we have to lead all these to safety. If the Chinese can break through, they'll need us to lead the retreat. How many men can we afford to lose?

SOLDIER I

>No more than three. Thompson's gone and that leaves two. If we can't save him with two more men then he's a goner.

NOBBY

>And we cannot be held responsible for it
>Even to ourselves.

SOLDIER II

>Not even to ourselves.

PAL

>O.K. Let's draw for who goes first

Nobby draws the long stick. He is visibly shaken

SOLDIER II

>We'll hoist the dummy over there. If you get him down and reach the hanging root, then whistle softly and we'll come out and help.

They start to hoist the dummy while Nobby walks to the front of the stage on the other side

NOBBY

>Oh God help me. I don't even like the man.
>If he hadn't have been so stupid
>They wouldn't have strung him up.
>It's one thing just to hate,
>But it's something else to be hated.
>Hatred grows because men let it grow.
>He felt so persecuted
>He invited persecution.
>And now I'm going to risk my neck
>To save his atheistic soul.

PAL *coming up behind him*

>You'll fail

NOBBY

>I know I will. Isn't it strange
>How you need a spark to kindle you,
>And that man leaves me cold.

PAL

> And yet if you don't go
> The torture will be with you

NOBBY

> I know, I know.
> I shall go mad. Dear God. I shall go mad.

PAL

> Let me go. Wait by the hanging root.
> If I succeed no one will ever know.

NOBBY

> And if you fail?

PAL

> Let's not talk of failure.
> I am a shepherd
> I cannot lose my men.

He disappears into the jungle. There is a shot, a scream from the same direction as before, followed by another agonizing cry. Soldier III jumps up.

SOLDIER III

> My turn.

He disappears into the jungle. The screaming continues but there it a momentary pause and a low whistle is heard. A couple of men run out and return with Soldier III and the victim. There is another scream.

SOLDIER II

> Who's that?

SOLDIER III

> Nobby's out there by the hanging root.

SOLDIER I

> I thought he got shot?

SOLDIER III

> Pal got shot but Nobby saved the day.
> When they heard him screaming they were sure
> Their victim was still strung up
> And fired on the dummy,
> And so I got him down.

There are shots, shouting and the Chinese national anthem is heard as several Chinese soldiers come grinning on stage. There is much handshaking.

CHINESE

> Come, Burma Road abandon.
> We must get out of here.

Exit and blackout

Scene 13

Deutschland Uber Alles

The Strains of Deutschland Uber Alles become clearer and clearer and end in a grand finale.

Complete blackout
Different voices come over the microphone.

VOICE
> Tell ye, and bring them near; yea let them take counsel together; who hath declared this from ancient time? Who told it from that time? Have not I the Lord? And there is no God else beside me; a just God and a Savior; there is none beside me.
> Look unto me, and be ye saved, all the ends of the earth; for I am God, and there is none else.

VOICE—CULTURED ABSTRACT
> The 'Final Solution' of the Jewish question meant the complete extermination of all the Jews in Europe.

VOICE—DISTANT *As if from another age*
> A war of extermination, in which
> Destruction of both parties and of all justice
> Can result, would permit perpetual peace
> Only in the vast burial ground of the human race.
> Therefore, such a war
> And the use of all means leading to it
> Must be absolutely forbidden.

VOICE—CULTURED WITH AN ACCENT—*scientific*
> I was ordered to establish extermination facilities at Auschwitz, in June, 1941.
> I visited Treblinka to find out how they carried out their extermination.
> He used monoxide gas and I did not think that his methods were very efficient. So when I set up the extermination building at Auschwitz, I used Zyklon B, which was a crystallized prussic acid which we dropped into the death chamber from a small opening.

VOICE—OBSERVER
> We knew when the people were dead,

Because their screaming stopped.
VOICE—POET
If I should die, think only this of me,
There are no memorials over Babi Yar,
And let the International ring out
The Warsaw Ghetto is no more;
Yet visit Zima Junction
And the Georgian Road
Of my Achilles Heart,
And Death shall have no Dominion.
VOICE—SCIENTIFIC
Another improvement we made over Treblinka was that we built our gas chambers
to accommodate two thousand people at one time, whereas at Treblinka their ten
gas chambers only accommodated two hundred people each.
VOICE—STATESMAN
Let us not break the Covenant
For bitter is the cup that passes then.
When Herr Hitler broke the Treaty of Versailles,
He undertook to keep the Treaty of Locarno
And when he broke the Treaty of Locarno
He undertook no further territorial claim:
And when he entered Austria for force,
He vowed that Czechoslovakia would be safe.
VOICE—SCIENTIFIC
Still another improvement we made over Treblinka was that at Treblinka the
victims almost always knew that they were to be exterminated, while at Auschwitz,
we endeavored to fool the victims into thinking that they were to go through a
delousing process.
VOICE—OBSERVER—RATHER DAZED
While the selections were made for the gas chambers,
A group of beautiful girls was singing
Tunes from the 'Tales of Hoffman'
VOICE—SCIENTIFIC
We have large collections of skulls of almost all races and peoples at our
disposal.—of the Jewish race, however, only very few specimens of skulls are
available. The war in the East now presents us with the opportunity to overcome
this deficiency. Following the subsequently induced death of the Jew whose head
should not be damaged, the physician will sever the head from the body and will
forward it . . . in a hermetically sealed can.
VOICE—SCIENTIFIC—FOLLOWER OR LAYMAN OF THE BEAST
I had no feelings in carrying out these things because I had received an order to kill
the eighty inmates in the way I already told you. That by the way was the way I was
trained. As a layman I could have no opinion in this matter. I merely transmitted
an inquiry from Professor Hirt. I had nothing to do with the murdering of these
people. I simply carried through the function of a mailman.

VOICE—FOLLOWER OF THE SHEPHERD

We are the Polish Underground Army. You may not know it but over half of the people gassed and destroyed in the Birkenau section of the Auschwitz camp are Gentiles. As a single race the Jews suffer, of course, the most, but every nation which the German attempts to crush—Polish, Czech, Creek, Bulgarian, Hungarian, French, Dutch and so on, yields its quota for Auschwitz. And the ovens and death pits ensure that about twenty four thousand of them do so every twenty four hours, a neat equation which appeals to the Germanic mind. We have established a column of our Resistance among the prisoners in the camp. We need your help.

VOICE—OBSERVER

The lofty chimneys soared up to the sky;
The thick black smoke
Rose high over the frozen countryside
With its taint of sickly sweetness
Clogging the air.
Three miles from this main factory,
The British camp of Monowitz.

VOICE—FOLLOWER OF THE SHEPHERD

We want you to get these things into the Buna factory at Birkenau

VOICE—COCKNEY—FOLLOWER OF THE SHEPHERD

I wondered what the hell was going on.
I've got the guns you gave the other chap,
Just tell me who to contact now.

He pauses then goes on jovially

Come on Fritzie, escort me back to camp,
We all have to do our little bit you know.

The lights go down and come up a little. Pal is left lying on the stage. Liberty enters.

LIBERTY

Where are you beloved?

PAL *very weakly*

Here, here

LIBERTY

Did they kill you beloved?

PAL

Yes, but why is it I cannot die?

She is bending over him and stroking the hair from his face

LIBERTY

Your spirit is not fulfilled, beloved.
They do not recognize you.
The vision of God to be anchored in men
Needs great strength in the thread between
So that the clouds do not obscure it
And it can still be seen.
And the spirit of shepherds guarding their sheep
Reaches out to the God on high,
But the strength is the strength of the lamb beloved,

215

And you cannot let it die.

PAL

But Germany is pagan.
And the beast is now all powerful.

LIBERTY

Her beast is the cry of freedom,
Armed with the sword of fear,
Surrounded by wild imagining.
That power is the all-powerful.

There is a pause

But you are your brother's keeper
And the shepherd of his men,
You cannot die beloved.
Your spirit is not fulfilled.

PAL *getting up quickly*

Then the horror that I dreamed of—
Is coming?

LIBERTY

Yes, beloved. It is here.

The finale of 'Deutschland Uber Alles' is played again and there is a tremendous explosion. The mushroom cloud is projected on a screen or else a picture or drawing of it stands on the stage. The lights are flashing on and off and 'Deutschland Uber Alles' gives way to the climax of 'Tanneheuser'. When the lights stop flashing a monster is standing on the stage. A soft light on the platform above shows the ghosts of the soldiers pacing around and staring at the huge beast on stage. The voice of the First Lord of the Admiralty of Scene Two of part One comes over the microphone.

VOICE

And if for this we fail, may the spirit of the men
Who die in their great love and trust in us,
Haunt ever our souls. And may that part of us
That will most surely die, should this our
Vision fail, still wander ghostly on this earth
Until our warlike spirits are all destroyed,
Or tamed by some great world catastrophe
That will with tongue of fire and more
Horrible presaging, cry to the worse
Than plague infested world, that man must live
In peace.

The beast is larger than a man. It is as big as it can be made, allowing that it has to move; for throughout the entire scene it moves slowly across the stage and then back again, just in front of the backdrop. The Japanese National Anthem is playing softly as a crisp voice comes over the microphone.

VOICE

On August 6, 1945, a U.S. army air force B-29 bomber dropped a single atomic bomb on Hiroshima.

The music of 'Anzac' strikes up vigorously, followed by 'Deutschland Uber Alles', then they are played simultaneously. There is a backdrop across the stage showing a landscape in ruins with brilliant explosives lighting the night atmosphere. As the two songs end at the same moment, figures are seen moving on stage. They are people covered with hessian, so that they are only in shapes. They are moaning, with an occasional weak scream. They cover the stage. There is still a soft light on the ghosts above and they have big black circles around their eyes. There is a rustling *in the aisles and the ghosts are also in the theatre wandering around the aisles searching for eyes in the audience and gazing fixedly at anyone who looks at them. While this is going on 'Nearer My God to Thee' is being played very softly. Pal comes rushing in from the back of the audience, asking the ghosts to please move out of his way as he rushes up on to the stage. When he gets up there, he recoils in horror. A man runs in from the wings.*

MAN

> Mea culpa, mea culpa . . . *kneels and wrings his hands*

OTHERS *running in*

> Mea culpa, mea culpa

A few actors are in the audience. They get up one at a time and run on to the stage shouting 'mea culpa'. The mad student enters from the wings groaning in agony. This time he has a long trail of flowers behind him. He writhes on the stage and tugs at the trail of flowers, pulling them up over him till finally there is one huge flower, big enough to cover his whole body. He draws it up and covers himself with it and sways underneath it groaning. The music for the hymn becomes stronger and the words are projected on a screen or written on a board.

> *Nearer, my God to Thee,*
> > *Nearer to Thee;*
> *E'en though it be a cross*
> > *That raiseth me;*
> *Still all my song shall be,*
> > *Nearer, my God to Thee*
> > *Nearer to Thee.*

> *Though, like the wanderer,*
> > *The sun gone down,*
> *Darkness comes over me,*
> > *My rest a stone;*
> *Yet in my dreams I'd be*
> > *Nearer, my God to Thee,*
> > *Nearer to Thee*

> *There let my way appear*
> > *Steps unto Heav'n*
> *All that Thou sendest me*
> > *In mercy given,*
> *Angels to beckon me*
> > *Nearer, my God, to Thee,*

Nearer to Thee.

Then with my waking thoughts
Bright with Thy praise,
Out of my stony griefs
Beth-el I'll raise;
So by my woes to be
Nearer, my God, to Thee,
Nearer to Thee

The ghosts begin to sing it softly as they motion to people in the audience to do the same. The voices grow louder until gradually the lights are all up and everybody is joining in the final stanza. The lights on stage have meanwhile become lower and lower except for those on the word of the hymn which are lit clearly to the end. Then a big sign is lowered or wheeled on stage. INTERMISSION. It is decorated with flowers. The ghosts move out with the audience. The ghosts are soldiers in uniform with any exposed flesh whitened and big circles around their eyes. They have a cloak over their shoulders which is simply a sheet or a piece of gauze with a hole cut out for the head. During the intermission they mingle with the audience. They try to get people to look at them with their eyes but they do not do it offensively and if anyone is unwilling to gaze at them they simply move on to someone else. If anyone attempts to talk to them they simply shake their heads gently or motion that they cannot speak.

INTERMISSION

CHRISTENDOM AFTER TWENTY CENTURIES

By far the most famous artist and cartoonist created by the War was Louis Raemaekers. Being a citizen of Holland, he was nominally a neutral, though his mother was of German birth. His earlier war-cartoons contained criticism of England as well as of Germany; but intense sympathy for Belgium gradually made him an impassioned supporter of the Allies' cause. Germany made every possible effort to supress the Raemaekers cartoons, realizing with what mighty force they were blazoning her shame before the world.

Scene 14

NUREMBURG

Pal, Shorty, Nobby and Darkie come on stage and begin arranging chairs. There is a raised platform the same as for the Treaty of Versailles and the same chair is placed on it and a small table to the side of it with a gavel. There is a large table this time and the names are printed in large letters and set at the foot of each group of chairs or stools. Eternal Justice and Justice in Bondage keep their same places, chairs and costumes. There is a group of chairs for Germany, a group for the U.S., England, France, Russia, Japan and Israel. Israel and the U.S. have brown cloaks on the chairs. The backdrop for the bomb remains as well as the monster who begins to pace up and down as soon as the lights go up. In addition, there is a tall figure of a shepherd, taller than the monster and a lamb which is about the size of a man. There is also a large wire frame which supports the following headings.

HOST OF THE LAMB	HOST OF THE BEAST
Shepherds	
! Philosopher	*!!! Nazi*
! Statesman	
!!! Poets	

Active Followers

of the Shepherd	Of the Beast
! Everyman	*! Layman*
!!! Everyman	

Passive Observers
! Anon
!!! Anon

At the signals, the lights flash, singly for one person and in clusters !!! for the collective designations. A voice is heard over the microphone.
VOICE

220

Look unto me, and be ye saved, all the ends of the earth; for I am God, and there is no-one else.

As this is being spoken, the top light goes on. It is a small red light surrounded by a white band. This light stays on throughout the scene. Eternal Justice enters and takes his place. He has on the same gown as he wore at Versailles. The other delegates enter and take their places on the stools. Moving from the right around Eternal Justice, England, U.S., Europe, Israel, Justice in Bondage, Russia, Germany and back to Eternal Justice. This time the flag of each country is not sewn on the backs of their garments but instead a large flag for each country is arranged among the group of stools. Some soft music is heard,

> *No rings on her fingers no bells on her toes*
> *But she shall have music wherever she goes.*

Young voices are heard singing at the rear of the audience and then they come down. First there is World Commonwealth dressed simply as a bride—the same as Versailles . . . She has a globe in her hands and sets it center stage where it lights up. She is followed by about six or eight young men who look as though they could be soldiers but they are bare-footed and have flowers dangling in a disorderly manner and give the impression of lack of military discipline. They make a gala showing on stage as they troup around cavorting. Suddenly there is a crash like thunder, a blackout and lightning. The only things lit up on stage are the red light and the globe. When the lights come on again World Commonwealth and her followers are gone. Eternal Justice hits the gavel.

ETERNAL JUSTICE

In the beginning was our language and our language was with God and our language was God. Let us take counsel together. Let us try to feel a sense of Justice in our Hearts.

Justice in Bondage rises and faces the audience, reading from a script.

JUSTICE IN BONDAGE

Ladies and gentlemen of the jury.
Our whole civilization has been torn asunder,
Our souls fractured to the very core.
We remember Versailles. How simple it was
To identify a man with his country's flag.
Those days are gone.
We have, for lack of better precedent,
Established for the judgement of our crimes,
Three categories of offences.
The first is crimes against the peace, the peace
Of world, and nations are responsible.
The second is war crimes; the crimes of war.
And under this is violation of law
Of any land involved in acts of war—
Devastation that is not justified
By military necessity.
For this the individual must be judged
And held responsible.
And if his government has forced his hand,
His nation will bear guilt unmitigated.

221

The man is guilty for himself alone,
And for the one who ordered him to act,
And for his nation who appointed him,
And for the victim that he raised his hand against,
And for the God whose image he has so defiled.

Pause

Yet will his guilt be mitigated
If he reveals the chasm in his soul
Of divided loyalties.
What young man ordered thus to fight
For honor and glory of his country's fame
Dares stand apart and raise his hand to God
And swear allegiance to his creator's covenant
Thou—shalt—not—kill
And thus defy his nation's gory flag?

Pause

To that young man our heart goes out in pain
A hero's death is his,
By bullet or by prison cell.

Pause

Yet will again his guilt be mitigated
If he takes up the dagger of the beast
And plunges it in blood,
For who are we to judge the inner soul of man?
The guilt we can define where man is wronged,
The judgement, never. That is God's domain.

Pause

The third of these offences here on trial,
Consists of all the crimes against humanity,
And all those acts that render man a beast,
Devoid of access to his eternal soul.
Not by their magnitude we number them
Though magnitude is a most awesome thing,
But rather by the quality of the deed.
Who takes a single life—is—guilty—
Who takes a million throws the grief on us
That we have let it happen,
That we *opening up his arms to the audience*
We, in all our millions
Have been so cowed down and unaware
Of where to halt the criminal act
Before it gains momentum

Pause

And now we shall attempt to clarify
The true significance of guilt, its root

222

And causes. Not just for retribution;
Retribution never can restore the life,
And punishment belongs to what is past.
But rather as the dead are lost and gone
So are their children entitled to a life
That is not cluttered up with deep remorse.

Each generation rises with the sun,
So let us now remove the haze of guilt,
Punish the guilty few and free the rest
That they may follow willingly the path
That leads them on to awareness of the self.

ETERNAL JUSTICE

The shepherd speaks, that will protect his men,
Heed him, philosopher, that loves his fellow man

VOICE—DISTANT *As from the previous scene*

My name is Emanuel Kant, born at Konisberg,
East Prussia. Native tongue, German.
Kings or kinglike peoples
Ruling themselves under laws of equality,
Should not suffer the class of philosophers
To disappear or remain silent.

The white light for Philosopher begins flashing

But should let them speak openly.
For true philosophers are by nature
Incapable of plotting and lobbying
And so above suspicion
When it comes to propaganda,
That oscillation from one side to the other
On the basis of expediency;
That agitation that is not rooted in
A solid faith but rather attempts to move
The other man by rhetoric alone.
And this I say—
A war of extermination, in which
Destruction of both parties and of all justice
Can result, would permit perpetual peace
Only in the vast burial ground of the human race.
Therefore, such a war
And the use of all means leading to it,
Must be absolutely forbidden.

The light stops flashing but remains on. The cluster of red lights for Nazi begin flashing

VOICE

Heil Hitler.
The 'Final Solution' of the Jewish question
Meant the complete extermination

Of all the Jews in Europe.

One of the group of men from the German section stands up. Eternal Justice motions to an attendant who gives him a red baton and he walks over and stands in front of the beast.

ETERNAL JUSTICE

Munich, 1938.

Would the Reich have attacked Czechoslovakia in 1938 if the Western Powers had stood by Prague?

VOICE

Certainly not.

ETERNAL JUSTICE

Hear the statesman, shepherd in wilderness,

The man whose vision launches the Dardanelles,

The man who never left his post,

Though followers deserted him.

The white light for statesman begin flashing

VOICE

Let me set down some principles of ethics

And actions which may yet the future guide.

First, the maintenance of every bulwark of defense;

Secondly, the gathering together

Of the collective strength of many lands,

And thirdly, making of alliances

And all within the Covenant of man.

Let us not break the covenant,

For bitter is the cup that passes then.

When Herr Hitler broke the Treaty of Versailles

He undertook to keep the Treaty of Locarno,

And when he broke the Treaty of Locarno,

He undertook no further territorial claim;

And when he entered Austria by force

He vowed that Czechoslovakia would be safe.

Pause, then pounding out

We have sustained a total and unmitigated defeat,

All, all is over now.

Silent, mournful, abandoned, broken,

Czechoslovakia recedes into the night.

We have broken faith,

We have sustained defeat without a war!

A member of the German group steps forward

MEMBER

Heil Hitler

I was ordered to establish extermination facilities at Auschwitz, in June, 1941.

The single red light under the beast is flashing. Eternal Justice looks over to the attendant who gives the man a red baton and he goes and stands in front of the beast. Another figure rises from the German section.

OBSERVER

>We knew when the people were dead,
>
>Because their screaming stopped.

A red and white light begins flickering under passive observer. The man turns to the audience and wrings his hands and appeals to them

ETERNAL JUSTICE

>You are not on trial here.

The man screams, walks over to the beast and recoils in horror, then tries to caress the lamb but cannot and grovels on the floor, center stage front. Eternal Justice stops looking at him and proceeds with the trial.

>The die is cast,
>
>The crime is unprevented
>
>And now it gains momentum.

A figure from the European group rises and the cluster of white lights under poets begin flashing.

POLE

>As a single race, Jews suffer most, but half
>
>The people gassed in Birkenau, Auschwitz,
>
>Are gentiles, Polish, Greek, Hungarian—
>
>We have established columns of resistance
>
>We need your help.

He steps back and another figure comes forward from the German section and the second cluster of lights under active followers of the beast begin flashing in red.

GERMAN

>We built our gas chambers to accommodate
>
>Two thousand people at one time

The attendant gives him a red baton and he goes over and stands in front of the beast. Another German rises and the cluster of lights under passive observers begins flashing red and white. The voice is questioning and bewildered.

GERMAN

>While the selections were made for the gas chambers,
>
>A group of beautiful girls was singing
>
>Tunes from the 'Tales of Hoffman'.

He turns and appeals to Eternal Justice who strikes the gavel.

ETERNAL JUSTICE

>You are not on trial here.

GERMAN

>Oh please, please, you must punish me,
>
>My soul is torn asunder.
>
>Oh God, I shall go mad
>
>I shall go mad. Dear God show me a way,
>
>Mea culpa, mea culpa, mea culpa . . .

JUSTICE IN BONDAGE

>Today, here in this place,
>
>We determine who bears public guilt
>
>Against his fellow man, that he has wronged.

But who can judge the quality of guilt
That severs man's immortal inner soul,
But he, himself, alone.

ETERNAL JUSTICE

Go from this place. You are not on trial here.

The man, wringing his hands in agony, jumps down from the stage and walks out of the theatre by way of the audience, wailing 'mea culpa', 'mea culpa'. A sprightly man from the British section jumps up as the single white light flashes by the side of everyman under the heading of active followers of the shepherd.

COCKNEY

I wondered what the hell was going on.
I've got the guns you gave the other chap,
Just tell me who to get in touch with now.

Eternal Justice motions to Pal who gives him a white baton which he takes over to the lamb, caresses it and look up at the figure of the shepherd and begins a silent discussion with the shepherd, changing positions, moving in a very comfortable and easy dialogue, all in silence. Another man rises from the German group and steps forward as the single red light begins flashing under active follower of the beast.

LAYMAN

I had no feelings in carrying out these things,
Because I had received an order to kill
In the way I already told you.
As a layman I could have no opinion in this matter.

Eternal Justice strikes the gavel

I had nothing to do with the murder of these people,
I simply obeyed my orders.

The gavel is struck again and an attendant gives him a red baton and he stands in front of the beast. The cockney is playing some antics with the lamb as all the lights are lowered except those on the diagram and the red and white cluster under passive observers is flashing.

VOICE

The lofty chimneys soared up to the sky,
The thick black smoke
Rose high over the frozen countryside
With its taint of sickly sweetness
Clogging the air.

Another German goes berserk, shaking other people pounding on the beast and finally exiting through the audience shouting 'mea culpa'. The lights flash on and off. The stage is dark except for the diagram and the light by philosopher begins flashing.

VOICE

My name is Emanuel Kant.
I would like to give to the world,
My treatise called, 'Perpetual Peace'.
Article.
No Treaty of Peace shall be held valid
In which there is tacitly reserved
Matter for future war.

The lights rise slowly but do not to up full. There is a heavy ticking like a slow clock. Israel rises, drops off the brown cloak, and steps forward to face the audience. The ticking continues. The man walks to the front of the stage. The lights flash on and off and he sinks to the floor next to the other man who fell there earlier. The lights go down again.

> No independent states, large or small
> Shall come under the comination of another state
> By inheritance, exchange, purchase or donation.

There is a heavy ticking again. The U.S. rises drops off the brown cloak and steps forward to face the audience. The ticking continues. The man walks to the front of the stage. The lights flash on and off and he sinks to the floor next to the other two.
Blackout
The only thing remaining lit is the single large red light surrounded by the white band.
VOICE

> Look unto me, and be ye saved,
> All the ends of the earth,
> For I am God and there is none else.

Scene 15

The Clubhouse—on Nuremberg

The ANZAC Clubhouse at Winton—On Nuremberg.
There is a bar at one end. There are three chairs on stage with a radio. Darkie. Nobby and
Shorty enter separately and sit down. They have some antics about who is to turn on or turn
off the radio. The men are middle aged by now and not well dressed.

DARKIE
>They are discussing the Nuremberg trials on the radio.

NOBBY
>Hm

DARKIE
>Eh, do you remember Versailles?
>Remember when China stomped out?
>We should have known then
>There'd be another war.

SHORTY
>Cripes, I can't forget Gallipoli.

DARKIE *Wiping his hand across his forehead then knocking his head*
>Poor little Tommie
>You know,
>I can't ever get those blokes out of my mind!
>Pal, Fred, Jimmie, Victor
>All the blokes from Charters Towers.

SHORTY
>Me neither.
>Remember when Enery met up with the Colonel
>After he'd been skinny-dipping in the bay?

DARKIE
>And Billo,
>Gawd blimey, Billo took the cake—
>What he said to that General

They all laugh

NOBBY

    Aw, stop it blokes

    I can't stand it

He is getting sad

    I remember the weir,

    And John Marshall

    And that little Kitty

SHORTY

    I liked that little sheila

    And Ilene that only had eyes for Jim

NOBBY

    And Jessica, and Kate

DARKIE

    And Millicent and Iris, the clever one.

NOBBY

    Aw blokes, come off it will 'yh

    I can't stand it.

    When my mind goes back on that

    It's as though I step on another planet

    And I go spinning and spinning

    And they all float before me

    And they smile and they laugh,

    Their faces taunting me.

    I go into another world blokes, really

    And everyone is there

    All me cobbers,

    All the sheilas we knew.

SHORTY

    Cripes Nobby

    You're getting me feeling all queer.

    The air is getting all clogged up in 'ere

    What are all these people doin'

    Millin' around.

    To hell with all this pain,

Talking to the air

    Eh blokes this is Winton, where Tommy was born

    Eh Tommy, Tommy

He stretches out his hand. The lights change color, Darkie comes to the center of the stage and Pal and the dead soldiers. Pal addresses his audience. The chorus is on tape.

PAL

    Distinguished friends,

    We are gathered here today in an attempt

    To understand the Trials at Nuremberg

    Since they affect us all.

CHORUS

    Hear, hear, good on yh. mate!

PAL

        Never since we all enlisted

        In 1914 and in 1939 have we had such a gathering.

CHORUS

        Cheers, cheers

The assembly begins to sing Nearer God to Thee, or Glory, Glory Halleluyah as they did in the Treaty of Versailles. While the hymn is being sung Pal enters with Eternal Justice. They move to the head of the table or to center stage. As the hymn tones down to humming they speak together.

ETERNAL JUSTICE and PAL

        In the beginning was our language

        And our language was with God

        And our language was God.

        Let us take counsel together.

        Let us try to feel a sense of Justice in our hearts.

ETERNAL JUSTICE

        I declare this meeting open.

He hands the gavel to Pal and steps back into the wings.

PAL

        If ye break faith with us who die

        We shall not sleep

        Though poppies grow

        In Flanders, fields.

CHORUS

        Cheers.

NOBBY *With a mug of beer in his hands*

        We are keeping the faith mates,

        We never forget you, never.

More cheers

JUSTICE IN BONDAGE

        Ladies and gentlemen of the jury,

        Our whole civilization has been torn asunder,

        Our souls fractured to the very core.

CHORUS

        Hear, hear,

SHORTY

        We fought with you

        We were ready to give our lives too

PAL

        We fought for Liberty and Justice

        But our lives were not enough.

ENERY

        It was all we had Mate.

        It was all we had.

        That first one was the war to end all wars.

        They slaughtered us on Gallipoli,

And if we survived Gallipoli,
They massacred us in France.
What else did we have to give?
We had our songs to sing
And they quieted our voices,
We had our joy, we had our love
And they buried us in mud.

FRED

And then they took our sons
And massacred them in Normandy,
North Africa, New Guinea,
All over the bloody globe
We died. For what?
And now the death camps,
The concentration camps,
The gas chambers, the trials.

DEATH *laughing and taunting them*

At the rate you are going
I will have your whole civilization before long,
Aha ha ha ha

CHORUS

Much shouting

No, no, no, leave us alone. Go away.

DEATH

Leave you alone, a ha ha ha ha
I do not have to come for you,
You have been coming to me
This whole century.
You hurl your bodies at me
You do not care about life—
I am so surfeited with your bodies,
I keep searching for places to disgorge them.
A ha ha ha ha
Now look at Auchwitz, Buchenwald,
Treblinka, Dachau, Nuremberg

The soldiers converge on Death. For a moment she appears terrified as she cannot get out of the circle of men.

CHORUS

Liberty, Freedom—*this becomes a chant*

At this moment Liberty comes in hurriedly spilling her flowers

LIBERTY *to Death*

I have watched you take my sons
War after war,
Confusing their minds
Gorging yourself on their young bodies,
And I am here to remind you,

> That you too have your place in this universe

CHORUS

> Cheers

LIBERTY

> And never again
> Will you take my sons from me!

DEATH

> They will forget you
> As soon as they go from here
> And they will be mine again
> Mine, mine, mine,
> More and more and more
> Till their whole civilization is mine.
> I will have them all,
> A ha ha ha ha

The men converge joyfully around Liberty and the chant begins again.

MEN

> We died for Liberty, Freedom, Liberty, Justice, Justice, Justice

ETERNAL JUSTICE reenters and there is a hushed silence. Everyone freezes.

ETERNAL JUSTICE

> You have indeed paid the price
> For the knowledge that will set you free.

He goes over to center stage, spreads out his arms and repeat for everyone to hear.

> Justice does prevail

DEATH

> They are mortal.
> Why do you tell them this?

ETERNAL JUSTICE

> Justice does prevail

Liberty joins him

> Show the yearning in your hearts,
> Act for justice always,
> And the new world shall be yours.

JUSTICE IN BONDAGE

> We remember Versailles. How simple it was
> To identify a man with his country's flag.
> Those days are gone.
> We have, for lack of better precedent
> Established for the judgement of our crimes,
> Three categories of offences.
> The first is crimes against the peace, the peace
> Of world; and nations are responsible.

TOMMY (Script I)

> Munich 1938.
> Would the Reich have annexed Czechoslovakia in 1938 if the Western Powers had
> stood by Prague?

JIM

      No, the western powers should have stopped them

VICTOR

      How could they have stopped them?

SOLDIER 1

      You have to have international law.

SOLDIER II

      You cannot expect nations to keep within their boundaries

      Without the guidelines laid down,

      And accepted by all nations.

PAL

      Let's have a show of hands

      Is this what we believe?

      The nation is guilty

      That invades another's sovereign soil!

      Gentlemen, gentlemen!

JUSTICE IN BONDAGE

      The second is war crimes; the crimes of war.

      And under this is violation of law

      Of any land involved in acts of war.

CHORUS

      Guilty

JUSTICE IN BONDAGE

      Devastation that is not justified

      By military necessity.

JIM

      Who dropped the bombs on civilian homes?

VICTOR

      Eh you can't blame the pilot.

BILLO

      If he joins the army or the air force, he has to obey his orders

The attendant beckons the next soldier to read a script

ENERY. (Script 2)

      Heil Hitler

      I was ordered to establish extermination facilities

      In Auschwitz, in June 1941.

NARK

      He's guilty

CHORUS

      Guilty, guilty. everyone is guilty, they are all guilty

JUSTICE IN BONDAGE

      He may be guilty,

      Yet will his guilt be mitigated

      If he reveals the chasm in his soul,

      Of divided loyalties.

      What young man ordered thus to fight

For honor and glory of his country's fame
Dares stand apart and raise his hand to God
And swear allegiance to his creator's covenant
Thou—shalt—not—kill
And thus defy his nation's gory flag!

CHORUS

Thou shalt not kill, thou shalt not kill.

BILLO

If everyone refused to kill
There would be no war

VICTOR

We never wanted to kill

FRED

We were happy on our farms

BILLO

In our homes

NARK

Rearing kids

ENERY

Working at jobs

TOMMY

We were not professional soldiers

FRED

We didn't want to kill

ANONYMOUS SOLDIER

There is only one true categorical imperative and that is GOODWILL.

CHORUS

Goodwill, goodwill

PAL

Now we've got something.
This is an important vote
The vote is for Goodwill around the globe
All in favor?

CHORUS

Aye, aye

JUSTICE IN BONDAGE

The third of these offences here on trial
Consists of all the crimes against humanity,
And all those acts that render man a beast
Devoid of access to his eternal soul.

BILLO (Script 3)

Still another improvement we made over Treblinka was that we built our gas chambers to accommodate two thousand people at one time, whereas as at Treblinka their ten gas chambers only accommodated two hundred people each.

NARK

They are guilty. They are all guilty.

CHORUS

        Guilty—its unthinkable, horrible.

They try to beat up the person who was just reading the script.

BILLO

        Eh get off me, get off

        I was only reading the bloody script!

        Eh. I don't want this part

        I didn't know that's what it was.

        To hell with this part!

He begins to tear the script up as the others back off.

ATTENDANT

        Stop, stop, stop. That is a historical document

        You can't destroy history.

        It's history man!

He retrieves pieces of the script and begins to put them back together.

PAL

        Move on to the next script

JIM (Script 4)

        We knew the people were dead because their screaming stopped.

BILLO

        Eh, what do you do about that?

JIM

        I dunno

VICTOR

        Eh mate, this is too tough for us

ENERY

        We are just ordinary men

        We can't understand all this

FRED

        Eh, let's go home

        We don't know what to do

PAL

        We can't go home.

        We've got to understand.

        We've got to vote on whether they are on trial.

SHORTY

        There 'e goes again

BILLO

        Not on trial, why shouldn't they be on trial?

VICTOR

        They let it happen didn't they?

ENERY

        They ought to have stopped it

JIM

        They could have tried to stop it

JUSTICE IN BONDAGE

> Who are we to judge the inner soul of man?
> The guilt we can define where man is wronged,
> The judgement, never. That is God's domain.

PAL

> Can we vote blokes?
> Come on now, let's vote
> We want to sleep fellas don't we?
> Aren't you tired of wandering the earth?
> We've had no peace since Gallipoli,
> None of us.
> We've got to be allowed to die blokes,
> We've got to understand.

GAVEL

> The vote is
> For acceptance of the pain.
> Acceptance without judgement
> On the human being.

DEATH *Laughing hollowly*

> You'll never learn.
> I tell you, I'll have your whole civilization
> Before you learn.
> Human beings learn?
> Ha, ha, ha, ha, ha

LIBERTY

> They WILL learn to recognize me

DEATH

> Never

PAL *Gavel*

> It carries

ETERNAL JUSTICE *Coming over to Death*

> Go from this place. Haven't they suffered enough?

DEATH

> They will never learn

Liberty raises her arms and begins singing Glory Hallelujah The dead soldiers join in and exit following Liberty

Scene 16

The Seance—The Palace of Justice

The home. Millicent is dressed in the long evening gown she wore for young Pal. She has an air of excitement as she checks the furniture etc. She is older of course and moves more slowly. She has a sheaf of paper in her hand and she checks something in it. Katie comes down the stairs also in her evening gown and with a sheaf of paper.

KATE

       Everything looks lovely Millicent

MILLICENT

       It does, doesn't it. I'm proud of it myself and this is a big occasion isn't it

There is a knock. Iris enters in her evening gown with a sheaf of paper

IRIS *Swirling around but in a slower way*

       Look at that!

       I could still get into it.

       How about you?

KATE AND MILLI *They are all pleased as they look at themselves*

       Yes, Yes

IRIS

       We've done alright for ourselves haven't we

She adjusts her dress as there is another knock and Kitty and Ilene enter also with paper. Ilene waltzes around in her evening gown

KITTY

       Thirty years in the closet—

       Thereabouts anyway—

       Not bad eh?

       Not bad for all of us really

None of them is going to let go their sheaf of paper but they waltz around a little. They pour themselves a drink if they feel like it then finally they settle down

ILENE

       Well now ladies, who would like to go first

IRIS

The lights rise and fall a little—she has much to read but only a little is heard here

237

I'll go first
I think I did the right thing,
In remaining with my friends.
I might have found a partner
Had our men returned
But not very likely.
Laughter and some exclamations
Many, many girls
Have passed through St. Gabriels
And I have tried to set an example
Of forthrightness and honesty,
Of courage to stand their ground
In a male dominated society.
Kate and Iris look directly at each other they then begin the same dance that they had together the day at the weir. They sit down.
KITTY *Lights rise and fall*
I have tried my best
To give my children
A little taste of the finer life.

KATE
You have done a lot Kitty.

ILENE
Your children adore you.
KITTY *Holding up her hand for silence*
I know if not for me,
Many little faces would not have smiled so much,
Many little voices would not have expressed their joy.
The life itself has been hard,
You all know that.
But I too, am glad I stayed.

Applause

ILENE

>Katie? Millicent?

MILLICENT *Lights rise and fall*

>I'll go.
>First of all I'm glad I stayed.
>This land is in my bones,
>My brothers' memories are here,
>My parents' graves.
>I have had only you and the children
>And the Sunday school, my Sunday school,
>And love has been the only thing
>I ever felt I had.

CHORUS

>Hear, hear,

KATE *going over to her, holding her shoulders and kissing her*

>The most important thing of all!

KITTY and ILENE lead the singing,

>Oh Millicent, Oh Millicent, Oh Millicent,
>We love you

They dance as they repeat it. Lights rise and fall.

KATE

>I'll go next
>We have to be really honest don't we?

CHORUS

>Yes, yes

KATE

>I thought so.
>Well, I have done my best.

applause and she motions silence

>I know that I had much more to offer,
>Than that I was able to give,
>And who is more the loser I don't really know.

IRIS

>Society is the loser, of course.

KATE *motioning silence*

>I have loved you all—very much.
>I have saved lives
>And some people say I have inspired them.

Applause

>But for me, in my soul,
>I am not fulfilled.
>I still yearn for Pal.

She rises as she speaks the following lines

>Oh Pal,
>The world is full, full of people,

Yet, some little time ago,
I walked those skies—with you
She turns back to the others
How is it I can never forget him?
MILLICENT
You will meet again Katie,
In paradise . . .
ILENE *trying to recover some joyfulness*
Sorry I'm late everyone.
My life at Eventide, oh, it's been so, so,
I never could take myself that seriously you know—
Laughter
I live each moment and try to enjoy it—
Whatever good I've done for others?
Well my old dears all love me,
And I love them,
I just pray to God when my turn comes,
I pop off just like that,
No Eventide for me,
No arm chairs, wheelchairs, bed pans——*hamming it*
I want to die on me feet I do,
With a glass of wine in me hand!
Lights change
And now my friends
You all promised remember—
CHORUS
Yes we did
ILENE
Over the years we have endeavored
To be part of the life force
With our deeds and with our thoughts.
Oh spirit of the eternal flame,
Reach out your hands to us.
IRIS
Great forces of the cosmic empire
Come to us now,
Penetrate the isolation of our lives,
ILENE
Reach out to us,
As we reach out to you,
IRIS
Show us we are not alone!
Transmit through death
ILENE
Through the unity of mortals,
And the dreams of mortals,

KATE
>The yearning of mortals,

MILLICENT
>The love of mortals,

ILENE
>Come to us now in whatever form —
>*There is a clatter. The lights go very dim. MADELINE appears*

MADELINE
>Hm. I don't see any violence here.
>I wonder what I'm doing here,
>It's so quiet
>Look, look at the horizon
>We are on a tip of the earth here
>And everything else is sky

ETERNAL JUSTICE enters with LIBERTY, JUSTICE IN BONDAGE, the Professor and the Black Intellectual

ETERNAL JUSTICE
>From the sky you shall know me.
>You all have been seeking me in your own way
>And so we have decided, Liberty and I
>To let you experience some proceedings
>In the Palace of Justice.
>Certain mortals have made steps
>Towards us
>In an understanding of our ways,
>And others are recalcitrant.

MADELINE
>Am I recalcitrant?
>I am not recalcitrant!
>I've been fighting against injustice
>All my life!

ILENE
>Who are you?

MADELINE
>I'm Madeline!

IRIS
>How did you get here?
>I mean, we don't even know you.

MADELINE
>Haven't you been conducting soirees?

CHORUS
>Yes, we have.

MADELINE
>Haven't you been thinking deeply
>About the injustices in this world?

KATE

       Well, yes we have.

MADELINE

       Well, so have I.

       I am here because you called me

       But what do we have to fight for now?

The women look at each other

KITTY

       There must be another way

MADELINE

       You think so?

       You really think so?

MILLICENT

       Yes.

BLACKOUT

After which the women sit still in a half light as the following dream sequence takes place. A sign is wheeled in or written somewhere THE PALACE OF JUSTICE.

LIBERTY

       Warm is the threshold where my people stand

       Before the Palace of Justice.

       Yet let us never break the covenant,

       And guilty stand beside our wrongful deeds:

       But rather gain our rightful place with love;

       No bitter cup for us; but crystal clear

       The fountain of our freedom's final quest:

       With dignity and discipline we seek

       Majestic heights for all mankind to reach,

VOICE OF MARTIN LUTHER KING

       For I have a dream that some day we shall see

       This world rise up, give meaning to that creed

       We hold these truths to be self-evident,

       All, all, are equal at the gate of God

ETERNAL JUSTICE

       You must come by way of questioning.

       You who follow the code of certainty

       To go not beyond, you have no need of me;

       For shepherd now, I come for my lost sheep

       That wander in the wilderness of change;

       Together we shall evolve new covenants

       To guide men onward through the path of love.

PROFESSOR

       Well am I thus excluded then?

ETERNAL JUSTICE

       He who lives within the bounds

       Knows not the agony of men that find

       Them antiquated and of no avail

In this new world that must be built from ruins,
He motions toward the bomb backdrop.

    For build we must, a new world where all,
    All, all, all mortals—defenseless—are!

The professor laughs incredulously

ETERNAL JUSTICE

    You do not recognize me.

PROFESSOR

    I obey the law,
    The law will protect and defend me.

He puts his arm around Justice in Bondage and together they walk back towards the wings. The lights grow dim. They walk very slowly and do not reach the wings to exit until the following voices stop speaking

VOICE OF MILLICENT

    Before the faith we were kept under the law
    Wherefore the law was our schoolmaster.
    But after faith we no longer need schoolmaster
    For we are all the children of God.

SECOND VOICE *African American*

    Then there is neither Jew nor Greek
    Nor bond nor free, nor male nor female
    Ye are all one and Abraham's seed
    And heirs according to the Promise.

ANOTHER VOICE

    For this Agar is Mount Sinai in Arabia
    And answereth to Jerusalem which now is,
    And is in bondage with her children.

VOICE OF MADELINE *in ecstasy*

    And Jerusalem which is above, is free
    And is the mother of us all.

Exit Professor and Justice in Bondage. There is a spotlight on a dark stage where the passive people from the Nuremberg trials are huddled together on the floor as they were at the end of that scene. They are the ones who did not act when they heard the people screaming, when they listened to the music of Hoffman at the gas chambers and when they saw the smoke from Auschwitz and smelt the bodies burning. Eternal Justice speaks to them.

ETERNAL JUSTICE

    Crush not your own soul, that it can never rise,
    But rather find the faith to live it through,
    Like some dark tunnel that moves out to light,
    If courage will but hold through depth of night.
    Seek out atonement: nor never cast a stone,
    And never look for one. Each separate heart
    It's balance holds if we but keep it still
    Till all emotion's surging tides abate,
    Go now alone. Seek out fresh hope in men,
    New hope, young hope, children of the soul.

They get up and go out up the aisles. They carry hope with them and are no longer afraid to look at the people of the audience as they move through them and exit. Eternal Justice then looks at a small path made out of pebbles next to which is a scarecrow with a tattered soldier's uniform on it and a bit of a bedraggled tent resembling the 'Hotel de Boulibif' from the beginning of the play. A couple of policemen enter from the wings stage left.

POLICEMAN

       I mean it's past a joke

They stare incredulously as John Marshall steps out of the tent almost naked as he throws handfuls of seeds on the ground.

ETERNAL JUSTICE

       What are you doing son?

JOHN MARSHALL

       These seeds. My girl. She gave them to me.

       But I can't make them grow.

The laughter of children is heard from the wings. John Marshall turns around bewildered and hurt.

POLICEMAN

       Get a blanket or something.

The other goes into the tent and comes out with a raggedy blanket which they wrap around him. He turns to Eternal Justice.

JOHN MARSHALL

       Don't let them take me away.

       I'm not hurting anybody.

       It was Beachy Bill,

       He blasted my mind

       And all that blood,

       I couldn't act. I couldn't.

       It was an accident.

       It was all a terrible accident.

       Tell them. Tell them.

       Not everybody is born to be a soldier,

       I couldn't face the guns,

       I couldn't.

       I cannot kill. I cannot kill.

       I—cannot—kill!

       The mad student who has been inside the second white gate, comes rushing out.

MAD STUDENT

       What can you do,

       What can you do for him?

ETERNAL JUSTICE

       Nothing

MAD STUDENT

       Nothing?

ETERNAL JUSTICE.

       Nothing. This man is given to the civil law,

       Formulated and written down,

And sacred in society of men.
And you, YOU have not evolved new covenants
To give protection when the circumstance
Extenuates. Come.

The policemen exit with John Marshall.
Eternal Justice enters THE NIGHT OF THE SOUL the space beyond the realm of codified
law and certain knowledge. The atmosphere is as other-worldly as possible with ferns and
flowers trailing from the ceiling He looks around.

ETERNAL JUSTICE

> The tree of mortals is no uncertain thing
> That grows up loveless in an alien world:
> Though parasites of war still suck its blood
> And draw their sustenance from its hidden springs.
> The tree of mortals a thing of beauty is
> And ready now to shake its branches free
> And seek its correspondences with God,
> Where extraneous relations cease to be.

VOICE OF MADELINE

> The covenant is characterized with blood
> Though pen of mortals then trace out its course
> And yield it up for all the world to see
> That they may read and follow as they can.
> For who but those of infinite faith will dare,
> To question thus the ancient rule of men,
> And shape new covenants with their mortal blood.

LIBERTY

> Children,
> Your blood is spilling over all the earth
> Enough, enough!

ETERNAL JUSTICE

> Honor thy mother and thy father still
> Thy sisters and thy brothers of the earth.
> Nor never cast them off; to sever roots
> Cuts off the life blood at the very source.

LIBERTY

> Nor never kill. Thou shalt not kill.
> That covenant most broken is. Each age
> Renews the character of that covenant
> With blood of its most beauteous sons of earth.

ETERNAL JUSTICE

> All other covenants in bondage are
> To civil codes for government of mortals
> Providing—that they do not violate
> These sacred characters described in blood.

Addressing those around him
>And now my children of the faith, explain
>Why you as sheep, instead of strong men, walk.

MAD STUDENT
>They have broken our spirit.
>They have set us apart from them,
>And we refuse to be a part
>Of institutionalized murder.
>But what can we do?
>We pick up this symbol
>And wear it always

ETERNAL JUSTICE
>Is that all you do?

MAD STUDENT
>I shout to all the world

ETERNAL JUSTICE
>Is that all you do?

MAD STUDENT
>I wear this symbol, man

ETERNAL JUSTICE
>Set that aside

STUDENT
>But it is all I have

ETERNAL JUSTICE
>Let us go back to the stormy ocean,
>Strike out in the raging waters
>And have faith in ourselves.

The student takes off his symbol and looks at it in is hands. Eternal Justice turns to the black intellectual.

BLACK INTELLECTUAL
>I am a black man that was born too free
>To tolerate that blasted hypocrisy.
>And so I burned with my language
>Their very asses, man,
>And they can NEVER sit down again
>Without feeling the sting of my brand,
>So they imprisoned and exiled me,
>They banned me from—

ETERNAL JUSTICE *Interrupting, smiling*
>Black is beautiful forever,
>Beautify your land.

Then he puts his arm on the shoulder of the young man and they walk upstage a little in deep close conversation. Eternal Justice gives something to the young man. Meanwhile two black panthers have marched on stage and taken up their posts just outside the white gate leading to the Palace of Justice. A couple of young men enter. One of them is wearing a cap.

YOUNG MAN
   Who yh waiting for?
Then he reads the sign THE PALACE OF JUSTICE
   Never heard of it.
PANTHER
   It don't exist, that's why.
YOUNG MAN
   Well why are you guys
   Standing here with guns?
PANTHER
   We're waitin' for somebody
   That's why.
YOUNG MAN
   Who?
The panthers shrug their shoulders
YOUNG MAN
   Who you plan on shooting?
   Who you plan on shooting
   With them guns?
PANTHER
   Who you plan on shooting
   With them concealed water pistols?
YOUNG MAN
   They're not water pistols!
PANTHER
   What are they then?
YOUNG MAN
   They're guns.
PANTHER
   Why you carrying guns, huh?
   Who's trying to bump you off, huh?
   They've had their turn at you
He turns to the young man with the cap
   The Jews are safe now
He looks curiously at the cap
   Why you wearing a damn cap anyway?
   Why can't you just be a man
   Like everybody else.
   You had a black skin man,
   You'd really have something to complain about.
YOUNG MAN
   I'm not ashamed of being Jewish
PANTHER
   I don't give a shit who you are,
   Just so long as you quit
   Lousing up my history books.

YOUNG MAN
>What on earth are you talking about?

PANTHER
>Look man, don't give me that shit,
>The whole educational system
>And all the military
>Is full of damn Jews.
>Look at your goddamn names.
>And if you can't tell by your damn name
>Then you plaster a picture in profile
>To show the damn nose
>And if you can't tell by the damn nose
>You stamp the shitty star of David.
>I'm sick of you damn Jews.
>Everywhere there's business,
>There's a Jew.
>Institutions are made up of you
>And if they're not full of Jews,
>Then they're full of Germans.

The young man is stunned.

YOUNG MAN
>That is the most outrageous accusation
>I've ever heard.
>You better go back to school
>And learn not to make
>Such sweeping generalizations.

PANTHER
>I don't need no education
>To know what's happening to me, man,

YOUNG MAN
>Our people have gone into the ghettos,
>We've written books about it,
>We've done everything we could to help
>Why should you turn on us?

PANTHER
>Man, when you're guts are empty,
>You look at those with their bellies full.

YOUNG MAN
>I'm so shocked
>There's nothing I can say.

PANTHER
>That's right. Turn away.
>Make a martyr out of yourself
>Well we're not taking that shit
>Anymore see?
>And if you'd picked up a gun

When you were threatened

You mightn't have been exterminated either

He pauses

It ain't going to happen to us, see.

The two young men walk away and into the center aisle, with the one with the cap speaking

YOUNG MAN

I'm shocked. It's not like that all,

You know it isn't.

We're doing everything we can.

It's not like that at all.

Young Pal appears. There is great excitement among the men but Pal does not see them at this moment. He sees only Eternal Justice and Liberty

ETERNAL JUSTICE

What are you doing to make new covenants?

Of all men on the earth,

The artist is most free.

The artist of all mortals can stand alone

And look with compassion on the rest of the world.

To the artist then a special charge is given,

To look beyond the strife of present things,

And feel the tranquil waters of the inner soul.

My son, what have you written?

YOUNG PAL

I was living in evil times

And I was taking the evil into myself

To try to understand.

I was studying government,

I wanted to write about government,

How to govern and be governed,

So the world could live in peace,

But power politics is so evil.

ETERNAL JUSTICE

My son, that have you written?

YOUNG PAL

How can I write their evil

When I don't know what it is?

ETERNAL JUSTICE

By not knowing

YOUNG PAL

I don't understand

ETERNAL JUSTICE

My son what have you written?

YOUNG PAL

Nothing

ETERNAL JUSTICE

Nothing will be taken down

   In evidence against you.
   My son, what are you writing?
YOUNG PAL
   Now, you mean NOW?
ETERNAL JUSTICE
   NOW
   For each age makes its call
   And molds the fabric of the shepherd's dress—
   My son, what are you writing?
YOUNG PAL
   I am writing of the eternal soul of man,
   That survives all tortures,
   That keeps alive the vision —
He looks up and sees the women for the first time
   Mother,
   Oh, thank God I've found you
   Thank God I've found you
He kneels crying. The lights fade on him and the women are left alone

A couple of stanzas of "Nearer my God to Thee" are sung by the chorus or are on tape. The women do not speak but, clutching their papers, say goodbye to each other. Iris, Ilene and Kitty leave. Millicent and Kate look at each other.

       LIGHTS

Scene 17

U.S.A, The 1960s

This is a typical election scene except that the name of the candidate does not appear anywhere, only the names of several states are being shaken up and down. People are wearing campaign hats with the stars and stripes. The bomb backdrop remains and the figure of the shepherd is moved back up close to it S.R. The figure is taller than a man so it's head and shoulders are still visible as the young people cavort on stage. Softly at first and hardly distinguishable over the noise of the campaign gaiety, one can distinguish the hymn, 'For those at Sea'.

> *Eternal Father strong to save*
> *Whose arm hath bound the restless wave*
> *Who bidd'st the mighty ocean deep*
> *It's own appointed limits keep.*

At this moment the chorus of soldiers' voices joins the band and rises up to a crescendo as they sing the next lines,

> *Oh hear us when we cry to Thee*
> *For those in peril on the sea.*

There is silence as a young man enters from the wings S.L.. He is dressed in the jungle uniform of a P.T. skipper and mounts a slightly elevated platform S.L. A soft light plays overhead to the high platform where the soldiers are looking down. The actor on stage mimes the speeches, but the voice coming over the microphone is that of John F. Kennedy.

KENNEDY

> My fellow citizens of the world—

There is great excitement at the back of the audience as World Commonwealth comes down the aisle followed by her young soldiers decorated with flowers. They are more disciplined now and the rhythm in their movement shows it. World Commonwealth sits on stage, spreads the folds of her bridal gown around her. One soldier places the globe center stage and it lights up. The soldiers range themselves round the girl and they all listen intently to the speaker.

KENNEDY

> My fellow citizens of the world
> Ask not what America can do for you
> But what together we can do
> For the freedom of man.

251

The lights flash and then grow dim on stage as another voice comes over the microphone very softly and distantly

VOICE

> To you, from failing hands we throw the torch
> Be yours to hold it high
> If ye break faith with us who die
> We shall not sleep
> Though poppies grow in Flanders fields.

The lights flash and then return to normal

KENNEDY

> Let the word go forth from this time and place to friend and foe alike, that the torch has been passed to a new generation of Americans—born in this century, tempered by war, disciplined by a hard and bitter peace, proud of our ancient heritage and unwilling to witness or permit the slow undoing of those human rights to which this nation has always been committed, and to which we are committed today at home and around the world.

There is wild cheering and shouting. Kennedy goes over and shakes hands with World Commonwealth and some of her soldiers whose uniforms somewhat resemble his own.

Blackout.

The next scene follows immediately.

Scene 18

A Guest of the Nation, U.S.A. 1963

The stairs are visible and the figure of the shepherd stands next to them. S.R. Downstage center, there is the slightly raised platform with the U.S. flag alongside it. Large photographs of Winston Churchill and Lafayette hang in front of the bomb backdrop S.L. with the sign underneath, 'A Guest of the Nation'. World Commonwealth is seated near the foot of the stairs and her retinue are sitting in formation across the stage with a row of small flowering rose trees between them. They form most of the audience at this presidential address although some other people are present. There is cheering and clapping as the president walks from the wings and stands on the podium facing the audience, with the microphone in front of him. He is dressed as the two Kennedy brothers are dressed at the funeral of John F. Kennedy, with pin striped pants and a dark jacket and is not the same actor as the one in the P.T. uniform from the earlier scene as this scene follows immediately.

PRESIDENT KENNEDY

>My fellow citizens of the world,
>My fellow Americans.
>We gather here to honor a great man,
>Sir Winston Churchill, shepherd of the free.
>In those dark days and darker nights
>When England stood alone, he took his pen
>And sent the English language into war,
>Marshaling the courage of the globe.
>He proved that zest for freedom and the faith
>Are truly indestructible in man.
>The Marquis de Lafayette we honored too,
>When Washington acclaimed him as his son—
>Symbol of freedom, hero of two worlds,
>Doyen of soldiers of liberty round the globe.

He speaks directly to the retinue of World Commonwealth.

>And both these men lived on to ripe old age,
>To serve this world in wisdom of their years.
>Six monarchs of his native land
>Sir Winston served and Lafayette survived

Both Revolution and Bonaparte
In honor and integrity of life.
Let us take heart that someday we too shall learn
That violence, though it kill the man,
Hurts more the land that bore him.
For others will pick up the torch,
But blood leaves stain forever.
And one more thing before we leave today,
Concerning now the gap between
The precept and the practice in our land,
In education of our citizens.
For the truly educated mind is wise,
And wisdom is the thing we need today
To steer our frail craft on to tranquil seas
Of freedom and equality for all.

In this, our twin goals must forever be
New and better standards of excellence
And availability of this excellence
For those who can and will pursue the truth;
Our progress as a nation hinges on
How we pursue and understand
That Truth and Justice are not easily found,
And invest in human beings, not cut them off,
Because their voices differ from our own.

For Churchill was a dullard in the school
Yet raised the English language to new heights
Of courageous eloquence. And Lafavette
Fought for independence of this our land
And sovereignty of the people and natural rights

Let us remember them.

There is clapping and everyone walks offstage as a ladder is lowered S.L. It is nearly touching the floor but not quite. Several rungs up, there is a sign to one side, A.B. Further up there is a sign M.A. and further up, Ph.D. On the top of the ladder but several feet to the side of it and at center stage, is a big white light. Madeline comes in and grips one of the lower rungs of the ladder and starts climbing. A few men enter, the same as the young men from the earlier scene.

STUDENT 1
    Hey Madeline, what are you doing there?
STUDENT II
    Madeline, we're on strike, didn't you know?

MADELINE

Oh are we?

She nearly loses her grip but keeps one arm around the rung of the ladder as she talks to the men

What are we striking for?

STUDENT I

The Third world. Come on now, Madeline,

The University's on strike.

Power to the people.

STUDENT II

Come on now, Madeline,

We're going to the picket line

MADELINE

What's your goal?

STUDENT I

To crush the system

MADELINE

But what's your goal?

STUDENT I

I told your to break the system

MADELINE

Well then, why don't you hire a demolition crew?

STUDENT I

Madeline, your sense of humor is in very poor taste.

I'm warning you.

STUDENT II

You're Third World aren't you?

MADELINE

You know I am

STUDENT II

Well put your body on the picket line

STUDENT I

Join us Madeline. We must end discrimination in employment. We must end reverse discrimination in Vietnam. Did you know that 40% of the men in Vietnam are black?

MADELINE looks shocked

We must end a racist ideology perpetrated through a white oriented curriculum.

STUDENT II

We must break the caste

That turns out iron men,

Inflexible in business,

Self-perpetuating in war.

STUDENT 1

We must break down research

That's geared to repression

Of Third World workers,

255

Rebelling to be free.
MADELINE
But what can I do?
STUDENT 1
Give us your moral aid
MADELINE
You've got that
STUDENT 1
Get down on the picket line
MADELINE
But what's your goal? I mean
I want to search for justice,
Do you know what that is?
STUDENT I
We know injustice, Madeline
And that's what we've got now.
STUDENT II
Look, I told you, it's no use talking to Madeline
MADELINE
But if I join you, will you leave me free,
To strike out for the white light,
The white light of justice
That I can see?
She points up to it
STUDENT I
It's all in your head, Madeline.
MADELINE
I know, I know,
But will you leave me free?
STUDENT I
We must unite, unite, unite
MADELINE
Look man, you exasperate me
STUDENT II
We must build a marxist-leninist party
To unite all those who struggle.
MADELINE
Are you still on that class thing?
Look man, Marx is dead
And so is the world in which he wrote
And so are the classes that he defined.
His labor theory is so outdated,
It's positively laughable.
I push a button. Is that worth my bread?
What's wrong with true reform,
Have you no faith in man?

Where is the craftsman gone?
The man that works for love of what he does?

Marx destroyed the craftsman
And I'll never forgive him for that,
Never. He took away men's pride
And men's joy in what they do.

STUDENT I

I told you it's no use talking to Madeline
Let faith in your so-called system set you free,
Traitor to our cause.
Go to your classes,
Find out for yourself.

MADELINE

I'm free already man.
No one can take that away from me.

They go out and she is alone

And I'm no traitor
Though you cannot see.

Madeline inches up the ladder with her back to the audience. A figure dressed in black tights comes in from the wings with an academic hat on. He watches her at a distance

FIGURE 1

That's not what I want

MADELINE

But I read everything
And I wrote truly.

FIGURE 1

That's not what I want

MADELINE

But this is what I believe

The figure comes over and tries to force her fingers off the rung of the ladder

Let me try again

FIGURE 1 *After a pause*

That's not what I want

MADELINE

But I am defenseless

The figure steps back and laughs hollowly. Another figure with full academic attire comes in

SECOND FIGURE

What in God's polka-dotted mind is this all about?
What you have written is completely incomprehensible
From beginning to end.

He pauses slightly as he passes Madeline and then continues walking across the stage and exits. The musicians play a couple of beats and the black figure goes into an erotic dance facing Madeline and the audience. He pauses momentarily.

FIGURE I

        That's not what I want.

He then continues dancing.

MADELINE

        Let me have an outside examiner.

        Let someone else read my paper—*He laughs hollowly*

        I'll take it to my representative

        I'll take it to the people—*He laughs louder*

SECOND FIGURE

        Don't try to buck the establishment Madeline

        That way disaster lies.

        Don't you know that the minute you appeal

        To someone else,

        The whole profession will unite against you?

        Do you think we can afford

        To let this giant edifice collapse? *They exit*

Madeline puts her head to the ladder and curls her legs around it. The second figure exits and the first hands her something. She takes it. It is a figure C. She holds it up so it can be seen. The black figure remains at a distance looking at her, then exits. The moment he does, she throws it to the ground. The lights are low. A drunk enters and looks at her struggling to keep hold of the ladder. He stands under her so her feet feel his shoulders. She stands there with one arm still around the ladder.

MADELINE

        Thanks

DRUNK *With a cockney accent*

        Oh that's O.K. dearie.

        I'd do more for you love if I could.

        Always lend a helping hand,

        That's me motto love.

        It's a cruel old world,

        And never pass up an opportunity

        For a bit of kindness,

        That's what I say.

        What are you doin' there love,

        If you don't mind me askin', that is.

        Seems a funny sort of occupation

        For a pretty little thing like you,

        Danglin' like an acrobat

        On a rusty old ladder

        That's leadin' up to no place

        What's up there love?

MADELINE

        It's a light

        A great white light,

        I'm rested now, thanks.

DRUNK

       Don't mention it love.

       It makes me old shoulders

       Feel strong again.

Madeline resumes her climb and the drunk topples over the stool he carried in and sits on it looking up at her, then ambles off stage. A big black man enters, full of fun. He. He tip toes up, piles up a couple of boxes, stands on them silently and looks at the girl as she grabs hold of the A.B. sign, tries to bite it and bend it. She turns it over and then throws it away. The man ducks and his white teeth show in a big grin till he gets behind Madeline and says.

BLACK MAN

       Boo

She nearly falls off the ladder but he catches her

MADELINE

       Man, you scared me.

BLACK MAN

       Hey, what you doin' up there chick

MADELINE

       You really and truly want to know?

BLACK MAN *Teasing her*

       Yeah, I do.

MADELINE *Very slowly*

       Well to tell you the truth

BLACK MAN

       Yeah

MADELINE

       I don't really know why I have to go through THIS in order to reach THAT

       She points to the white light

BLACK MAN

       You don't know, you don't know,

       Madeline don't know

       What she's doin' up the ladder,

       She don't even know what the ladder is

       Most likely.

       She don't know it's crooked and ugly

       And rusted rotten. *He dances around*

       She don't know it's a decrepit old ship

       Drifting in a contaminated sea.

       Madeline don't know nothin'.

       All she sees is that big white light. *He looks at her*

       Do you know you look real comical, chick,

       Them fancy legs in horrible contortions

       Instead of doin' their thing.

MADELINE

       I'm rested now.

BLACK MAN

       Now I've got to take you back?

She nods

> Madeline's a screwball, an egg head
> A real nut,
> Goin' after a pie in the sky.

He takes her back

> Save a piece for me.

He lifts her up as high as he can. She grabs the rung and he dances off stage. She moves higher painfully—The lights are very low.

FIRST TEMPTER.

> Take it Madeline,
> Keep it Madeline,
> It will open many doors for you.
> These days a degree
> Is your very bread Madeline.
> Take it Madeline.
> Keep it Madeline. *She turns it around and inches on*

SECOND TEMPTER

> If you really believe
> That you understand poetic justice
> Then let go Madeline,
> Let go Madeline.
> For all the artists that have been destroyed
> By the system,
> You will be saved Madeline,
> Poetic justice will save you
> When you fall,
> Let go Madeline.

She clings to the ladder and inches up

THIRD TEMPTOR

> It's the Ph.D. Madeline,
> It's a great distinction child,
> Just look what you can do Madeline,
> You can get a professorship in a University,
> You get tenure,
> Nobody can kick you out,
> You're there for life.
>
> Go for the Ph.D. Madeline
> Give up the lonely fight
>
> And all these things will be given you,
> A home in the hills, secure, serene,
> Out of the common plight.
> A view out over the city,
> No rioting, no tear gas,

No student demonstrations,

Peaceful, tranquil nights . . .

Madeline screams and doesn't stop screaming until she inches up and turns the Ph.D. sign around. She is now just below the white light. She puts one arm over the last rung and breathes heavily while she leans over to the side to grip the horizontal ledge just beneath the light. She closes her eyes and turns her head so she is partly facing the audience. Visible to the audience the feet of a giant in army shoes (only the feet are visible) step across the ledge and approach her. She remains motionless except for the breathing. The big foot comes down on her hand and Madeline falls. "Gaudiamus Igatur" plays very brokenly. Then Madeline gets up. The net that held her when she fell was held by four stage hands. She realizes that she is not hurt, looks at the stage hands, grins first and then they all laugh delightedly as a flute plays,

The Bells of hell go ding-a-ling-a-ling

For you but not for me,

Oh Death where is thy sting-a-ling-a-ling

Oh grave they victory?

They all dance around the stage singing and then go out through the wings.

Strains of the 'Horst Wessel' song are heard and a harsh masculine voice comes over the microphone.

VOICE

We must have law and order in the land.

ORDER above all.

The soldiers come back on stage near the shepherd S.R. Some in bell bottom trousers with army shirts, others in army pants and colorful tops. The mad student is there too. Pal is trying to draw their attention to something. It is Liberty entering from the wings lower S.L, all bruised and her clothes all torn. They put flowers around, bathe her as before and bring her a new gown and cape. They are looking around to see who has hurt her. They go out through the wings and the audience and then come back leading the power politicians. They carry the tubs for them. The men arrange themselves in a circle, the way they were just before 1915. The soldiers put the tubs near them and they place various objects in front of themselves—a tank, a plane and other objects of war. One looks at another's pile. He turns to the toy people in his own tub and grabs a handful (some are made of plasticene, others the same as before). He crushes them between his hands and puts this object in front of himself. Another one steps over to look at someone else's pile. He picks up a missile and looks at it then goes to his own tub and shapes a long projectile which he sets in front of himself then looks very smug and self-satisfied. The stage is in half darkness. The voice of the actor who plays Bismarck originally speaks over the microphone

VOICE OF BISMARCK

I'll have a military budget.

We must be first in the race for arms.

First, first, first, *echoing to silence* first

Slowly a soft light plays on the soldiers on the high platform and then halfway between them and the floor, another landing is seen. Liberty is there looking with interest at what is going on below because bits and pieces of men still stick out from whatever the power politicians try to mold and some toy figures are made of celluloid. She motions silence and then beckons to some people beyond he wings. Soon a group of young people including children, come

261

near her, all dressed in very pale pink tights. They are the unborn children. They look intently at what is going on and see to be completely unable to comprehend it. They finally look to her for an explanation. Liberty points to the advocates of power politics on stage although her hand also ranges over the audience and makes her most stern speech of the play,

LIBERTY

> They are tampering with your inheritance,
> Not content to lay waste their own age
> They plan to mutilate yours.

A child's voice comes over the microphone

CHILD'S VOICE

> But what are they doing, beloved,
> I do not understand,
> Why they are killing men like that,
> And crushing them in their hands?

LIBERTY

> They are doing it because we allow them, child
> We—our silent band
> *She ranges her arm in an arc over the audience*
> We beat on the drums of suicide,
> We crucify YOUR land.

CHILD'S VOICE

> But is there no halt?

LIBERTY

> Yes child, there is a halt.

Children's voices resound all over the theatre.

VOICES

> Halt, halt, halt . . .

The lights flash on and off. The figures on the stage hurl everything they have at each other, tubs as well, and end up bruised and beaten in a big heap on the floor. The lights stop flashing and the children go over to them and pull them apart and take off all their clothes so they too are left naked wearing only pink tights which are a darker shade than those of the children

CHILD'S VOICE

> But they are only men.

The children are helping the power politicians to sit up

LIBERTY

> Yes child

The children then sweep away the mess and leave the men naked and without their objects of war. They turn the tubs upside down and make the men sit on them with their backs to the audience. A blackboard comes down in front of the bomb backdrop. The smallest child prints

BEING IS	*SURVIVAL IS*
LOVE IS	*JOY IS*

CHILD

> What is being?

The child points to one of the men

MAN

> Being is

A child attendant hangs an A on his back

CHILD

> What is love?

MAN

> Love is

An attendant hangs an A on his back

CHILD

> What is survival?

MAN

> Survival is.

Another A. The children then turn the tubs right way up, fill them with the toy people and set the men in front of them again. The men look at each other and they look so ridiculous squatting naked that they burst our laughing. One picks up one of his men and looks at it. Another does the same. They toy men are all different colors. One of the children brings in a frame that looks like a tree. One man sets a toy on one of the branches. Soon they are decorating it with toy men. One looks in his own tub and can't find what he is looking for so he goes over to another—asks permission and is given a toy man from another tub. He puts it in a place. They are all very engrossed. One man wants to change the position of a toy. He goes to take it off. Another stays his hand. They scowl at each other. A third man comes over. They go into a huddle, miming the aesthetic effect. They can't agree so they get a couple more who are interested in the discussion (some are not). There are three toy men involved. They take a vote and decide against one toy color. They take another vote and put one of the toy men in the place. They all stand back and admire their handiwork, nod at each other, clap each other on the back. The children bring in flowers. Pal's voice comes over the microphone.

PAL'S VOICE

> Who are you?

LIBERTY

She is now back on the platform

> I am Liberty beloved.

PAL'S VOICE

> How shall I recognize you?

LIBERTY

> Recognize me by my shadow,
> The shadow of goodwill
> That my children know as flowers.

> > *Blackout*

The figure of the STATUE OF LIBERTY is on stage, in the manner in which she appears at the beginning. She has a pronged crown on her head, holds a torch in her right hand and a gold book in her left. A woman's voice comes over the microphone.

> Give me your tired, your poor,
> Your huddled masses yearning to breathe free,

The wretched refuse of your teeming shore,
Send these, the homeless, tempest-tossed, to me
I lift my lamp beside the golden door.
Pal comes stumbling on stage in the darkness.

PAL

  I am the world,
  I am the soldier,
  Every man that ever bore a gun
  Is me. Oh God,
  Why have you forsaken me?

  I stood upon the beach at Anzac Cove
  And gazed out over the glistening Dardanelles,
  Yearning, yeaning yearning
  To walk upon the golden plains of Troy,
  As if amid that rubble I might find
  The covenant that man must live in peace.

  As Hector was, so then am I
  But Kemal stood for me,
  And I thrust with my bayonet
  The man that stands for me.

  I murdered with my very hand
  My kindred, my own blood,
  Oh Hera, mother of the gods, have mercy
  For I have betrayed and slain my own.

  The monster carnage welled up in my veins
  And tore my soul in two
  Oh—is—there—no—vision
  Higher than the circumscrib-ed man
  To halt the wandering of my ghostly soul
  And let me die in peace?
  Is there no one in all the world?

The light which has been very, very, dim, rises a little to show Pal in his striped bellbottom trousers and kaki army shirt pleading to the audience and then half turning toward the Statue of Liberty. The figure of the shepherd remains further back near the stairs. He addresses Liberty.

PAL

  Why do you haunt me, woman?

LIBERTY

  I am Liberty beloved

PAL

  Can you put Humpty together again?

LIBERTY

    No, beloved

PAL

    Then weep with me

LIBERTY

    No, beloved

PAL

    No?

LIBERTY

    I live in gardens beautified by men,
    Some men rise up great heights and then they fall;
    For fearing what may someday threaten
    Their radiance in the sun,
    Attempt thus to exterminate the all
    Of what may yet offend,
    And let the weeds go on unchecked
    No threat to them;
    And so the ground lies fallow for a time
    Till God once more with love replenishes
    What man has broken, putrified, destroyed.

PAL

    Will that go on forever?

LIBERTY

    Oh no beloved. The call is out
    And echoing in orbit around the earth,
    God needs assistance. Man's monster grows too bold.
    From mass destruction now he turns to one,
    One single life, one lover of mankind
    Struck down thus in his prime,
    Cuts deeply at the very roots of man,
    Severs the life blood at its very source.

PAL

    Oh I have dipped my hands in blood

LIBERTY

    You warrior now?

PAL

    The warrior gained ascendance when I broke faith
    And murdered my own brother.

LIBERTY

    Beloved, give me leave,
    Give me leave to wander on the earth,
    All now is sunset. The dragon guards the night,
    Yet God is waiting with the morning dew.
    Hold my torch.
    Let me, a woman, look upon this world
    That men have made alone.

Pal takes her torch and steps back stiffly then to the side. The mad student enters with flowers trailing from his hat and the very large one dragging behind.

LIBERTY

>Why do you not tend your garden, beloved?

He caresses his flowers

MAD STUDENT

>I tend them—in my own way

LIBERTY *Going up to him*

>I pick a flower
>
>And it changes color in my hands,
>
>What kind of vision is that?

MAD STUDENT

>A vision that is afraid

LIBERTY

>Why are you afraid beloved?

MAD STUDENT

>I am afraid because I know
>
>That if my peers taunt me
>
>And say it is not so,
>
>I will collapse beneath them,
>
>And I will broken go.

LIBERTY

>No beloved

MAD STUDENT

>Oh yes, I know

LIBERTY

>No beloved,
>
>They hold not the standard.

MAD STUDENT

>Who holds it then?

LIBERTY

>Those that will re-write it,
>
>For it is buried now
>
>In the rubble of your youthful dream.

MAD STUDENT *trance-like*

>In a conflict of two categorical imperatives, a hierarchy of values must be established
>which is acceptable to all the world.

LIBERTY

>Yes beloved

MAD STUDENT

>They would not listen then

LIBERTY

>They will listen now.

Musicians have come on stage and play softly. The Mad Student exits and the black intellectual comes on stage with the two panthers on either side of him bearing guns. The man in the center is shaking his head.

266

INTELLECTUAL
  I don't get it. I don't get it.
PANTHER
  It sure was a strange thing to give you man.
The man in the center looks at the gold object in his hands and begins to speak as if repeating something that has been told to him.
BLACK INTELLECTUAL
  At last, a passport to the world.
  The sick man does not know the remedy
  But there are those who do.
  Keep faith with new world covenant,
  And trace it with the blood
  But—shed—not—any.
He looks at the two men with him and touches a gun
  Goodwill precedes the law
  Where new covenants are in making.
  Great issues begin with knowledge of the self,
  Decisions are not made by governments but by human . . .
Liberty approaches them
LIBERTY
  Are you not free beloved?
He looks at her and continues half trance-like
BLACK INTELLECTUAL
  True freedom is a state of mind.
  In physical bondage were your ancestors
  For hundreds and hundreds of years, yet were they free
  In their high reaching souls to give to you
  The strength this day to plant your foot on earth
  And write with burning pen your heritage
  And destiny in the annals of humankind. *then he turns to Liberty*
BLACK INTELLECTUAL
  But I am an exile
LIBERTY
  Does your country have monopoly on ink beloved?
  No alien from the world of men is he
  Who has a pen and ink. No exile is,
  But he who chooses of his own free will
  To hate his native land. Stoop not to fools,
  And waste not breath on them that are not just,
  But think of me. Your word is stronger far,
  Than voice of them who would prevent your tread
  Upon a little stretch of God's own ground
  That some men call America and some call free . . .
  Write it then,
  Trace out the blood
  But—shed—not—any.

A businessman enters, sees Liberty and goes over to her.
BUSINESSMAN

Ah Liberty, we're selling bonds

For Israel. Help us. Help our people

LIBERTY

Yes beloved I will help you.

But not as you expect. Forgive me.

Free—your—bonds.

You are in greater bondage now

Than you have ever been,

For now you have defined your boundary

And placed it before all men

And you hold it with the sword beloved

Beware!

BUSINESSMAN

But it was promised us

LIBERTY

Obtain your brother's sanction

For the promised land!

He is shocked and puts his two hands up in front of his face as if to shield himself from her. She steps back.

Live by boundaries if you desire,

But abide by them,

Or you compromise your race beloved,

And justify the men

That massacred the soul of an age

To annihilate your sons.

She begins to move away. The lights are very low and there is a little musical accompaniment to the pauses

Heed me or heed me not, beloved

My debt is paid to the yet unborn

By utterance of the word,

For it is the unborn that will judge me.

She moves further away. The music picks up the tone

Seek out your own judge beloved

The spotlight fades from her and the business man, bent over, staggers off the stage. A few bars of martial music play and an American General enters on stilts. He comes over to Liberty. He holds the cat-a-nine-tails that Bismarck held in Scene one. She does not move. The music builds up. He holds the whip high in the air. The music stops.

GENERAL

You are not afraid?

LIBERTY

No, beloved.

He drops the whip to his side.

LIBERTY

Throw it away beloved

It is nearly dawn.

GENERAL

But what will I do?

How will I survive?

LIBERTY

In the sun

There are places for everyone.

GENERAL

But look at my height!

Arn't you impressed?

She shakes her head

Well what are your standards then?

I am an important man

Don't you at least respect me?

LIBERTY

Respect goes out to the great in heart

But not the great in power

Unless they be the same.

He who kills his fellow man

A murderer is.

He who treads another's sovereign soil

Betrays his native land.

The General falls off his stilts and crawls off the stage as the musicians laugh at him and play 'The Bells of Hell'. Then the music stops and Liberty comes to center stage. A group of vandals bring in a statue of Lincoln from the wings and begin to deface it. At the same time the figure of Death enters from the back of the audience and comes down the aisle. He is the same as before with his long black gown and cream colored facial mask. He speaks very loudly and clearly as he walks down the center aisle.

DEATH

November nineteenth, nineteen—correction—eighteen sixty three. Our fathers brought forth on this content a new nation, conceived in liberty and dedicated to the proposition that all men are created equal. We are met on a great battlefield. We cannot dedicate—we cannot consecrate—we cannot hallow this ground. The brave men living and dead who struggled here have consecrated it far above our poor power to add or detract.

As he speaks this last he is standing next to the vandals. Then he reads the rest from the inscription underneath the statue.

We here highly resolve that these dead shall not have died in vain—that this nation under God shall have a new birth of freedom—and that government of the people by the people and for the people shall not perish from the earth.

He begins to laugh eerily. Then he turns and sees Liberty and crouches down.

LIBERTY

I know who you are, and why you're stalking me—

Come, why are you afraid of me?

DEATH

I have no jurisdiction.

The earth is drenched with blood
And covered with a carpet of flowers.

Liberty turns to the vandals

LIBERTY

Why do you fear charisma
And the flowers of goodwill?
Why do you vent your anger
On image, when the soul is free?
Do you not know beloved
That you cannot destroy me?
The torch will pass. The torch will pass.
How many times does he have to tell you
He has no jurisdiction?

Death shrivels up and backs off the stage. The boys are shaken and try to make repairs while the musicians play something resembling Bob Dylan's 'Blowin in the Wind', and if they play 'Blowin in the Wind', a soft voice comes over the microphone, 'Bob Dylan', 'Bob Dylan'. The lights fade except for a soft light on Liberty. She sits down almost dejectedly. Pal comes over and bends over her stiffly because he is still holding the torch.

LIBERTY *Turning to Pal*

I had to tell them things—
I had to speak beloved,
And tear the veil from their eyes.

PAL

Did you speak justly?

LIBERTY

Yes I did.

PAL

Well then you have the golden apples

LIBERTY

Yes I have

PAL

Are they beautiful?

LIBERTY

They are very beautiful,
VERSAILLES, SAN FRANCISCO, NEW YORK

PAL

And what about me?
Shall I be free?
Shall I be free?

LIBERTY

Your spirit will soon be fulfilled beloved.

PAL

Then the horror that I dreamed of
Is coming?

LIBERTY

Yes beloved, it is here.

The light goes up on John Kennedy and Robert Kennedy
JOHN KENNEDY

> Let us take heart that someday we too shall learn
> That violence though it kill the man
> Hurts more the hand that bore him,
> For others will pick up the torch,
> But blood leaves stain forever.

"Let the word go forth from this time and place to friend and foe alike, that the torch has been passed to a new generation of Americans—born in this century, tempered by war, disciplined by a hard and bitter peace, proud of our ancient heritage and unwilling to witness or permit the slow undoing of those human rights to which this nation has always been committed, and to which we are committed today at home and around the world.".
There is wild cheering and shouting.   *SHOTS*
                              LIGHTS

Scene 19

The Valley of the Shadow of Death U.S.A. 1963

There is complete darkness on stage. Three pistol shots are heard clearly. A woman's voice comes over the microphone. It is the same as in the Gallipoli scene
VOICE

And last night in my dream
I felt the joy of all your childhood years,
I saw you standing in a blaze of light;
A dove was flying toward your open hand;
And Tommy dear, you looked so beautiful.
But then I heard the shots and from the sky
A winding sheet was drawn around your head
And they led you stumbling, Tommy, up to heaven.

The lights go on. There is light on the elevated platform where the soldiers are standing as well as on the stairs leading up to it. Close to these stairs and slightly backstage a figure stands in his P.T. skipper's uniform with the whole of his head covered with white bandages. Jackie stands slightly in front of him with her pink dress splattered with blood. Her dress could be an exact copy of what she was wearing on November 22, 1963. A pace or two in front of her, closer to the audience, Robert Kennedy stands in his pin striped pants and jacket. Edward Kennedy is closer to the wings and backstage slightly to that he and John Kennedy are the same distance from the audience. The model of a small child dressed in white and saluting, standing almost center stage in front, facing the audience. The others are all facing S.L. so that they are seen in profile by the audience. They are facing S.L, where there is a big rocket with 'Cape Canavarral' in front of it and a flag pole. The soldiers are lined up all along the platform and also all the way down the stairs. They are holding a long white winding sheet. Almost center stage, immediately in front of the platform, is the figure of the shepherd. The bomb background remains but it is not lit up. As soon as the lights go up a young girl moves quickly in front of the soldiers, along the platform and down the stairs. She is wearing a simple white chiffon gown. She takes the end of the winding sheet from the soldier at the foot of the stairs and holds it in her hands as she directs her attention toward John Kennedy. Everything is silent then some sobbing is heard as two or three groups of people all in black, come from the wings and huddle together. The girl inches towards John Kennedy. As soon as she reaches him she attaches the winding sheet to the back of his head and takes his arm. Five more shots ring out. Robert Kennedy falls backwards. A young man springs out from behind a group of mourners and holds his head which is covered with blood. The young man is wearing black pants and a white jacket. He holds Robert Kennedy's head in his arms and stares incredulously but Jackie and Edward remain as statues. The spotlight comes up on the shepherd and there is a patch of blood on the white gown over his heart and it is also splattered as though it has been shot with a pistol full of blood. The sobbing and hysteria become very loud with the sounds of many african american voices. They slowly calm down. There is dead silence and the main actors on stage remain rigid. Then Jackie slowly raises her arm and points toward the rocket. A stage hand enters and changes the sign 'Cape Canavarral' to 'Cape Kennedy'. Edward Kennedy makes a slight movement as though he is going to step forward but as he does so, there is a humming sound of children and the unborn children on the earlier scene come running in, in their pink tights with their arms full of flowers. They run to him. A couple grip his legs and put their heads close to him and prevent him from moving. They all sit and kneel in a circle around him and he remains rigid. The sobbing and the humming continue. A telephone rings loudly and music plays one stanza of 'Nearer My God to Thee'. A stage hand comes and unfurls the American flag and tries to raise it. He pulls it up to half mast but it sticks there. He hauls and tugs but it will not move. Another man enters and another. Soon there is a pile of men sprawled on top of each other, and the flag remains at half mast. Then the national anthem is sung by the rest of the people on stage and they are sobbing as they try to sing it and cannot because they are crying.

> Oh say can you see by the dawn's early light
> What so proudly we hailed at the twilight's last gleaming
> Whose broad stripes and bright stars through the perilous fight
> O'er the ramparts we watched were so gallantly streaming
> And the rockets' red glare, the bombs bursting in air,
> Gave proof through the night that our flag was still there.

There is a pause and then a complete stop.

> Oh say, does that star-spangled banner yet wave
> O'er the land of the free, and the home of the brave.

They sing it through to this but they are crying while they do it. Meanwhile many men have been hurling themselves on the pile by the flag trying to raise it but they cannot. Then as the last two lines are playing a big african american, naked to the waist, comes down the aisle and throws his weight on the pile and to the last sound of the national anthem, at the weight of this man, there is a loud boom from the rocket and a streak of light flares up from it as the flag goes up.

Blackout

The voice of an african american woman sings,

> My country 'tis of thee
> Land of sweet liberty

She sings several stanzas while the stage is blacked out and her voice is joined by those of children who are really singing 'God Save our Gracious Queen' in Perth, Australia and the next scene follows without a break

273

Scene 20

Perth, Australia

After all the voices mingle for about a stanza, the children's voices fade and the woman's voice continues as a large colorful drop is lowered showing the moon with the men landing on it and the earth in the distance. It can be hand painted, or an artist's impression, providing that it reveals details about the actual landing. The bomb backdrop remains.
A voice comes over the microphone.

VOICE

    Rise up great bird from the searing heat of earth,
    Gather the globe into your flaming pyre
    And soar onward, upward.
    Seek ye out your God,
    The life blood of this daring enterprise.
    Your nest is fashioned with the spice of men,
    Aroma of the ages permeates the boughs,
    And flower of our youth, the oil for fire.

    Rise up great bird. Shining projectile rise.
    Rise up from world's inferno;
    Leave here the fiery monster of the earth
    And gather artifice into eternity.
    Sing out the song that man shall reach the moon
    And leave his footprint on eternal time.

    Miraculous bird, fly high and higher still,
    Fear not to give what has been given you,
    For God alone dispenses melody
    And takes not back the hand in punishment
    For godlike aspiring in the soul of man.

    Scarlet your plumage of the earth great bird,
    And golden is the temple of the sun:
    Eternal, the white hot light of God,
    The meaning of man's music on the earth.

Fly on great bird until you reach the moon.
Trace out the justice of man's life on earth;
Plot well your course. One little step of man
Beyond his present self to great unknown
Lifts up the soul divided, gathers it
To giant leap, eternity of man.

Rejoice you children of the earth this day to feel
The rebirth of the phoenix soul of man:
Gather up your ashes each and every one,
Embalm them in a golden egg of myrrh
And place them on the altar of the sun.

For you today have felt the hand of God
Sanction aspiring man in quest for peace,
Where every planet glorifies the whole,
Rejoicing in the music of the spheres.

The stage is in darkness but people are entering with torches and placing them on what is beginning to look like a big tree, broad at the base with a big white light at the top which comes on as many touches are brought into place. A little stage lighting comes on, just enough to reveal a group of men and boys and girls dressed in scout uniforms. A sign is placed on S.L. where 'Cape Kennedy' was in the previous scene, reading 'Perth, Australia'

DARKIE

Do you think he'll see us?

SHORTY

Well if he doesn't see us, he won't see anybody else.
The whole world is in darkness to him,
Except for us.
A man must have a lot of courage
To fly up there alone.
Turn it on.

Someone tunes into a portable transmitter they have brought with them.

VOICE ONE

Friendship 7, this is Muchea cap com. How do you read me?
Over.

Then a whole series of children's voices are heard in many different languages saying "America is coming in Friendship'.

VOICE TWO

Loud and clear. How are you doing Gordo?
We're doing real fine up here.

VOICE ONE

John, shortly you may observe some lights down here. You want to take a check on them? Out to your right.

VOICE TWO

I do have some lights in sight. On the ground. Over.

275

VOICE ONE

Roger, understand they are just off to your right.

VOICE TWO

That's affirmative, just to my right . . . I can see a big pattern of light, apparently right on the coast. I can see the outline of a town and a very bright light just to the south of it.

VOICE ONE

Roger. That's Perth and Rockingham you're seeing there.

VOICE TWO

Roger. The lights show up very well. Thank everybody for turning them on will you?

VOICE ONE

Sure will, John.

Everyone has been listening with great suppressed excitement. When the microphone is switched off, the girls and boys stand together in formation and begin to sing softly, 'God Save our Gracious Queen', while simultaneously the african american girl's voice predominates with 'My Country Tis of Thee'. Then they make a camp fire at the base of the tree of lights while some climb up on it.

DARKIE

Is the billy boiling?

SHORTY

Well did you ever think fifty years ago when we were on the Dardanelles that in our lifetime, in our lifetime, a man would walk on the moon!

PAL

Remember the Zeppelins flying over the Menin Road?

Like bats they were.

DARKIE

Technology has sure made fools out of a lot of people hasn't it. Take Marx for instance.

SCOUT ONE

Marx is the great savior of the working class.

DARKIE

Oh, I don't doubt that. But that's not my point

SCOUT ONE

Without Marx where would the worker be today

I ask you.

SHORTY

He'd be a craftsman son, and maybe a happy one.

DARKIE

Tommie will you listen to the point of my argument?

SCOUT

I don't want to listen. You never have a conversation without knocking Marx.

DARKIE

I'm knocking Marx and if you can't join in an intelligent conversation intelligently then whose mother's son are you? Come to think of it your mother was just like that too. Get some tea will you Tommie? Two spoons of sugar for me please.

PAL

You know it's not that much over 50 years since we became a Commonwealth.

DARKIE

Wonder when we'll get a Commonwealth of the World?

SCOUT TWO

Never

PAL

Why not?

SCOUT TWO

Reconcile China and the U.S.? You must be daft, man

DARKIE

I wasn't talking about reconciling ideologies but about living in peace.

SCOUT TWO

Oh man, you're naive.

DARKIE

Is that a sin?

SCOUT TWO

Nobody said it was a sin but you have to have a more sophisticated world view than that these days.

DARKIE

Look who's talking

Tommie returns and sits next to Darkie

DARKIE

When Marx was writing, people were being forced to sell their labor for their daily bread and they used arithmetic and calculated what they produced by hand. But that's all old hat now. The great idea of equality for all is always a great idea, but the bourgeoisie is dead and in its place we have semi-literate intellectuals who study truth but not its meaning and so they never understand what justice is.

SHORTY

Perhaps they are afraid.

PAL

Everybody is afraid but fear is like the sound barrier,
Pass through it and a whole new world
Is opened up; balk at it
And the devil takes your soul,
Look at those men up there on the moon,
They've broken through!
Till one small step accomplishes
What's been man's aspiration
Since he ate the forbidden fruit
And had to go out on the quest alone
To find his certain pathway back to God.
And now he's done it.

SCOUT TWO

How do you figure that?

PAL

He's done it in encircling the earth.
In doing that he demonstrates
Community of man,
In doing that he demonstrates
Futility of fear,
In doing that he proves
That man though monster,
Still aspires to his God.

SHORTY

Gee you really waxed poetic Pal

PAL

These are poetic times
Madeline was going to sing a song of Pete Seeger's
Where is she?

DARKIE

Pete Seeger? Any relation to Alan Seeger,
The American poet who wrote,
'But I've a rendezvous with Death'?

PAL

I don't now, but he's a troubadour of the twentieth century, if ever there was one.
And Bob Dylan too.

The scouts have been climbing up and around the fir tree in the half darkness.

VOICES *From the tree*

Where's Madeline?

A young girl comes over. She could be a child and she begins to sing with the others accompanying her,

Where have all the flowers gone
Long time passing
Where have all the flowers gone
Long time ago
Where have all the flowers gone?
Young girls have picked them everyone
Oh when will they ever learn
Oh when will they ever learn . . .

Where have all the young girls gone . . .
Gone for husbands everyone . . .

Where have all the husbands gone . . .
Gone for soldiers everyone . . .

Where have all the soldiers gone . . .
Gone to graveyards everyone . . .

Where have all the graveyards gone . . .
Gone to flowers everyone . . .

Where have all the flowers gone . . .
Young girls have picked them everyone . . .

The words should be visible to the audience which should be encouraged to join if possible, with an actor or two located in the audience and singing. The young people have been grouped around Madeline for the song and when it is over they go back to cavorting on the tree.

DARKIE

    It'll be daylight soon.

PAL

    And the earth will never be the same again,
    It's like turning on a light,
    Once you have seen the vision
    You can never forget what it looks like

DARKIE

    Come on you kids
    Put out the campfire and let's get back to town.

As the scene changes, a flute plays over the microphone, "There's a long, long trail a-winding into the land of my Dreams".

Scene 21

The Fiftieth Anniversary, 1965, The Earth

The stage is blacked out except for spotlights on very intense little girls sitting on stools in brown tights nursing dolls. All races are represented and mixed. A black child has a white doll, cooing, kissing and hugging it: a yellow child a black doll etc.. A woman's voice comes over the microphone.

VOICE

> I am the earth; I bore you, oh my babe,
> I held you in my body close and warm,
> I saw your eyes before they opened up,
> I loved you more than you can ever know.
>
> They gave you toys to play with, guns
> They dressed you as a solider—oh my son,
> They taught you in their schools—the art of war,
> They taught you hatred, my little one—my blood.
>
> It happens thus and so it's true my son,
> You are a murderer; for you have slain
> Your brother; oh my babe, my little one,
> When will you learn from me what justice is?
>
> The vision of eternal time is yours
> If you but raise your eyes beyond the self,
> Look backwards to the mists of ancient times,
> And forward to gigantic leap to moon.
>
> In this eternal spectrum, oh my son,
> Locate your little time upon this earth;
> Locate in infinity of space
> The infinitesimal mark of your small step.
>
> It happens thus and so it's true, my son,
> A little truth, that you a murderer are;

Each little truth, a fallen leaf on me,
The earth that bore you, oh my son, my blood.

Can you alone count all the little truths
That make up creative nature's pulsing heart
Into the infinite eternal Truth
That is not yet completed, nor will be?

And if you cannot comprehend the all,
The reason for its being thus, is lost,
Buried in its own eternal law,
And you do not even seek it, oh my son!

You look for truths, the little certain things
That fall upon my breast in drops of blood;
Oh my babe, when will you raise your eyes
And seek out Justice in the heart of man?

The spotlight fade and the girls exit. The stage is dimly lit with a spotlight upstage R. where there is a raised platform supporting a coffin with the Union Jack draped over it. The lid rises slowly and a short plump figure emerges in a while gown and gives the traditional V sign with his fingers. He then sits down next to the coffin, still on the platform and begins to smoke a big cigar. It can now be seen that the bomb backdrop is still there but in front of it is a kind of screen of hanging tinsel to give the effect of a haze resulting in a distancing from what is painted on the backdrop. If possible, a sound track recording of the death of Winston Churchill is played. If the recording is not available, it goes as follows. A band plays the funeral march then a voice speaks.

VOICE

The queen is there and so are the kings, queens, presidents, prime ministers and leaders of one hundred and twelve countries.

The funeral march continues

VOICE

Sir Winston helped arrange his own funeral under a plan with the code name, 'Operation 'hope not''. One hymn he asked was his favorite, 'The Battle Hymn of the Republic' and so an American hymn was sung by the kings, queens, presidents and leaders of the world.

All the words of this hymn are visible to the audience. While the hymn is playing, Eternal Justice comes in via the raised platform S.L. and steps down on to the stage and sits on the stool which is now center stage. Liberty comes in from the wings and sits at his feet. He strokes her long hair which falls over his knees but there is no light on them. You are just aware of their presence, nothing more.

Mine eyes have seen the glory of the coming of the Lord

He is trampling out the vintage where the grapes of wrath are stored,
He hath loosed the fateful lightning of His terrible swift sword,
His truth is marching on,
Glory, glory, hallelujah,
Glory, glory, hallelujah,

Glory, glory, hallelujah,
His truth is marching on.

I have seen Him in the watch-fires of a hundred circling camps;
They have builden Him an altar in the evening dews and damps;
I can read His righteous sentence by the dim and flaring lamps;
His day is marching on.

He has sounded forth the trumpet that shall never call retreat;
He is sifting out the hearts of men before his judgment seat;
Oh! Be swift my soul, to answer Him! Be jubilant, my feet!
Our God is marching on.

VOICE

General Eisenhower speaks a tribute

GENERAL EISENHOWER'S VOICE

In the coming years, many in countless words will strive to interpret the beliefs, describe the accomplishments and extol the virtues of Winston Churchill, soldier, statesman and citizen that two great countries were proud to claim as their own. Among all the things so written or spoken there will ring out through all the centuries, one incontestable refrain, here was a champion of freedom. May God grant that we and the generations who will remember him, heed the lessons he taught us in his deeds, in his words, in his life. May we carry on his work until no nation lies in captivity, no man is denied opportunity for fulfilment. And now to you Sir Winston my old friend, farewell.

Bagpipes play and a light flickers up the stairs and along the high platform. On the steps are Adlai Stevenson, Robert Kennedy, John Kennedy and all the ghosts of the soldiers. The figure of the shepherd remains by the side of the stairs in front of the new screen which has come down for this scene. A flute plays 'There's a long, long trail' and the spotlight falls on a young soldier standing lower S.L. leaning out over a wall. Throughout the scene he listens intently to the woman's voice which should be that of an older person, the actress being chosen for her clear articulation.

SOLDIER

The fires are lit once more around the world,
And little conflicts ravage many lands.

WOMAN'S VOICE

Oh when will they learn beloved,
That arbitrator is not partisan?

SOLDIER

We must take sides. We cannot sit on fence
And watch the things we cherish fall away.

WOMAN'S VOICE

Recognize your just allegiance, son
Allegiance to the common cause of man
Exemplified by citizens of the world

All nations know that their best men will serve
The common cause of man and there no conflict is
Between the common cause and national decree.

SOLDIER

But I am real. I am alive.
I'm flesh and flood.
Where is reality in all of this?

VOICE

Reality is this,
Give not the power of arbitrator
To a single land, The burden is too great.

The soldier now speaks as if in a trance, remembering what he has heard before.

SOLDIER

First we recognize allegiance to the world,
And we enjoin all nations of the globe
So they our brothers are
But what about their separate civil codes?

VOICE

Leave all intact, except where they concern
Their brothers of the earth in other lands.
Eternal Justice lives in every heart
In language yet unwrit, though traced in blood,
Write out these tracings.
Give Justice in Bondage the appointed task
Of weighing out men's actions by this code
And power of true enforcement for the peace
With soldier citizens of every land;
And all men are treated equal by this law.

SOLDIER

You talk of an ideal my mother,
That cannot be attained.

VOICE

Eternal Justice in its purity
Is unattainable by any man,
But he can still approximate
With Liberty at his right hand:

For freedom gives him choices
And freedom gives him calm
To recognize his brother
And the fallibility of man.

All men are fallible
Yet are they noble still.

Where citizens of the world approximate,
Goodwill surrounds the word
And Liberty brings mercy
When men of goodwill err.

The ghost of Churchill has put his cigar aside and has been also listening very intently

SOLDIER

Oh mother, it is impossible

VOICE

No, son, no . . .

A telephone rings sharply and the tinsel screen is violently drawn back from the bomb backdrop. The soldier turns and looks at it as it slowly comes across again. The lights fade slowly as the voice echoes.

VOICE

Write new covenants, new covenants, new covenants . . .

Blackout

Scene 22

Peace on Earth

The figure of the shepherd remains by the stairs. The tinsel remains in front of the bomb backdrop. Upstage L. is a tall white triangular column surrounded by a small white fence with a gate facing the audience. A children's chorus begins to sing 'Let There be Peace on Earth' by Miller and Jackson and about a dozen children tumble on stage coming from the R. wings. There are white children, brown, black, red and yellow dressed in the national costumes of many countries and all singing the song. Two officials enter from S.L. both carrying lists of names. Pal enters from the wings S.L. and stands by the small white gate. The children finish singing. All the words of the song are shown on a screen or blackboard lowered at the beginning of he scene.

> *Let there be peace on earth*
> *And let it begin with me,*
> *Let there be peace on earth*
> *The peace that was meant to be*
>
> *With God as our Father,*
> *Brothers all are we,*
> *Let me walk with my brother*
> *In perfect harmony.*
>
> *Let peace begin with me,*
> *Let this be the moment now,*
> *With ev'ry step I take,*
> *Let this be my solemn vow:*
>
> *To take each moment and live each moment*
> *In peace eternally*
> *Let there be peace on earth*
> *And let it begin with me.*

One of the officials comes forward

OFFICIAL

OFFICIAL

To commemorate the passing of one of our great champions of freedom, Commonwealth scholarships are to be awarded to all children of goodwill who come with open hearts to pay tribute to those who gave their lives for freedom and won for them this heritage of peace.

The following names are called out and as each name is called a child steps forward, one of the officials checks the name off and the child goes over to the cenotaph and is welcomed by Pal and then takes his or her pace inside the white fence. Algeria, Australia, Belgium, Canada, Ceylon, Congo, Czechoslovakia, Ethiopia, France, Ghana, Greece, India, Iran, Italy, Japan, Mexico, New Zealand, Pakistan, South Africa, Turkey, U.S.S.R., United Arab Republic, United Kingdom, United States of America. Two children are left. One is the most beautifully dressed of all in oriental red brocade and the other a raggedly little boy of indeterminate color who has been playing with his dog all the while and seems to be carrying a stuffed owl. The officials come over to the beautiful oriental child in the red costume. The child bows ceremoniously and the officials bow awkwardly back.

OFFICIAL

What is your name child?

CHILD

Yao Shun Wen Wu

They write it down. The child bows ceremoniously and they bow back. He walks over to Pal and bows and Pal bows back. He enters the white gate. The two officials then begin checking the lists because they cannot account for the raggedy boy still on stage. They look at Pal as if if to say that that is everybody on the list but he only smiles at them and holds the gate open. The Mad Student enters from the wings S.L. decked with flowers which are a little more orderly now and he is dragging the gigantic flower that he used to cover himself with at Hiroshima.

CHILD

Why are you wearing all those flowers?

MAD STUDENT

Because I am beautiful

CHILD

You mean because you love beauty

MAD STUDENT

I mean because I am beautiful
And why are you so curious anyway?

CHILD

Because I am curious

MAD STUDENT

Well for the curious, I have Shimi.

He takes off the gigantic flower and gives it to the child

CHILD

But that is your most beautiful flower

MAD STUDENT

Beauty is not measured by size
But that is my most curious flower.

286

The child puts his hand over it and draws up a cover as if covering an umbrella. The Mad Student looks at the child incredulously

MAD STUDENT

Never give it away

CHILD

No, I never will

The child fastens it to his belt. The Mad Student walks off stage. Meanwhile the officials come over.

OFFICIAL

What is your name child?

CHILD

Pal, sir.

The older Pal straightens up and gazes very fixedly at the child. Meanwhile at the rear of the audience, a girl's voice calls out delightedly but softly and there is much suppressed excitement. The official continues.

OFFICIAL

What is your country of birth?

CHILD

I dunno sir.

OFFICIAL

Where were you born?

CHILD

I was born of woman sir.

OFFICIAL

And what is her name?

CHILD

Liberty sir.

OFFICIAL

Mother, Liberty

The other writes it down.

And your father

What is his name?

CHILD

God sir

OFFICIAL

Father, God.

God who?

CHILD

Just God sir.

The other writes it down

OFFICIAL

What is your native tongue?

CHILD

My what sir?

OFFICIAL

What language do you speak?

What is your language?

CHILD

Equality sir.

OFFICIAL

Native tongue, equality.

The other writes it down. A stage hand takes his dog and the child moves over to the white fence. As he reaches the gate and is greeted very affectionately by Pal there is a movement from the back of the audience and World Commonwealth comes down the enter aisle in her bridal gown, complete this time with headpiece and bouquet. She is followed by her soldiers who are now very well disciplined, marching rhythmically. She stands downstage R. and the soldiers give a demonstration, marching across the stage and back in perfect harmony. Then they take up their places across the front of the stage and sit down. The boy and World Commonwealth gaze at each other. The officials notice it and so does Pal who taps the young man on the shoulder and he walks inside. Pal then gives him his keys and the closes the gate. The young man looks at them and holds them in his hands. From the wings S.L. two stage hands wheel in a dress suit with a white carnation on it and set it near the white gate. A flute plays 'There's a long, long rail a-winding', Pal walks across the stage to the steps and pauses there as a voice comes over the microphone.

VOICE

Let us observe a moment of silence
For those who have laid down their lives
To bring our heritage to its fulfilment;

Where men recognize from whence they came
And who their brothers are upon this earth;

And let us pray for guidance now
In this our new world, phoenix risen
From the ashes of the old.

Pal mounts the stairs as low lights play over the soldiers and "Anzac' is heard softly.

Then these lights go out, a screen is lowered with all the words of the "Battle Hymn ". The white gate is opened, the children come out singing and join with the young soldiers. They motion to the audience to join in the singing.

Scene 23

Gallipoli Revisited

Eternal Justice and Liberty are waiting on the shore. There is the lapping of water on tape. Pal in semi-darkness is coming ashore. Death is there also. "A Long Long Trail" plays softly.

LIBERTY

       I am the earth; I bore you, oh my babe,

       I held you in my body close and warm,

       I saw your eyes before they opened up,

       I loved you more than you can ever know.

VOICE 0N TAPE

       Cast off and drift astern . . .

LIBERTY

       They gave you toys to play with, guns,

       They dressed you as a soldier—oh my son,

       They taught you in their schools—the art of war,

       They taught you hatred, my little one—my blood.

VOICE 0N TAPE

       Company ten over the side . . . .

LIBERTY

       It happens thus and so it's true my son,

       You are a murderer for you have slain

       Your brother; oh my babe, my little one,

       When will you learn from me what loving is?

VOICE ON TAPE

       Easy does it . . .

LIBERTY

       The vision of eternal life is yours

       If you but raise your eyes beyond the self,

       Look backwards to the mists of ancient times,

       And forward to gigantic leap to moon.

VOICE ON TAPE

       Company eleven over the side . . .

LIBERTY

> In this eternal spectrum, oh my son,
> Locate your little time upon this earth.
> Locate in infinity of space
> The infinitesimal mark of your small step.

VOICE ON TAPE

> Cast off and drift astern . . .

LIBERTY

> It happens thus and so it's true my son,
> A little truth, that you a murderer are;
> Each little truth, a fallen leaf on me,
> The earth that bore you, oh my son, my blood.

FATHER'S VOICE ON TAPE

> He wants a hundred pounds down . . .

LIBERTY

> And if you cannot comprehend the all,
> The reason for its being thus, is lost,
> Buried in its own eternal law,
> And you do not even seek it, oh my son.

FATHER'S VOICE ON TAPE

> A hundred pounds and the farm will be ours, ours . . .

LIBERTY

> You look for truths, the little certain things
> That fall upon my breast in drops of blood;
> Oh my babe, when will you raise your eyes
> And seek out Justice in the heart of woman?

The splashing of water becomes louder as Pal emerges from the shadows and sits down on the shore. "Nearer My God to Thee' plays very softly. Eternal Justice, Liberty and Death have been huddled together, waiting.

PAL

> Oh God, you must let me die!
> How long will it take?
> Have I not suffered enough?

ETERNAL JUSTICE

> We thought you would never get here.
> It's a desolate place, Gallipoli.

PAL

> Why here?

ETERNAL JUSTICE

> To close the gaping wound.

PAL

> I am so tired

DEATH *Seductively*

> Rest here, stay here
> Have I not loved you always?
> Was I not here, right here at Wire Gully

Did we not meet at the Somme?
And on your journeys around the world?
Did you not see my work in America?
Aha ha ha ha . . .

PAL *bewildered*

But my journey is not done

DEATH

Aha, ha, ha, stop right here . . .
Were you not betrayed
Here on Gallipoli?
They betrayed you then
They will betray you now . . .

PAL

But I cannot stop now . . .

DEATH

Why not? Why not?

PAL

If I stop now
Everything will be for naught

DEATH

Ah ha ha it will be for naught anyway,
They will not listen,
They will not hear you . . .

Pal looks over at Liberty and Eternal Justice

LIBERTY *smiling*

The choice is yours, beloved.

PAL

I will go on

DEATH

Agh. What is there about you
That you will not die!

PAL

I want to die.
Do you think I enjoy
Wandering the earth?

DEATH

Well stay here then with me.
You will be mine forever.
They will not hear you,
But I'll hear you.

PAL

We have achieved nothing,
War and war and more war
Korea, Vietnam and now Terrorism,

DEATH

Aha ha ha and so on and so on and so on,

> To the end of time,
> And everything shall be mine,
> Aha ha ha
> Your whole civilization will be mine . . .

Pal looks over to Eternal Justice who holds up a set of keys.

DEATH

> They will say to you
> "Who do you think you are?"

PAL

> But I have suffered
> Haven't I?

DEATH

> Suffering. Aha ha ha
> Mortals are always suffering.
> They will say to you.
> "Why are you so arrogant?
> Greater than you have tried and failed!"

Pal looks again to Eternal Justice and the keys

DEATH

> World peace. aha ha ha ha
> Peace and conflict are flip sides of the coin
> You haven't even learnt that.
> Who are you to take the keys?

PAL

> I live on because I must,
> But the wars, oh God the wars
> They go on and on and on . . .

DEATH

> Aha ha ha ha

Pal begins toward Eternal Justice and the keys. He pauses next to Liberty and kneels.

LIBERTY

> They must learn beloved
> That arbitrator is not partisan.

PAL

> But we must take sides.
> We took sides here on Gallipoli

LIBERTY

> You erred, here on Gallipoli.
> Recognize your just allegiance, son,
> Allegiance to the common cause of mortals
> Exemplified by citizens of the world.

ETERNAL JUSTICE

> All nations know that their best will serve
> The common cause of mortals and there no conflict is
> Between the common cause and national decree.

PAL

    You talk of an ideal
    That cannot be attained.

ETERNAL JUSTICE

    Eternal Justice that I represent
    Is unattainable by human beings,
    Yet they can still approximate
    With Liberty at their right hand.

LIBERTY

    For freedom gives them choices
    And freedom gives them calm
    To recognize their siblings
    And the fallibility of man.

LIBERTY

    Mortals are fallible
    Yet are they noble still.

ETERNAL JUSTICE

    Where citizens of the world approximate,
    Goodwill surrounds the word,
    And Liberty brings mercy
    When mortals of goodwill err.

PAL

    It is impossible

LIBERTY

    Oh, no

ETERNAL JUSTICE

    It needs new covenants, new covenants,

PAL

    But I just want to die
    Have I not suffered enough?

ETERNAL JUSTICE

    Your rest is coming,
    And your love awaits you.
    Only one thing more remains.

PAL

    What is it?

DEATH

    This knowledge will die with him.
    Aha ha ha

ETERNAL JUSTICE

    Return to your love

DEATH

    She is dying even now ha ha . . . .

ETERNAL JUSTICE

    There you will find
    The next shepherds.

Give them the keys and they will know me.
And one is coming even now
With artifice to all eternity . . .
Your price is paid . . .
Listen, listen . . .
They are waiting for you . . .
ON TAPE the soldiers' chorus "They were sons of Australia"

LIGHTS

Scene 24

ANZAC DAY, Charters Towers

There are banners and balloons decorating the town. Darkie, Nobby and Shorty enter, rather old by now, wearing their ANZAC medals and feeling quite uncomfortable in ill fitting suits. Eventually they settle themselves on a bench on the front porch.

DARKIE

    This is the place

SHORTY

    Right on the main street. We'll get a real good view from here.

NOBBY

    This place still gives me goose pimples. All me mates from here that never came back.

DARKIE

    Well they'll be with us today
    You can be sure of that.

SHORTY

    Cripes. Do you think we should knock or somethin'.

DARKIE

    Nah. They know we're comin'.
    Anybody gonna march?

SHORTY

    I might march a bit
    What about you Nobby?

NOBBY

    I can't. It's me gammy leg.

SHORTY

    What about you Darkie?

DARKIE

    I might. If those flamin' kids
    Ever get 'ere
    That boy Pal's a wild one.
    Have you heard about 'im?

SHORTY

    Yeah,

I'ere 'es givin' this old ghost town
Somethin' to yak about

DARKIE

'e goes around insistin'
That God's 'is father

NOBBY

Well that's Millicent's damn Sunday school influence
Right there

SHORTY

Well 'e never knew his real father

DARKIE

Or 'is grandfather for that matter

PAUSE

SHORTY

Cripes. 'es a Legacy kid
'es our responsibility.
What's wrong with 'avin God for a father?
Maybe 'ell stop him from gettin' killed
Like the others.

DARKIE

Well maybe there's nothin' wrong
With God for a father but get this
'es got Liberty for a mother!

Much laughter

NOBBY

Wot 'is mother's got to say
About all this mularky?

DARKIE

'is Mum's a little pommie lass
She gave up long ago.
'e 'angs around with the abos,
'es quite spiritual I 'ere

SHORTY

My God is that 'im?

BOY PAL *entering barefooted, bare-chested in cut off shorts*
Good-day blokes,
Me name's Pal
Are yh here for the parade?
I'm sure there are people
From all over the world
"Back to Towers" and all that stuff
Do you know me grandmothers?

DARKIE

We knew yh grandfather too

BOY PAL

Yh did?

> Well stone the crows!
> 'Yh can't be from these parts then.

DARKIE

> We come from the far west,
> Winton really.

NOBBY

> Well I was born 'ere
> But I never came back
> After the war—the first war—
> Till now—not till now!

The front door opens. Millicent appears

MILLICENT

> Darkie is that you?

Boy Pal gives her a squeeze and a kiss

DARKIE

> Yes Milli. Yh got me letter OK?

MILLICENT

> Oh yes, we've been looking forward to seeing you
> Is that Shorty? And Nobby?

NOBBY

> Yes Millie

SHORTY

> Gdday Millie

MILLICENT

> Would you like to come in?

DARKIE

> Nah Millie,
> We might march a bit.
> Sit down a while

Young Pal gives them tea that Milli has prepared. She sits and Boy Pal sits on the step and whistles looking curiously at the old men

PAUSE

> Old Winston kicked the bucket finally.

SHORTY

> I 'eard 'e died
> The scholarships are a good thing for world peace.

PAUSE

Looking up in a trance

> Eh there's your little buggar
> Isn't that Tommie?

DARKIE *Peering out into space*

> Yeah. I think it is
> 'Ell be here.

PAUSE

MILLICENT

> Boy Pal might get a scholarship

297

SHORTY

       Yh might? Gawd blimey.

BOY PAL

       I'd 'ave to put me shoes on.

DARKIE

       'yh could put shoes on for a scholarship couldn't yh'?

BOY PAL

       I dunno.

DARKIE

       Yh damn well better

BOY PAL

       'Yh think I should?

CHORUS OF OLD MEN

       Course yh should, streuth, gawd blimey

DARKIE

       Stone the flamin' crows!

       Ain't we got suits on?

       Where's yh father's medal?

SHORTY

       And yh grandfather's medal?

BOY PAL

       Oh I march every year,

       For Legacy.

MILLICENT

       He always marches every year

       He never misses

She hands him the ANZAC medal which he hangs around his neck

DARKIE

       Damn well better not!

       How's Katie and the others?

MILLICENT

       The others are coming

       But Katie

She begins to sob

BOY PAL *gently*

       Cut it out Milli. Now cut it out.

       Think of all the things we've been teaching each other.

SHORTIE

       What 'ave yh been teaching each other?

       Who's that?

BOY PAL

       That's Madeline *he takes her hand*

The band begins to play

The lights rise and fall

       Here comes me mother

       Everybody's gonna be here

Liberty enters with all her men following her. Ilene is marching, and Kitty. Iris bespeckled, conducting the band. Mother and father are there arm in arm. Eternal Justice enters. They keep marching. Pal comes in looking around expectantly. He is at the back of the stage (or he comes through the audience) when he catches sight of Boy Pal and Madeline. Holding his arms high in the air he weaves his way through the crowd. He has a set of keys clearly visible. He reaches Boy Pal and Madeline who lift up their arms and take the keys. As they exchange the keys, Kate emerges young, in a simple white gown, wearing her pendant and comes directly to Pal. They link arms as the "Battle Hymn of the American Republic" begins to play.

Epilogue

Slowly and indiscernibly at the beginning, a didgeridoo is heard. As the Battle Hymn fades away the didgeridoo becomes louder, then continues quietly through the following. The lights dip and on the stage are Boy Pal and Madeline with the didgeridoo and its player at one side.

MADELINE.
>In the beginning

BOY PAL
>In the beginning, was the word
>And the word was with God
>And the word was God.

MADELINE
>The word is mortal.

BOY PAL
>Yes it is

MADELINE
>Before the beginning is beingness,
>The bond of birth,
>The responsibility of woman,
>The right of the womb.
>Beingness is immortal.
>From beingness I come

VOICE OF ETERNAL JUSTICE
>I am the Force of Life,
>The force of beingness,
>I am the Life Force,
>Call me what you will, God, Allah, Yahwah,
>Sexless, remorseless, I do prevail.
>Words, words are mortal,

I am immortal.
BOY PAL *Turning to Madeline*
    God didn't write anything?
    Is that what you are saying?

MADELINE
    Yes.
    Mortals are gifted
    With language,
    And the writing of language,
    The writing of the word.
    They try to describe
    The Immortal,
    Eternal Justice.

    But man's laws are in bondage to the word,
    To the language
    Man wrote in the beginning.

BOY PAL
    And woman?

MADELINE
    Woman is beingness

BOY PAL
    And the laws of man?

MADELINE
    After the silence of the word of God
    Came the word of man,
    They called them laws

BOY PAL
    The laws of man
    Man's laws.

MADELINE
    Yes,
    Man's laws are Justice in Bondage
    To the word.
    But women's laws are the laws of beingness
    They are the force of beingness
    The Life Force
    Before the word was uttered,
    Before the word is uttered,

Before the laws of man.

During this time in the shadows there are figures moving to the almost inaudible sounds of the didgeridoo.

BOY PAL
Is there a difference?

MADELINE
Oh yes.

Man's laws approximate
Women's laws ARE

The will of God is the force of beingness,
The Life Force.
Before the beginning
In the womb of mother earth
Dwells the spirit of all life,
Languageless, wordless,
Beingness,
The Life Force, the communal source
The common root,
Of all life, everywhere.

In the beingness
Is belongingness
With the life force
With each other,
With all existence.
And the great spirit requires
Cherishingness, lovingness,
Understandingness,
The honoring of beingness,
The honoring of belongingness.

Woman's laws are voiceless covenants
Unspoken until now.

The essence of every being
In the womb of beingness
Is the essence of the self,

Evolving with Mother Earth

COVENANT

Honor self, trust self, believe self, always
    COVENANT
Honor the Earth our Mother
Look upon her with goodwill
In our hearts
    COVENANT
Honor every woman,
Honor the bond of birth,
The responsibility of woman,
The right of the womb.
    COVENANT
Honor every child,
Cherish every child.

FINALLY, THE COVENANT
OF UNDERSTANDING

Any harm to mother earth—
To any who emerge from her womb
Is harm to our own self,
Is loss of honor to our own self.
To kill another,
Is to kill our self

    REMEMBER THE COVENANTS
And the gift of goodwill.

The Life Force prevails
As Goodwill
Tempers justice . . .

The didgeridoo and its player, Boy Pal and Madeline are silhouetted against an expanse of sky and gums.

. . .

LIGHTS

f i n i s